CW01064335

'Wynter-Vincent has written a luminous and deep
will appeal to anyone with an interest in cı
psychoanalysis. It is both a wonderfully clear i
Bion's work, and a series of enthralling encounte
in contact with Freud, Stevie Smith, B.S. Johnson, ͺ
and other writers, to remarkably illuminating effect.'

Nicholas Royle, *Professor of English, University of Sussex*

'This book will change how you think about thinking. Naomi Wynter-
Vincent's tremendously enlivening study draws on significant, conse-
quential affinities between Bion's ideas and the work of literary writers.
We come to understand how Bion thought and how he considered
thinking. In the process, we benefit from clear, searching accounts of his
idiosyncratic and highly influential psychoanalytic inventions (alpha-
function, beta-elements, bizarre objects, O, and the Grid, to name a
few). *Wilfred Bion and Literary Criticism* reminds us how exciting,
inventive, necessary and sometimes maddening thinking can be, and
how courageous and important a thinker Bion is for us today.'

Sarah Wood, *Reader in English Literature and Literary Theory at the
University of Kent (retired); Psychoanalytic
Psychotherapist in private practice*

Wilfred Bion and Literary Criticism

Wilfred Bion and Literary Criticism introduces the work of the British psychoanalyst, Wilfred Bion (1897–1979), and the immense potential of his ideas for thinking about literature, creative process, and creative writing.

There is now renewed interest in Bion's work following the publication of his *Complete Works* but the complexities of his theory and his distinctive style can be forbidding. Less well-known than Freud or Lacan, the work of Wilfred Bion nevertheless offers new insights for psychoanalytic literary criticism and creative writing. For newer readers of his work, this book offers an engaging introduction to several of Bion's key ideas, including his theory of thinking (the 'thought without a thinker'), the container/contained relationship, alpha-function; alpha-elements, beta-elements, and bizarre objects; K and -K; the Grid, O, and the caesura. It also offers a way in to Bion's astonishing and challenging experimental work, *A Memoir of the Future*, and explores the impact of his devastating personal experiences as an officer during the First World War. Each chapter of *Wilfred Bion and Literary Criticism* draws on one or more specific aspects of Bion's theory in relation to creative texts by Sigmund Freud, Stevie Smith, B.S. Johnson, Mary Butts, Jean Rhys, Nicholas Royle, J.G. Ballard, and Wilfred Bion himself.

The first full-length study to explore the potential of Bion's ideas for literary criticism, *Wilfred Bion and Literary Criticism* introduces his complex and extensive work for a new audience in an accessible and engaging way, and will be of great interest to scholars of creative writing, literary criticism, and psychoanalysis.

Naomi Wynter-Vincent holds degrees from the University of Cambridge, University of Sussex, and University College London. She completed her PhD at the University of Sussex. She has presented her work on Wilfred Bion at conferences in the UK, Italy, Finland, and Brazil. Naomi works in private practice in London and Luton as a therapist and coach.

Wilfred Bion and Literary Criticism

Naomi Wynter-Vincent

LONDON AND NEW YORK

First published 2022
by Routledge
2 Park Square, Milton Park, Abingdon, Oxon OX14 4RN

and by Routledge
605 Third Avenue, New York, NY 10158

Routledge is an imprint of the Taylor & Francis Group, an informa business

© 2022 Naomi Wynter-Vincent

British Library Cataloguing-in-Publication Data
A catalogue record for this book is available from the British Library

Library of Congress Cataloguing-in-Publication Data
Names: Wynter-Vincent, Naomi, 1978- author.
Title: Wilfred Bion and literary criticism / Naomi Wynter-Vincent.
Description: New york : Routledge, 2021. | Includes bibliographical
references and index. |
Identifiers: LCCN 2021013094 (print) | LCCN 2021013095 (ebook) |
ISBN 9780367439460 (hardback) | ISBN 9780367439453 (paperback) |
ISBN 9781003006619 (ebook)
Subjects: LCSH: Bion, Wilfred R. (Wilfred Ruprecht), 1897-1979. |
Psychoanalysis. | Creative ability. | Creative writing--Psychological aspects.
Classification: LCC BF173 .W96 2021 (print) | LCC BF173 (ebook) |
DDC 150.19/5--dc23
LC record available at https://lccn.loc.gov/2021013094
LC ebook record available at https://lccn.loc.gov/2021013095

ISBN: 978-0-367-43946-0 (hbk)
ISBN: 978-0-367-43945-3 (pbk)
ISBN: 978-1-003-00661-9 (ebk)

DOI: 10.4324/9781003006619

Typeset in Bembo
by MPS Limited, Dehradun

For Dan and Edith, with love.

Contents

Citations

Citations from *The Standard Edition of the Complete Psychological Works of Sigmund Freud*, translated from the German under the General Editorship of James Strachey; London: The Hogarth Press and Vintage, are given throughout as *Standard Edition* volume number, page number.

Acknowledgements

Ideas are born if they are given a chance.[1]

Many people have encouraged, supported, or otherwise accompanied me in bringing this work to publication. Looking through old emails with Professor Nicholas Royle, subsequently my doctoral supervisor at the University of Sussex, I am struck both by how little my eventual thesis resembled my original proposal, but also by how a number of resonant themes – the germs of an idea – are already there. Here's to enquiries *in K*, and to not knowing exactly how your research will turn out. Thank you, Nick, for keeping faith with me, even when (especially when) there was not much to show for it: I have very much enjoyed our conversations and correspondence.

I would also like to thank the Arts and Humanities Research Council for a grant that enabled me to become a doctoral candidate. The public funding of creatively critical thinking is a 'luxury' we can ill afford to lose. Additionally I am grateful to both the Faculty of English and the Doctoral School at the University of Sussex. I also extend my gratitude to the staff of the British Library, to Karnac Books, Myriad Editions, the Estate of W.R. Bion, and to Hannah Wright at Routledge.

Along the way I have received practical help, moral sustenance, and chocolate from a great number of my friends, colleagues, and clients. I send heartfelt thanks to Robert Adamson, Adelaide the cat, James Burt, Jenny Chamarette, Konni Deppe, Ann Fielding, Johannah Flaherty, Peta Freestone, Florian Gliksohn, Leda Glyptis, Tilly Hawkins, David Landau, Ros Maprayil, Dinésha Mendis, David Pritchard, Angela Rayner, Sophie Rollins, Randeep Sidhu, Helena Smith, Rachel Smith, Isabel Stainsby, James Sumner; my mother, Christine Warren-Mercer; and Andrew Wyld. I am deeply grateful to Professor Peter Boxall and Dr Sarah Wood for examining my thesis in 2016, and would especially like to mark my appreciation of Chris Mawson's generous and attentive review of my book proposal and manuscript. I was very saddened to learn of his passing in late 2020.

I could not have achieved the completion of this book without Dan Smith's love, encouragement, and delicious cooking, and I also thank his parents, professors Angela and Grahame Smith, for their support and interest over several years. My discussion with Angela Smith about *Wide Sargasso Sea* was very helpful. It has been especially sustaining to meet people who consider writing and thinking to be important, necessary work.

It was an honour to correspond with Dr James Grotstein (1925–2015) in 2012.

Finally, in a more spectral way, I am indebted to the inspiration of two, very different people, both of whom died in 1979, the year after I was born. The first of these is Wilfred Bion, and I am grateful to the Estate of W.R. Bion for licenses allowing me to cite his work without restriction. The second person is Dr Ida Rolf, the founder of Rolfing® Structural Integration, whose work and ideas accompanied the creation of my thesis, and this publication, as I trained to become a Certified Rolfer® in 2014, an Advanced Rolfer® in 2017, and a Rolf Movement® Practitioner in 2019. In very different ways, and in different fields of enquiry, they have both nevertheless deeply affected the ways in which I think about the world.

Notes

1 Bion, *Complete Works*, 9:25 (*The Tavistock Seminars*, 22).

1 Selected facts: introducing the work of Wilfred Bion

> I have experience to record, but how to communicate this experience to others I am in doubt; this book explains why.[1]

The work of the British psychoanalyst Wilfred Bion (1897–1979) is beginning to emerge from a position of relative obscurity, even within clinical psychoanalysis. A number of publications in recent years[2] suggest that Bion's oeuvre, in its bewildering entirety, is enjoying renewed interest. In 2014, the first complete edition of his works (comprising sixteen volumes) was published under the general editorship of Chris Mawson. Viewed as a whole, it becomes clear that the scope and breadth of Bion's writing demands detailed commentary and bears comparison with that other great 'standard edition' within the psychoanalytic field, the complete works of Freud.

In this book I will argue that the work of Wilfred Bion offers a rich and valuable resource for thinking about writing (and writing about thinking). While a number of writers have drawn on his work to explore literary themes (see, for example, work by Jacqueline Rose,[3] Mary Jacobus,[4] and Steven Connor[5]), the relative difficulty of his writing, in some places replete with apparently mathematical symbols, and a style that hovers undecidably between clinical detachment and dry humour, has perhaps hindered the wider circulation of his ideas among literary critics and critical theorists. R.D. Hinshelwood has written of Bion that 'his writings appear gnomic, irritating and intensely stimulating, and this style has been responsible for a tendency to sanctify him while not really understanding him'.[6] Some of his more approachable texts, such as the collections of his transcribed seminars and lectures, have only been available in print since 2005 (*The Italian Seminars* and *The Tavistock Seminars*) or in the past decade (*Los Angeles Seminars and Supervision* was published in 2013). With the exception of his important early paper 'Attacks on Linking', his work has not been anthologised, which is surprising given how concise some of his papers are, although a recent book by Nicola Abel-Hirsch[7] brings together and provides commentary on 365 Bion quotations (one for each day of the year), and moreover draws our attention to how very quotable Bion is. His two remarkable 1977 essays about the 'stray' or 'wild' thought, improvised onto a dictaphone and posthumously transcribed by Francesca Bion, have been in print since 1997, but in a minor edition that has not

DOI: 10.4324/9781003006619-1

yet succeeded in bringing these gems of his thinking to a wider audience. More recently, one volume of the *Complete Works* has brought a number of additional essays and his 'Further Cogitations' to light, including the provocative essay 'New and Improved'.

Bion also left a rich collection of autobiographical resources. His war memoir, written immediately after his return from the First World War, was intended to serve belatedly in lieu of unwritten letters to his parents; episodes from this period are revisited and enriched by later accounts that appear in *The Long Week-End*, which offers a biographical account from birth through to the end of the war. A further autobiography, *All My Sins Remembered*, picks up the story of Bion's life from after this period through to the immediate aftermath of his first wife's death, though the volume has been more happily rounded out with a selection of his letters and illustrations to his second wife Francesca, and their children. The collected volume of his 'cogitations', as he called them, provides an extensive theoretical journal offering glimpses into the development of many of his ideas over a number of years. Finally, his strange three-volume 'novel', *A Memoir of the Future*, launched Bion late in life into a wildly creative, experimental kind of autobiography, drawing on personal history, theory, and the exercise of his 'speculative imagination'.[8]

Part of the reason for Bion's relative neglect derives, I suspect, from the not unreasonable tendency by commentators to position his work as a footnote to Melanie Klein. Bion entered into analysis with Klein after the period of the 'Controversial Discussions' (between the followers of Anna Freud and the followers of Melanie Klein in the 1940s), although he was involved in psychotherapeutic training at the Tavistock Institute from the 1930s. His theoretical approach undoubtedly builds on Melanie Klein's highly original reading of Freud, and he is usually named in the group of post-war psychoanalysts described as Kleinian and post-Kleinian, alongside others such as Hanna Segal, Betty Joseph, Elliott Jaques, and Esther Bick. Indeed, the central Kleinian concepts of projective identification and the (paranoid-schizoid and depressive) positions are a *sine qua non* for Bion's best-known idea, the container-contained relationship.[9]

His clinical specialism in treating psychotic patients also benefitted from Klein's extension of psychoanalysis to children, for whom new ways of thinking about and practising psychoanalysis were needed. The language of object relations (splitting, part-objects, the 'good' and 'bad' breast, unconscious 'phantasy'[10]) is strongly evident in his work, although his formal use of 'Kleinian' terms comes to be supplemented with new, wholly 'Bionian'[11] concepts, such as alpha-function, beta-elements, and bizarre objects; and existing words and phrases used to new effect, such as the selected fact, transformations, and the caesura. Over time, the recognisable elements of Kleinian theory are also modified in subtle but distinctive ways: the paranoid-schizoid and depressive positions become PS ↔ D (drawing attention to the oscillation *between* the two states, and their continued operation throughout the life span), and where the two positions are further glossed as 'patience' and 'security', respectively, when applied to the psychoanalyst's experience of feeling successively bewildered by – and making sense of – the analysand's material.[12]

While Bion's work proceeds from his grounding in Kleinian metapsychology, it is Freud's short 1911 essay, 'Formulations on the Two Principles of Mental Functioning',[13] that serves as starting point and inspiration for Bion's highly original speculations in *Learning from Experience*, as well as for the labels he gives to the different 'uses' of a statement along the vertical axis of the 'Grid', his observational tool for the practising analyst, first described in 1963.[14] His recourse to Freud can also give rise to a comparison of Bion with that other 'inspired bizarre analyst',[15] Jacques Lacan, whose work, unlike Bion's, has enjoyed considerable posthumous attention within the world of critical theory and literary and film criticism.

Bion was himself keen to stress that he did not necessarily wish to challenge existing psychoanalytic theories, being chiefly concerned with the refinement of psychoanalytic *observation*. This modesty on Bion's part has also, perhaps, contributed to the overlooking of his work beyond the clinical field: he has been seen as a specialist primarily in what at first (and second) sight can appear to be an overly abstracted or technical approach to psychoanalytic work. Although the later seminars and lectures did much to round out that picture, his laconic style of responding to audience questions confirmed his 'difficulty' even as he was at pains to dismantle and ironise a position of authority. In this respect, too, he bears comparison with Lacan, who sought to bring into question the presumed authority of the analyst. Unlike his French counterpart, however, it is clear from Bion's frequently scathing self-commentary that he considered himself to have achieved nothing more than making 'the best of a bad job'.[16]

Wilfred Bion's life was a remarkably eventful one,[17] marked by a number of traumatic events that included serving in the First World War and losing his first wife very shortly after the birth of their first child, Parthenope. The son of a British civil engineer and a woman of Anglo-Indian heritage, he was born in north-west India in 1897 and spent his infancy there. His childhood memories of India – of brilliant sunlight and searing heat amid the ever-present vigil against wild animals – made a profound of impression on him. At the age of eight, he was abruptly sent away to a public school in England, an experience he found profoundly painful: in his view, he survived the ordeal chiefly by cultivating his skill in sports and developing a personality structure that he later described as a 'shell'.[18] His interrupted childhood was compounded by the more traumatic interruption of his early adulthood by the First World War. He joined the Royal Tank Regiment in 1916, serving as an officer in Flanders and Ypres until the end of the war; was decorated for his bravery with a DSO (Distinguished Service Order) medal by the British government, and awarded membership of the French *Légion d'Honneur*. After the war, he read history at the Queen's College, Oxford, and after graduation briefly entered school teaching (before a false allegation of misconduct prompted his resignation); thereafter he embarked on medical training at University College London in 1924, already intent on pursuing a specialism in psychoanalysis. In the 1930s he studied psychotherapy at the Tavistock Clinic, and began a training analysis in 1938 that was, again, subject to interruption: the onset of the Second World War. During the first part of the 1940s he began the experimental group work (known as the Northfield Experiment) with demobilised and injured soldiers that would form the basis of his first (and, during his lifetime, most successful) book, *Experiences in Groups*.

His personal life was also marked by false starts and interruptions. After a disastrous love affair and broken engagement with a young woman after the First World War (recounted in *All My Sins Remembered*), he married Betty Jardine, a successful stage actor. War work took him away from home shortly before she was due to give birth to their first child; he received the good news of Parthenope's birth while he was away from home, only to learn of his wife's death a few days later. Thus Bion found himself a widower and a new father at a point when his career as an analyst was only just beginning and his financial situation was precarious. Later, he went into analysis with Melanie Klein, and was in due course married a second time, to Francesca, going on to have a further two children. His first fully psychoanalytic work, *Learning from Experience*, came out in 1962, following *Experiences in Groups*, his work on group therapy, in 1961. Bion was by then already in his mid-sixties, entering relatively late in life into the most productive, ground-breaking and distinguished phase of his career. He was made Director of the London Clinic of Psychoanalysis from 1956 to 1962, and then President of the British Psychoanalytical Society from 1962 to 1965, and published two further books in quick succession (*Elements of Psychoanalysis* in 1963, and *Transformations* in 1965).

We can all take heart from the long gestation of Bion's career. On entering his seventies, he surprised everyone with a decision to leave the UK. He moved to Los Angeles along with his family, leaving behind the leadership roles that threatened to see him 'loaded with honours and sunk without trace',[19] and choosing instead to begin again with a new set of clients and students. He went on to publish *Attention and Interpretation* in 1970, and to begin to publish the original three parts of *A Memoir of the Future* between 1975 and 1979. It was also in that year that he finally returned to the UK, settling in Oxford but planning an extended trip to India to which he had not returned since his childhood. But his intended return to the land of his birth never took place: he died a few months after arriving back in the UK, at the age of 81.

Bion worked with many highly disturbed patients, and he emphasised that the development of the capacity to *think* is a precarious, hard-won achievement that, analogous to Freud's enquiries into sexuality, cannot be taken for granted. His elaboration of Melanie Klein's concept of projective identification into a two-mind model of thinking (the 'container-contained' relationship) reframes the analytic space as a place of 'being-two-to-think' or – put another way – two to *dream*, as James Grotstein describes:

> Put another way, as the analysand shared his dream with me, it had been incompletely dreamed. As I listened to him, I unconsciously entered his continuing dream and 'became' his 'dreaming co-pilot' in order to complete the dream.[20]

Dream is central to Bion's work, as it is for Freud, but differently: he writes that '[Freud] took up only the negative attitude, dreams as 'concealing' something, not the way in which the *necessary* dream is *constructed*'.[21] The question of how we process experience is taken up in the first of his four metapsychologies, *Learning from Experience*, where he develops a number of remarkable and perhaps intimidating theoretical concepts – alpha-function, alpha- and beta-elements, bizarre objects, the contact-barrier and the beta-screen, the L[ove], H[ate] and K[nowledge] links, and their 'minus' coun-terparts (chiefly, -K). The distinction between the conscious and unconscious parts *of* the mind outlined by Freud becomes less important than the question of how experience is made available for use *by* a mind, and whether the personality that develops can grow by what it learns. Bion found it helpful to suggest that thoughts are ontologically prior to the thinker, and he describes the 'thought without a thinker' that places a demand on the subject to develop an apparatus able to 'think' the thought through. He reoriented Klein's for-mulation of the paranoid–schizoid and depressive positions to the process of learning: borrowing the phrase used by the French mathematician, Henri Poincaré, it is the 'selected fact' that drives the change from the paranoid-schizoid to the depressive state, by making it possible to 'unite elements long since known, but till then scattered and seemingly foreign to each other'.[22] In Bion's work, the positions (paranoid–schizoid and depressive) are usually in-dicated as PS ↔ D, indicating a continuing, lifelong process of movement between the two states of mind that are both normal aspects of learning.

In some ways the 'analyst's analyst', Bion was deeply concerned to develop observational and analytical tools for the working practitioner. He created the Grid (Figure 1.1) in an attempt to provide a framework for noting and de-scribing the analysand's statements and the analyst's interpretations, and within the clinical community he is perhaps best known for his dictum that analysts should work without 'memory and desire'.[23] The analyst should cultivate her or his ability for observation untainted as far as possible by preconceived theories, focusing not on what is already known, but on what is unknown. Unlike Freud, whose project it was to uncover and integrate the experiences of the past, Bion was concerned with the future and what might yet emerge.

Psychoanalysis and literature

The use of psychoanalytic ideas to think about literature is not new. Psychoanalytic literary criticism has developed along the path of a twofold 'return to Freud' that went first via the post-structuralist 'linguistic turn' sti-mulated by the work of French psychoanalyst Jacques Lacan (e.g. his 'Seminar on *The Purloined Letter*'[24]). His best-known ideas – the mirror stage, the 'un-conscious structured like a language', the three orders of the symbolic, the imaginary, and the real – have been deeply influential in inspiring a vast in-dustry of 'Lacanian' criticism in fields such as film theory (especially Laura Mulvey's paper, 'Visual Pleasure and Narrative Cinema'[25]) and culture (e.g.

	1 Definitory Hypothesis	2 Ψ	3 Notation	4 Attention	5 Inquiry	6 Action	...n
A β-elements	A1	A2				A6	...An
B α-elements	B1	B2	B3	B4	B5	B6	...Bn
C Dream Thoughts Myth, Dream, Model	C1	C2	C3	C4	C5	C6	...Cn
D Pre-conception	D1	D2	D3	D4	D5	D6	...Dn
E Conception	E1	E2	E3	E4	E5	E6	...En
F Concept	F1	F2	F3	F4	F5	F6	...Fn
G Scientific Deductive System		G2					
H Algebraic Calculus							

Figure 1.1 The Grid.

Replicated from Bion's 1971 paper, 'The Grid', in *Two Papers: The Grid and Caesura.*

Slavoj Žižek's *The Sublime Object of Ideology*), to the extent of having being taken at one time more or less as *the* psychoanalytic criticism, *tout court*.

More recently, a second pathway to Freud inspired by the work of Jacques Derrida (and also by work alert to Freud's achievements as a writer, such as that by Patrick Mahony[26]) has led to a new Freudian criticism via clinically 'marginal' texts such as *The Uncanny* and themes such as telepathy (for instance, in work by Jacques Derrida[27] and Nicholas Royle[28]). Yet both of these pathways to (and from) Freud have overlooked the considerable contribution of post-Freudian thinking stimulated by the 'British turn' of psychoanalysis associated with the work of Melanie Klein and her followers, and in the various strands of Independent psychoanalytic thought associated with Sándor Ferenczi, the Balints, Donald Winnicott, Marion Milner, and others (though see, for example, the volume edited by Peter Rudnytsky[29]). The work of Julia Kristeva, drawing on Kleinian preoccupations with the maternal body and primary destructiveness (as well as drawing on Lacan), is a notable exception to this trend. In part, this reflects the more practical, clinical orientation of the British psychoanalytic school (with a greater focus on working with children), as well as the notion, now outdated, that their approach to art might be 'unsophisticated' compared to thinking based on French psychoanalysis. The basis for a 'Kleinian aesthetics' resides chiefly in the work of Hanna Segal, who brought Klein's idea of *reparation* to bear in creative work: art as the working through from the paranoid-schizoid to the depression positions.[30]

The psychoanalyst and feminist theorist Juliet Mitchell, having previously advocated a feminist 'return to Freud' in 1974, made the case for a fuller consideration of Melanie Klein, editing and introducing a selected volume of her papers that appeared in 1986. She concluded her critical introduction by stating that 'Klein change[d] the terrain and thereby change[d] the task',[31] noting that Klein's characterisation of the unconscious as a primarily descriptive, rather than dynamic repository or realm of experience, accounts for the diminution of its conceptual importance among her followers, including Bion: 'In a way it [the unconscious] has become uninteresting; after all, in what way can we say a baby phantasising a breast is unconscious of it?'[32]

Klein's reading of *Beyond the Pleasure Principle*[33] and Freud's conception of a death drive foregrounds primary destructive impulses at the heart of the child's psychical landscape. In literary criticism, the effects of the Kleinian turn are seen in work by, among others, Jacqueline Rose,[34] Lyndsey Stonebridge,[35] Mary Jacobus,[36] and Steven Connor[37] in relation to his work on Samuel Beckett. In *Why War?*, Jacqueline Rose argued that a critical reconsideration of Melanie Klein's attention to that which was repressed in Freud's theory – namely, the primacy of destructive impulses and the death drive – was overdue. Klein's supposed weaknesses as a writer should not, she suggested, be so easily taken at face value, for 'Klein does theory *otherwise*'.[38] For Rose, engaging seriously with the question of the death drive can puncture the phantasy of mastery at the heart of theory, and reorients the critical project to what is 'creatively unmasterable'. The re-emergence of UK state-funded aggression in the 1980s and 1990s (in the Falkland Islands and the first Gulf War) under the government of Margaret Thatcher required a critical theory, Rose argued, based precisely along Kleinian lines to account for the ubiquity of destructive impulses observed in political and popular culture. Rose asks: 'Why [...] has there been no rereading of Melanie Klein?', suggesting that 'a post-Lacanian orthodoxy has blocked access to Klein'. In a later collection, *On Not Being Able to Sleep*, Rose draws on Bion's theory of the bizarre object (from his early essay, 'On Hallucination'[39]) to identify moments in the work of Elizabeth Bowen and Mary Butts where 'the relationship between history and perception' is rendered 'objective and odd',[40] as in the example she gives from Bowen's *The Heat of the Day*:

> Louie repeatedly stopped to touch petals, her raspy finger-tips being every time entered by their smoothness.[41]

While Rose's instinct in her selection of texts is unerring, her analysis of the representation of history within modernist texts is stronger than her immersion in Bion's theory.[42] Nevertheless, her essay offers an interesting, if under-developed, illustration of the possibilities of reading Bion in connection with literature. Her consideration of the writer Mary Butts led me indirectly to the discovery of Butt's short story, 'With and Without Buttons', which forms the subject of chapter five; her identification of the bizarre object in Bowen's work provided the theoretical focus of chapter six, which addresses a scene from Jean Rhys' *Wide Sargasso Sea*.

Mary Jacobus' work to develop a specifically Kleinian (and post-Kleinian) literary criticism has gone further in exploring Bion's work both as theorist and writer. In *The Poetics of Psychoanalysis: In the Wake of Klein*, the entire third section of the work ('Transformations') is devoted to detailed critical readings of Bion's work, including the autobiographies and *A Memoir of the Future*. Jacobus writes:

> Bion's way with his psychoanalytic constructions is to read them aslant, against the grain of their received meaning. This tendency illustrates the swerve that makes him a strong reader of Klein rather than her follower, even as he continues to work with the basic tools of Kleinian concepts such as splitting and projective identification.[43]

Bion was also Samuel Beckett's first analyst (from 1933 to 1935) at an early point in both men's careers. Their relationship forms the central interest of Ian Miller's and Kay Souter's study of Beckett and Bion, published in 2013.[44] In *Beckett, Modernism and the Material Imagination*, Steven Connor reflects on aspects of Beckett's use of language in terms of Bion's early paper, 'Attacks on Linking'.[45] In his chapter 'Making Flies Mean Something', he writes: 'Beckett's work often seems driven by the urge to atomise, to slice, split and divide, in pursuit of the ideal of maximal disarticulation, or what Wilfred Bion (1993) calls an 'attack on linking'.[46]

Bion and literature

> Poets have found a method of communication. Milton invents a new word, 'pandemonium'; Shakespeare strings together ordinary words in a way that starts things vibrating inside countless generations of people. Why? How is it done?[47]

While Bion did not address himself directly to literary questions, it is clear that he was closely attentive to language and sensitive to literature and poetry. What at first sight seems so austere in his earlier theoretical style – such as the elaboration of a distinctive, ostensibly algebraic terminology – attests to a concern that his enquiry into certain psychical mechanisms should remain free of pre-conception, 'unsaturated',[48] for as long as possible and in such a way that the curiosity underlying the question might avoid being arrested by a premature answer. He frequently recalls the phrase by Blanchot: '*la réponse est le malheur de la question*'.[49] Alpha-function, in particular, is a 'placeholder' term: designed to free his investigation from the 'penumbra of associations'[50] that might attach to another word more closely related to conventional speech or Freudian terminology.

Bion received a classical, English public school[51] education, and remained a voracious and catholic reader all his life. His writing makes liberal and frequent use of a range of both literary and philosophical references, returning frequently to two or three quotations from Milton's *Paradise Lost* ('So much the rather celestial light', 'void and formless infinite'), as well as Shakespeare's *Macbeth* and *Cymbeline* ('Golden lads and girls all must/ As chimney-sweepers, come to dust'[52]). He also references Virgil (in the story of Palinurus), Tolstoy (noting the translated word, 'sooth', to indicate the truth-seeking instinct), Stendhal, Hugo, Valéry, Bagehot, Bennett, Manley Hopkins, Joyce, Pound, Kipling, Coleridge, Tennyson, Shelley, Byron, and Keats, whose phrase, 'negative capability', he takes up enthusiastically in *Attention and Interpretation*. Lewis Carroll's *Alice in Wonderland* provides an important intertext for *A Memoir of the Future*. He also draws on an eclectic range of philosophers of science, historians and spiritual thinkers, including Kant, Hume, Descartes, Tacitus, Frege, Russell, Popper, Meister Eckhart, Isaac Luria, Bishop Berkeley, Buber, and Teilhard de Chardin. He quotes from both the Bible and the Bhagavad Gita.

Much of the apparent complexity of his thinking in *Transformations* and *Attention and Interpretation* stems from his eager and detailed discussion of Euclidean geometry; aside from Poincaré, Heisenberg and Fraunhofer provide additional scientific references. He refers frequently to Leonardo da Vinci's depictions of swirling currents and hair, seeing in them an attempt to represent the experience of the emotional turbulence of change.[53]

In their preface to *Bion's Sources*, Hinshelwood and Torres compare Bion to Freud:

> To some extent [Bion's] intellectual breadth resembled Freud, but whereas Freud wrote in a linear narrative style [...], Bion wrote in a non-linear, labyrinthine and enigmatic style [...]. His style is more Beckettian than Shakespearean.[54]

Bion himself never mentions his former analysand, but (as Connor has noted), Bion's work provides a way to think about fragmented or non-linear modes of expression as an 'attack on linking'. In a short passage in *Cogitations*, the homophony that is endemic to the French language prompts an intriguing discussion of 'disarticulate' language, language in transition from the paranoid-schizoid to the depressive position:

> The people of this district [the Dordogne, France] speak of a 'crise de foie'. It seems to be that this would be quite appropriate if it were spelt 'crise de foi' or 'crise deux fois'. There is no need to suppose that the language being spoken, the appropriate language, is an articulate one rather than, say, a language that is a transition from paranoid-schizoid to depressive, from part objects to whole objects.[55]

Bion's development of projective identification emphasises its communicative role, but this is not to suggest that he returns language to a narrowly re-presentational function. His work is exquisitely concerned with the trans-mission and cultivation of the *thought*, posited as logically prior to the mechanism of thinking. For Bion this is both developmentally true, when the pain of hunger and the absence of the breast in infancy generates a problem to be solved (what to do with the 'bad' feeling of hunger), and structurally true for the adult equipped with a mind who nevertheless needs some *thing* to set off the thinking process.

He introduces time into the process of projective identification by sug-gesting that it is the sojourn of the split-off, evacuated object in the mother's mind that enables the infant to take back and *bear* the thought, and he reflects that Klein's clinical style – offering immediate and direct interpretation of the analysand's unconscious phantasy – may have the unintended consequence of stimulating even greater anxiety if it does not promote an increasing capacity to bear the frustration that is the parent to the thought. The effect of art, Bion suggests, is produced over time: new literatures seed ideas and thoughts that may germinate in other minds and in other times:

> It is very difficult to give expression to the wild idea. If people can possibly bear to have a wild idea and allow it to germinate, then they might be able to put it into a form that made it more communicable. In *Finnegan's Wake* Joyce says that you would have to spend your life reading it to acquire the language or the capacity to understand it. I don't think anybody is likely to do that. But then you get this curious effect: perhaps in another fifty years people will be able to read *Finnegan's Wake*; what has happened to the wild ideas that are triggered but not expressed, we cannot tell. But they *are* communicated[56]

Bion's work has attracted a small but dedicated academic following that has until recently focused on a few key names. The late James Grotstein, who was ana-lysed by Bion in Los Angeles, oversaw the essay collection prepared in com-memoration of Bion's life in 1981,[57] and wrote a detailed theoretical exposition of Bion's work in *A Beam of Intense Darkness: Wilfred Bion's Legacy to*

Psychoanalysis. Donald Meltzer devotes part three of *The Kleinian Development* to Bion's clinical significance. Rudi Vermote has more recently published *Reading Bion*, which offers a clear and accessible introduction to key themes within Bion's oeuvre for new readers.[58] *Bion's Dream*, by the poet and writer Meg Harris Williams, is the result of her detailed and creative engagement with *A Memoir of the Future*, including her role in an unfinished film dramatisation, itself the subject of *The Becoming Room: Filming Bion's* A Memoir of the Future, published in 2016. The Brazilian psychoanalyst Paulo Cesar Sandler has also written extensively on Bion, including one of two dictionaries of Bionian terms (the other is by Rafael E. López-Corvo), and a projected three-volume commentary on *A Memoir of the Future*. The late psychoanalyst and writer Parthenope Bion Talamo, Bion's daughter by his first marriage, brought her father's ideas to a wider audience in Italy, where she lived and worked until her untimely death (in a car accident) in 1998. The Italian analysts Antonino Ferro and Giuseppe Civitarese have written a number of books that develop Bion's ideas under the guise of 'analytic field theory'. In the UK, R.D. Hinshelwood and Nuno Torres have edited a volume of essays devoted to exploring Bion's philosophical and theoretical sources, and Chris Mawson, editor of the *Complete Works*, previously edited *Bion Today*. Francesca Bion, who edited a number of Bion's works for posthumous publication and wrote the 'Key' to *A Memoir of the Future*, remained closely engaged with Bion scholars until her death in the spring of 2015. More recently, Carla Ambrosio Garcia[59] and Kelli Fuery[60] have brought Bion's theory of thinking to bear on film and visual culture theory. Other noteworthy developments of Bion's ideas can be found in work by clinicians Duncan Cartwright, David Bell, Annie Reiner, Célia Fix Korbivcher, Howard Levine, and Lawrence Brown. Bion's theory of the container-contained relationship is a key theoretical underpinning of the 'Solihull Approach' (to parenting and health visiting) developed by Dr Hazel Douglas MBE[61]; his work is also taken up in the coaching model ('relational coaching') developed by Erik de Haan.[62] The 'thought without a thinker' has also been brought into a productive relationship with Buddhist teachings in a book by Mark Epstein.[63]

As my doctoral thesis, this work was originally titled 'In the Penumbra of Bion: Possibilities for Literary Criticism'. That title recalled Bion's frequent use of that unusual word, *penumbra*, which appears on over thirty occasions in his *Complete Works*, and seven times alone in *Learning from Experience*. The word appears almost exclusively as part of the phrase 'penumbra of associations', and most frequently in relation to that which Meltzer describes as Bion's 'empty concept'[64] of alpha-function, so named as to avoid the associative ideas that might accrue unhelpfully to words borrowed from conventional language. The penumbra is the area of 'partial or lighter shadow round the perfect or darker shadow' (*Chambers*); the word is derived etymologically from the two Latin words *paene* (almost) and *umbra* (shadow), the latter shared with another word that Bion frequently uses: 'adumbrate' (or 'adumbration').

Bion's penchant for the penumbra appears to have gone largely unremarked by his commentators, which is the more surprising given Bion's frequent invocation of light and darkness as metaphors for the psychoanalytic enterprise. Referencing both John Milton's blindness and Freud's letter to Lou Andreas-Salomé, in which Freud writes 'I know that in writing I have to blind myself artificially in order to focus all the light on one dark spot', Bion proposes to bring darkness, rather than light, to bear on obscure problems, the better to discern any faint 'light' (clarity or pattern) immanent within the object under investigation:

> Instead of trying to bring a brilliant, intelligent, knowledgeable light to bear on obscure problems, I suggest we bring to bear a diminution of the 'light' – a penetrating beam of darkness: a reciprocal of the searchlight.[65]

I was also alert to what Bion would call the 'implicit model'[66] of the original title. Being 'in' something implies, as Bion made clear, a 'container and something to put in it'.[67] The penumbra (that is also *not quite* an umbrella) may be a place of refuge, as well as a place defined by a relationship to a light source with the potential to cast new and other shadows. In medical terminology, where it refers to the area just outside the place of a stroke, the 'existence of a penumbra implies that salvage of the cells is possible'.[68] It is, therefore, a precarious but hopeful place. Even under a different title, the project of this work stands *in the penumbra* of Wilfred Bion, since it meets his ideas in the half-shadow that they cast, in my mind at least, over questions of 'creatively critical' writing and the literary representation and transformation of thinking and thoughts.

I also finally decided against a title that would include the word 'Bionian', recognising that that word is a problematic (if convenient) shorthand to indicate 'based on the ideas and work of Wilfred Bion'. In this I was guided by Bion's discussions of the group and the mystic in *Attention and Interpretation*, where he describes the tension between the new idea represented by the mystic (or genius) and the group's efforts to assimilate (and thereby suppress) the new idea.[69] Bion wanted thinkers, not followers. I was also guided by Bion Talamo's essay, 'Why We Can't Call Ourselves Bionians: Notes on the Life and Work of W.R. Bion',[70] in which she identifies the 'quality of mental freedom that made Bion such a disconcerting person, and an academic who could not, by his very nature, "found a school"'.[71] Though used sparingly, I do retain the word's use as a reasonable abbreviation. The term is also used straightforwardly by a number of notable Bion commentators, including Grotstein, Meltzer, Ferro, and (surprisingly) Bion Talamo herself.[72]

In what follows I aim to demonstrate that a number of Bion's ideas can be read productively alongside a range of literary texts, and also alongside texts by Freud and Bion himself. Each of the following chapters is designed to illustrate one or more facets[73] of Bion's work, and to introduce the reader unacquainted with Bion to the breadth of his ideas while drawing attention to his own status and interest as a writer. This last point echoes Patrick Mahony's reappraisal of 'Freud as a Writer'. It is indeed chiefly Freud, rather than Klein, whose work offers a spectral counterpoint to Bion in the chapters that follow.

A further note about my intention and approach: Bion's work is complex, subtle, and quite often strange. In the course of my research I came to admire Bion's work a great deal, but I also remember very distinctly the first time I encountered one of his texts (it was probably *Learning from Experience*) on a library shelf at the University of Sussex. The slim, austere volume in no way seemed to me like the psychoanalytic texts I had previously read and 'enjoyed' for their insights into the human condition, the fascinating vignettes of particular patients, and yes (recalling Freud's perspicacious comments about his 'Fragment of an Analysis of a Case of Hysteria', better known as the case of 'Dora'), their occasionally sensational, prurient quality. By contrast, Bion's writing seemed absurdly dry, technical, even boring (there is very little sex in his theory); whole books were composed as numbered paragraphs, seemingly recalling the style of a mathematical or philosophical treatise. The Grid, often printed into the inside cover of Bion's books, seemed as improbable a psychoanalytic tool as I could imagine – far removed from the sensitivity to feeling and emotion that I associated with the practice of psychotherapy or my enjoyment of literature. In what follows I hope that you, if you are new to his work, may be persuaded to see beyond these kinds of first impressions. Repeatedly I found that my bafflement and discombobulation gave way to moments of surprise, even laughter, at Bion's characteristic capacity for emotional honesty and understatement, such as the line from *Learning from Experience* with which this chapter opens, or the drily amusing opening paragraphs of *Experiences in Groups*. His writing often has this disarming quality that reminds you that he only believed himself to be 'making the best of a bad job' where the task was simply to remain able to think clearly in the face of adversity and the seductions of excessive credulity in one's own assumed knowledge. There is also, in quite a lot of his writing, a strand of dry, facetious humour that may be thought particularly (or at least stereotypically) 'British': consider again the first paragraph of *Experiences in Groups*, or the ninth of his *Italian Seminars*,[74] or the author's note to *Bion in New York and São Paulo*[75]. For the reader completely new to Bion, I suggest that the following texts may offer interesting ways in: *Learning from Experience* is undoubtedly essential, a primer to almost all the key aspects of his theory, despite its remarkably compressed quality; the transcribed audio essay '28 May 1977' found in *Taming Wild Thoughts* makes for a differently strange but delightful chaser, strange perhaps especially suitable for students of creative writing and literature; meanwhile his 1958 account of his experience at the Battle of Amiens (included in the same volume as his war memoir as 'Amiens') offers a deeply affecting insight into Bion's inner world.[76]

Throughout this book, I have placed Bion's work alongside very close readings of a number of texts that may themselves be strange (to everyone) or unknown (to you). Some of the texts that follow are better known than others, and it may be worth accessing these in order to make sense of some more detailed points in my analysis; I have quoted at length (where I could) in order to enable close textual analysis, but also at the limits of copyright conventions around 'academic fair use'. The novels (Smith, Rhys, Johnson, and Royle) and the short story by Butts are the most straightforwardly 'readable';

Freud's *Project for a Scientific Psychology*, Ballard's *The Atrocity Exhibition*, and Bion's *A Memoir of the Future* are notably stranger and more complex texts. I include these comments (both about Bion and the writers that I place in connection with him) only to encourage the wary reader to persist with a thinker whose relevance to literary criticism may initially seem obscure.

In 'Freud's 'excessively intense idea': the *Project for a Scientific Psychology*', I propose a Bionian reading of Freud's early and unpublished neuropsychology.[77] It may be read, I suggest, as a purely creative work designed to enable him to advance a series of 'wild' thoughts, in line with Bion's theory of thinking in which the thought precedes the thinker, and furthermore places a demand on an available mind to become capable of thinking it.

Freud's spectral presence continues in the next chapter, 'Pompey's thought-worm: Stevie Smith's *Novel on Yellow Paper*', in the form of a marginal reading of *Beyond the Pleasure Principle* alongside Stevie Smith's début novel, *Novel on Yellow Paper*. The figuring of thought as an intestinal worm that 'works at her' from the inside resonates with Bion's digestive model of thinking and in turns helpfully dramatises Bion's paradox of the 'thought without a thinker'. Attention to the trope of parasitism within the novel also enables a re-reading of the book's disturbing antisemitic themes. Furthermore, a Bionian reading of *Novel*'s subtitle, 'Work it out for Yourself', enlarges a reading of the story's possibly suicidal subtext by arguing that what Pompey seeks is not simply an attentive reader to 'work out' the true meaning of her story, but a collaborative mind that does some of the work. The chapter closes with a consideration – using one aspect of Bion's Grid, 'column 2' – of Bion and Stevie Smith as tonally distinctive writers.

In 'Restoring the lost container: B.S. Johnson's *The Unfortunates*', I draw attention to an aspect of B.S. Johnson's famous 'book in a box' that has been overlooked in earlier criticism; namely, the box itself. Where previous commentators have read Johnson's experimental work primarily in terms of the unbound *contents* (as a metaphor for the experience of chaos and disintegration), I seek to demonstrate that the *box* relocates *The Unfortunates* as an elegiac work of reparation of the container-contained relationship that has been lost through the death of B.S. Johnson's (real-life) mentor, Tony Tillinghast. Bion's conception of thinking as something that is developed through the proxy of another person's mind (the relationship of the container to the contained) provides a valuable tool for thinking anew about book, box, and all.

The next chapter, 'With and without Bion: supplementing an uncanny reading of Mary Butts', enacts a close reading of the short story, 'With and Without Buttons', by the English modernist writer, Mary Butts. While the story can be understood in terms of the Freudian 'uncanny', I suggest that a number of Bion's ideas – beta-elements, the protomental space, and O – deepen a reading of the story that traces unthinkable – rather than repressed – sexual desire in the relationship of the narrator, her sister-double, and their sceptical neighbour, Trenchard.

The figure of the telescope in *Wide Sargasso Sea* provides the focal point for the next chapter, 'Jean Rhys' bizarre telescope: a Bion-emic/-etic reading of

Wide Sargasso Sea'. I develop Jacqueline Rose's productive suggestion that Bion's theory of the bizarre object opens a way to read dissociative, psychotic effects in literature. The telescope in *Wide Sargasso Sea* can be seen both as a form of link between characters and communities, and as a bizarre object that figures the disintegration of Rochester's mind.

The theme of psychosis is continued in 'Efficient psychosis: notes towards a Bionian Ballardian breakdown', which develops a Bionian reading of J.G. Ballard's experimental novel, *The Atrocity Exhibition*. Bion's theorisation of psychosis, through the ideas of beta-elements and beta-space, provides ways to think about Ballard's experimental use of form to depict a 'psychotic' landscape. Moreover, both Bion and Ballard seem to gesture toward the possibility of a positive, sane, or 'efficient' conception of psychosis that would take seriously its potential to disrupt existing modes of thinking.

In 'Becoming ray: transformations in Nicholas Royle's *Quilt*', I read Royle's début novel through Bion's 1965 metapsychology, *Transformations*. The novel's darkly suggestive conclusion evokes the possibility that the main character and narrator – the unnamed son living in the aftermath of his father's death – undergoes a radical transformation that can be explored in a more detailed way by reference to Bion's four kinds of transformation: the rigid-motion transformation, the projective transformation, the transformation in hallucinosis, and the transformation in O.

Finally, in 'Dream I Tell You: Bion's *A Memoir of the Future*', I turn to Bion's own creative writing through his experimental work, *A Memoir of the Future*. Part-experimental autobiography, part-fiction, part-theoretical exposition, Bion's three-volume *Memoir* defies analysis at the level of genre and stands as an exemplary instance of that which Theodor Adorno and Edward Said have described as 'late style'. Bion's initial readership – chiefly practising psychoanalysts who had known Bion during his leadership of the London Clinic of Psychoanalysis and the British Psychoanalytic Society[78] – were not only baffled but embarrassed by this last efflorescence, with many dismissing the work as evidence of Bion's senility. With the exception of work by Meg Harris Williams,[79] *A Memoir of the Future* has, at the time of publication, received little attention in terms of its specifically literary aspects. Though I do not attempt an exhaustive study of it here, I suggest that it merits a close reading as an attempt, through writing, to construct the 'necessary dream' that would give birth to the thought without a thinker, and to integrate Bion's traumatic wartime experiences.

Notes

1 Bion, *Complete Works*, 4:263 (*Learning from Experience*, v).
2 For example, Harris Williams, 2016; Levine & Civitarese [eds.], 2016; Sandler, 2015.
3 Rose, *On Not Being Able to Sleep: Psychoanalysis and the Modern World*.
4 Jacobus, *The Poetics of Psychoanalysis: In the Wake of Klein*.
5 Connor, *Beckett, Modernism and the Material Imagination*.
6 Hinshelwood, *A Dictionary of Kleinian Thought*, 232.
7 Abel-Hirsch, *Bion: 365 Quotes*.

8 Bion, *Complete Works*, 9:142 (*The Italian Seminars*, 47).
9 This is sometimes referred to as 'containment'. I follow Mawson in avoiding this, due to the way it leads the term to be confused with Winnicott's concept of 'holding' (Bion, *Complete Works*, 4:250).
10 The spelling of phantasy references this unconscious dimension, and is differentiated from the conventional spelling, 'fantasy'.
11 Though see my further discussion of the term 'Bionian' in this chapter.
12 Bion, *Complete Works*, 6:326 (*Attention and Interpretation*, 124).
13 Freud, *Standard Edition*, vol. 12.
14 Bion, *Complete Works*, vol. 5 (*Taming Wild Thoughts*).
15 Phillips, *On Flirtation*, 136.
16 Bion, *Complete Works*, 10:136 (*Clinical Seminars and Other Works*, 321).
17 Drawn from Bion's own accounts, and from the essay by Francesca Bion, 'The Days of our Years' (Bion, *Complete Works*, 15:91–111).
18 Bion, *Complete Works*, 1:95 (*The Long Week-End 1897–1919: Part of a Life*, 81).
19 Bion, *Complete Works*, 15:102.
20 Grotstein, *A Beam of Intense Darkness: Wilfred Bion's Legacy to Psychoanalysis*, 286.
21 Bion, *Complete Works*, 11:39 (*Cogitations*, 33).
22 Poincaré, *Science and Method*; quoted in Bion, *Complete Works*, 4:339 (*Learning from Experience*, 72)
23 Bion, *Complete Works*, 6:205 (*Wilfred Bion: Los Angeles Seminars and Supervision*, 136).
24 Lacan, *Écrits: The First Complete Edition in English*.
25 Braudy and Cohen, *Film Theory and Criticism: Introductory Readings*.
26 Mahony, *Freud as a Writer (Expanded Edition)*.
27 McQuillan, *Deconstruction: A Reader*.
28 Royle, *The Uncanny*.
29 Rudnytsky, *Transitional Object and Potential Spaces: Literary Uses of D. W. Winnicott*.
30 Segal, 'Notes on Symbol Formation'.
31 Klein, *The Selected Melanie Klein*, 32.
32 Klein, 24.
33 Freud, *Standard Edition*, vol. 18.
34 Rose, *Why War? Psychoanalysis, Politics and the Return to Melanie Klein*.
35 Stonebridge, *The Destructive Element: British Psychoanalysis and Modernism*.
36 Jacobus, *The Poetics of Psychoanalysis: In the Wake of Klein*.
37 Connor, *Beckett, Modernism and the Material Imagination*.
38 Rose, *Why War?*, 139.
39 Bion, *Complete Works*, 6:112 (*Second Thoughts*, 65).
40 Rose, *On Not Being Able to Sleep: Psychoanalysis and the Modern World*, 93.
41 Rose, *On Not Being Able to Sleep*, 193.
42 Rose's essay, as it appeared both in *Critical Quarterly*, and later as a chapter in *On Not Being Able to Sleep*, includes two small errors in respect of Bion's name and the title of one his books – mistaking Bion's *Attention and Interpretation* for the critical theorist Frank Kermode's *Forms of Attention*; moreover, she suggests that the bizarre object should be understood as deriving from a 'particular form of attention' rather than from the psychotic failure of alpha-function.
43 Jacobus, *The Poetics of Psychoanalysis: In the Wake of Klein*, 201.
44 Miller, *Beckett and Bion: The (Im)Patient Voice in Psychotherapy and Literature*.
45 Bion, *Complete Works*, 6:138 (*Second Thoughts*, 93).
46 Connor, *Beckett, Modernism and the Material Imagination*, 55.
47 Bion, *Complete Works*, 8:296 (*Bion in New York and São Paulo*, 59–60).
48 Bion, *Complete Works*, 5:44 (*Elements of Psychoanalysis*, 48).
49 'The reply is the question's misfortune' (my translation). Blanchot, *L'entretien infini*; quoted in Bion, *Complete Works*, 9:33 (*The Tavistock Seminars*, 30).

50 Bion, *Complete Works*, 4:270 (*Learning from Experience*, 2).
51 For readers outside the UK, it is worth noting that the meaning of the term 'public school' is counterintuitive. A public school is not, in fact, a publicly-funded school (these are called state schools), but one of the country's most élite private schools.
52 Shakespeare, *Cymbeline* (Act 4, Scene 2); quoted in Bion, *Complete Works*, 14:11 (*A Memoir of the Future*, 436).
53 Bion, *Complete Works*, 7:28 (*Brazilian Lectures: 1973 São Paulo, 1974 Rio de Janeiro/São Paulo*, 23).
54 Torres and Hinshelwood, *Bion's Sources: The Shaping of His Paradigms*, xv.
55 Bion, *Complete Works*, 11:342 (*Cogitations*, 370).
56 Bion, *Complete Works*, 9:40 (*The Tavistock Seminars*, 37).
57 Grotstein, *Do I Dare Disturb the Universe? A Memorial to W.R. Bion*.
58 Vermote, *Reading Bion*.
59 Ambrósio Garcia, *Bion in Film Theory and Analysis: The Retreat in Film*.
60 Fuery, *Wilfred Bion, Thinking, and Emotional Experience with Moving Images: Being Embedded*.
61 See, for example, https://solihullapproachparenting.com/about-us/ [accessed December 2020], and Douglas, *Containment And Reciprocity: Integrating Psychoanalytic Theory and Child Development Research for Work with Children*.
62 de Haan, *Relational Coaching: Journeys Towards Mastering One to One Learning*.
63 Epstein, *Thoughts without a Thinker: Psychotherapy from a Buddhist Perspective*.
64 Meltzer, *The Kleinian Development*, 389.
65 Bion, *Complete Works*, 7:25 (*Brazilian Lectures: 1973 São Paulo, 1974 Rio de Janeiro/São Paulo*, 20).
66 Bion, *Complete Works*, 4:344 (*Learning from Experience*, 78).
67 Bion, *Complete Works*, 5:11 (*Elements of Psychoanalysis*, 6).
68 http://multiple-sclerosis-research.blogspot.com/2015/04/education-inflammatory-penumbra.html [accessed December 2020].
69 See, for instance, Bion, *Complete Works*, 6:284 (*Attention and Interpretation*, 74).
70 Bion Talamo, *Maps for Psychoanalytic Exploration*.
71 Bion Talamo, 7.
72 Bion Talamo, 100.
73 Meltzer, *The Kleinian Development*, 396. Another implicit model. Meltzer notes the letter that Bion wrote to him following his review of his work. He offered the model of 'the diamond cutter's method of cutting a stone so that a ray of light entering the stone is reflected back *by the same path* in such a way that the light is augmented'.
74 See my brief discussion of this in chapter ten.
75 See chapter three.
76 See my discussion of this in chapter nine.
77 Freud, *Standard Edition*, vol. 1.
78 Bion, *Complete Works*, 15:114.
79 Harris Williams, *Bion's Dream: A Reading of the Autobiographies*.

2 Freud's 'excessively intense idea': the *Project for a Scientific Psychology*

> In writing this I have to start somewhere and this produces difficulties because the start of a discussion tends to impose an appearance of reality on the idea that the matter discussed has a start.[1]

Where and how to *begin*? Edward Said tells us that 'the problem of beginnings is one of those problems that, if allowed to, will confront one with equal intensity on a practical and on a theoretical level'.[2] To begin to situate Bion within psychoanalytic literary criticism undoubtedly requires a reference to Freud and Freudian theory. Bion's daughter, Parthenope Bion Talamo, considered the question of how and to what extent Bion might be considered a strong reader of Freud:

> Rarely, or perhaps never, have I been asked whether Bion read Freud, since I suppose that it is taken for granted that he did; and yet the ways in which Freud's thinking permeated Bion's, and the degree to which it did so, are neither so obvious nor so automatic – there is not too much 'of course' about it.[3]

The psychoanalyst and writer Adam Phillips places Bion in comparison with Jacques Lacan: for him they are both 'bizarre' and 'inspired' psychoanalysts, and challenging in different measure. Like Lacan, Bion experimented with the use of mathematical (or algebraic) symbols, potentially alarming to the uninitiated, and professionally they shared a particular depth of experience in working with severely ill and psychotic patients. They also both stand in an interesting, oblique relationship to Freud: Lacan, famously, declared that his work performed an essential 'return to Freud'[4] in the face of American-led ego psychology. While Bion claimed no such project, it is to Freud, more frequently than Klein, that he directs his theoretical commentary, especially in relation to Freud's theory of dreams, his comments on the 'caesura' between intra-uterine life and early infancy, and, in *Learning from Experience*, Freud's short essay, 'Formulations on the Two Principles of Mental Functioning'.[5]

A re-reading of Freud's early essay, *Project for a Scientific Psychology*,[6] alongside Bion's *Learning from Experience*, unearths unexpected resonances between the very

DOI: 10.4324/9781003006619-2

early, pre-psychoanalytic Freud and aspects of Bion's theory. Additionally, a reading of the *Project* informed by Bion makes possible a fuller appreciation of Freud as a writer, by drawing attention to the *Project*'s purely *creative* aspect. I propose that the *Project* may be productively read as a piece of creative writing; that is, as a work that seeks to generate or express a new idea. While the *Project* benefits from a contextualised reading that locates it as a part of the pre-history of psychoanalysis, a sustained reading of the *Project for a Scientific Psychology* as creative writing demands that we pay closer attention to its quirks and contrivances. This chapter takes its title from the phrase, 'excessively intense idea', that appears in the *Project* on five occasions, at the beginning of the first and second parts. 'The emergence of the excessively intense idea,' Freud writes, 'brings with it consequences which, on the one hand, cannot be suppressed and, on the other hand, cannot be understood'.[7] Bion's theory of thinking offers new ways of approaching the *Project*, and I suggest that we can see the 'excessively intense idea' that drives Freud to write the *Project* as the 'thought without a thinker': that is, the wild or stray thought 'awaiting a sufficiently mature mind [...] to be thinkable, thoughts pressing for the development of an apparatus to think them'.[8]

Written over several months in 1895, the *Project for a Scientific Psychology* is Freud's attempt to 'furnish a psychology that shall be a natural science: that is, to represent psychical processes as quantitatively determinate states of specifiable material particles, thus making those processes perspicuous and free from contradiction'.[9] It is a wildly ambitious task, impossible within the confines of neurological knowledge in Freud's time. Although the text seems to draw heavily on neurological concepts, Freud's use of scientific ideas is suspect, tendentious. As Mark Solms and Michael Saling have made clear, the 'neurology' that Freud invokes in the *Project* bears only slight comparison to the contemporary research that Freud himself wrote about in some of his early neurological papers (which are not included in the *Standard Edition*), such as 'Gehirn' ('brain') and 'Aphasie' ('aphasia'). They suggest that Freud 'ignored almost completely the complex gross structure of the nervous system, the knowledge of which he demonstrates and communicates so skilfully in 'Gehirn''.[10] In the *Project*, Freud will invent several classes of specialised neurones and modes of interaction to explain reflex actions, cognition, and memory, resulting in a text that is bewildering in its convolution and complexity.

Not published in Freud's lifetime, the *Project for a Scientific Psychology* also stands as a pre- or proto-psychoanalytic curio that has nevertheless attracted influential readings by Jean Laplanche and Jacques Derrida. Its memorable single case study of Emma, a young woman traumatised retroactively (*nachträglich*) by a sexual assault in childhood that she only later understands, offers a complex account of the sexual determinants of hysteria. The two-stage model of trauma at the heart of this episode forms the basis for Jean Laplanche's later recuperation of a 'generalised' seduction theory,[11] in which the infant is the unwitting recipient of the adult's enigmatic 'signifier' (or message) that is only understood *après-coup*.[12] In his 1966 essay, 'Freud and the Scene of Writing', Derrida traces Freud's recourse to a metaphorics of writing at work in his conception of the psyche. He draws attention to two ostensibly marginal texts by Freud over the thirty-year period 1895–1925 demarcated by the *Project for a Scientific Psychology*, at one end, and the 'Note on the 'Mystic Writing-Pad'',[13] on the other, to uncover in Freud's texts 'the structure of the psychic apparatus [...] represented by a writing machine'.[14] Derrida's discussion centres on the translation of the curiously productive word *Bahnung* (translated in the *Standard Edition* as 'facilitation'), for which he proposes the word *frayage* in French, variously translated as 'breaching' or 'fraying'.[15] This reading will inform my own, different focus upon that same term to support a reading of the *Project* as a work *in transit*.

Freud's letters to Wilhelm Fliess, his close friend and correspondent, leave us in no doubt as to his own difficulties and frustrations in its composition. In a series of letters between April and November of 1895,[16] he veers between devotion and despair, alternately taking up and abandoning the work before eventually beginning to write the final version in late September. In April, he is 'positively devoured by it, till I am really overworked and have to break off. I have never experienced such a powerful preoccupation'.[17] A month later he describes devoting 'every free minute of the last few weeks' to writing, spending 'the night hours from eleven till two with imaginings, transpositions and guesses'; not stopping before he is 'truly and seriously overworked'. By mid-June, the project is *in embryo*: 'To make an announcement on this now would be like sending the six-months' foetus of a girl to a ball'; but the gestation that is progressing well in early August is then beset by difficulty:

> I have had a queer experience with my ΦΨω.[18] No sooner had I made my alarming announcement and called for your congratulations after climbing a secondary peak, than I met with fresh difficulties and found I had not enough breath left for the new task. So I quickly made up my mind, threw down the whole alphabet and persuaded myself that I took no interest in it whatever.[19]

A visit to Fliess in September proves reinvigorating, and on the 23rd he writes that his 'rested brain now makes child's play of the difficulties that were left over',[20] beginning to write again while 'still in the railway carriage' on his return journey. Yet by October he writes again of his continued frustration as he describes himself alternately 'proud and happy [...] ashamed and wretched', and beset by mental torment that the project 'does not fit together and perhaps never will'. A fortnight later, things are again looking up: 'Everything seemed to fit in together, the gears were in mesh, the thing gave one the impression that it was really a machine and would soon run of itself'. But November returns Freud to his earlier despair, such that he throws the writing into a drawer, declaring 'I can no longer understand the state of mind in which I hatched out the 'Psychology''. Left unfinished, the *Project* will, in fact, spend the next several decades confined to Freud's drawer prior to posthumous publication in 1950 (in German) and 1954 (in English translation).

Freud's correspondence with Fliess suggests that there are two aspects to his problem. What is beyond question is that Freud has an *idea* that he is struggling to express in writing, where writing is both the expression of the idea itself *and the machinery or apparatus* that would enable its expression. The idea that, as Stevie Smith's character, Pompey, will put it in the next chapter, 'works at [Freud] like a worm', is a thing both inside and outside Freud: it is a 'six months' foetal idea, gestating within Freud; it is a parasite or a canker (he is 'positively devoured by it'); it is something that nevertheless eludes him despite 'beckon[ing] to [him] from afar from time immemorial',[21] and which, in his view, he will finally fail to capture in writing.

Bion develops the idea of the 'thought without a thinker' from the time of his early paper, 'A Theory of Thinking', although the term does not appear in his published work until the late audio-essays of 1977 (published posthumously in *Taming Wild Thoughts*), *A Memoir of the Future*, and in his published lectures and seminars where the idea is referred to interchangeably as the 'stray' or 'wild' thought. In 'A Theory of Thinking' he describes two distinct components in the process of thinking and places the 'thought' ontologically prior to 'thinking':

> It is convenient to regard thinking as dependent on the successful outcome of two main mental developments. The first is the development of thoughts. They require an apparatus to cope with them. The second development, therefore, is of this apparatus that I shall provisionally call thinking. I repeat – thinking has to be called into existence to cope with thoughts.[22]

Something of Bion's thinking is echoed by Georges Perec, the French writer and leading member of the experimental writing group, the *OuLiPo*.[23] Perec, whose interests ranged widely between formal experiments in constrained writing, occasional essays, and novels, was also a devoted crossword setter. In his preface to a volume of his crosswords, he offers an analysis of the *cruciverbiste*'s art that resonates with Bion's theory of thinking to a remarkable degree. Perec identifies two discrete operations involved in compiling a crossword puzzle: 'The creation of a crossword is composed of two operations which are completely different, and, at the limit, perfectly independent of each other: the first is the construction of the grid, the second the writing of clues'.[24]

Perec is detailed and explicit in locating these two phases of work in quite different, even 'contradictory', states of mind. Constructing the grid is 'a fastidious, meticulous, maniacal task',[25] while making up clues can be carried out in any idle hour, while strolling, 'without thinking';[26] he can even imagine a crossword being created by two writers: one providing the grid; the other, the clues. In a similar vein, Bion writes: 'the thinking used in the development of thoughts differs from the thinking required to use the thoughts when developed'.[27] Perec goes on to identify the starting point for the new crossword as the *potence*, the combination of the first vertical and first horizontal words that stimulates the creation of the grid. Outside of this context, the word *potence* also means a post and brace (as in a scaffolding), the thing from which some other thing hangs (as in a gallows), but it also 'carries' the idea of potency and potential.[28] Freud's 'excessively intense idea' is, I suggest, the *potence* on which the *Project* hangs, a first conjunction of ideas (that which Bion called the 'definitory hypothesis', marked in column 1 of the Grid,[29] and which is placed, like the *potence*, in the top left-hand corner). It is the thought without a thinker, the wild or stray thought that requires the construction of some thinking apparatus enabling it to be apprehended and developed.

Bion describes the way that the writer must await the thought without a thinker with a combination of patience and guile. Paraphrasing Keats,[30] he imagines sitting in his armchair and thinking preparatively 'in case that strange creature should exist and should it swim into my ken'; he also evokes the distress of the thinker who must find 'some sort of network' in which to 'catch' his thoughts:

> I find myself in the state of mind with which I am distressingly familiar – the state of mind in which I can only say that I am abysmally, literally and metaphorically, ignorant. That is one reason why it is a matter of some urgency to me to be able to find some sort of network in which I can catch any thoughts that are available.[31]

Freud's evident torment in composing the *Project* goes some way, perhaps, to conciliate the modern reader faced with the task of making sense of his frequently specious neurology. Highly speculative concepts such as Q, abstractly denoting 'quantity' (of stimulus), beget related terms used unclearly or inconsistently ($Q\acute{\eta}$[32]); classes of neurones proliferate to meet Freud's changing requirements: permeable Φ– [phi] neurones are supplemented first by impermeable Ψ– [psi] neurones (that provide the physical basis of memory) located more deeply inside the organism. The perceptual neurones, ω [omega], make a relatively late appearance, *deus ex machina*, to account for consciousness and 'qualities'. Finally, 'secretory' or 'key' neurones, mentioned only briefly towards the end of part one of the *Project*, evoke the tantalising prospect of the influence of endogenous Q by mysterious internal secretions.

A striking aspect of the *Project for a Scientific Psychology* is the way that Freud uses neurology to build an argument that tends elsewhere. Many of the ideas that will become tenets of psychoanalysis are there *in embryo*, from the primary and secondary processes, drives, dreams, repression, and the role of sexuality in the formation of hysteria. Yet this is a text on the way to becoming a different kind of work that will not subsequently require a neurological scaffolding. Within five years, Freud will publish the *Interpretation of Dreams*; within ten, his *Three Essays on the Theory of Sexuality*. Freud assembles an impressive and distracting array of pseudo-neurological concepts not to defend but to construct a scientific account of psychology. The *Project* builds in complexity from two principal ideas:

> (1) What distinguishes activity from rest is to be regarded as Q, subject to the general laws of motion. (2) The neurones are to be taken as the material particles.[33]

With these two planks in place, Freud takes a surprising number of steps forward. I suggest that he builds the apparatus of his argument 'on the fly', in a manner similar to 'booting' (from 'bootstrapping'[34]) into a computer pro-gramme. Bootstrapping describes the self-starting process that proceeds through a series of steps that install instructions of increasing complexity to a point where the overall programme can run independently. It offers a tech-nique or a response, if not a complete answer, to the question of how to begin. Even the first lines of the text suggest a progressive initialisation from a strikingly telegraphic style (requiring substantial work on the part of the translator to render the first paragraph in readable English) that gradually opens out into full and connected sentences. Freud's translator into English, James Strachey, noted that his chief difficulty in translating the text was Freud's striking use of abbreviation, most notably in the *Project's* opening lines: 'de-finite and indefinite articles omitted, sentences without any principal verb. Here, for instance, is a literal translation of the first sentence of the work: 'Intention to furnish natural-scientific psych., i.e. to represent psych. processes as quantit. determinate states of specifiable material particles, thus to make perspicuous and free from contradiction".[35]

Bion has written that 'the start of a discussion tends to impose an appearance of reality on the idea that the matter discussed has a start', a concern that is perhaps most evident in the opening pages of *Learning from Experience*, which begins (and continues) in a telegraphed, halting style in which he also writes: 'I have experience to record, but how to communicate this experience to others I am in doubt; this book explains why'.[36] Where Bion has 'experience' to record (and learn from), Freud has as yet only the intuition that the anxiety neuroses are in some way traceable to the question of sexual functioning, as he describes in his correspondence with Fliess as early as 1892.[37]

Freud's letters to Fliess provide a richly suggestive account of the process of writing that resonates in parallel with the themes of the *Project* itself. A text *about* mechanism (the various mechanisms of psychological processes in re-sponse to Q), and its success or failure, is described *in terms of* a mechanism that Freud hopes will 'run of itself' and which will facilitate or impede the flow of the explanatory demands placed upon it. An associative nexus of words and ideas speaks to a concern both for mechanism and flow, coalescing in the word 'facilitation' (*Bahnung* in the original).

A few remarks of exposition are unavoidable before we continue, because Freud's pseudo-neurology quickly becomes difficult to follow. Two classes of neurones initially emerge from Freud's first and second principal theorems to account for a neuronal system that receives and gives off Q (that is, quantities of external stimulus). Beyond an initial trend in the neurones to 'divest themselves of Q' (immediate and complete discharge of external stimulus in the form of reflex action), there arise 'endogenous stimuli' from within the organism itself, giving rise to 'the major needs: hunger, respiration, sexuality'[38] (the antecedents here of Freud's drive theory), requiring purposive action and a store of energy available to meet the 'exigencies of life'. Needing to account for the structure of 'cathected' neurones pre-loaded with endogenous Q (or Qή), Freud hypothesises the existence of contact-barriers around each neurone, offering varying resistance to the passage of external Q.

His neurone theory must now account for the 'main characteristic of nervous tissue [...] that is, quite generally, a capacity for being permanently altered by single occurrences',[39] or what we might also call a simple kind of 'memory' (or learning). At the same time, the organism must retain its ability to receive new stimuli. 'It would seem, therefore,' he writes, 'that neurones must be both influenced and also unaltered, unprejudiced [to further external stimulus]. We cannot off-hand imagine an apparatus capable of such complicated functioning'.[40] He accordingly *invents* a distinction between Φ-neurones, which are and remain permanently permeable to new sensation, and Ψ-neurones, which come 'loaded with resistance' and are thus in effect impermeable to Q, but which can be 'permanently altered by the passage of an excitation' in the direction of greater permeability and similarity with the Φ-neurones from which they are originally distinguished.

Freud's conception of contact-barriers evokes a neuronal reticulum comprised of barriers of varying resistance, relative to their surrounding neurones. The passage of Q from the Φ-neurones meets resistance from the contact-barriers that may nevertheless yield to quantities of stimulus that surmount their particular resistance. The modified pathway that this leaves behind he calls 'facilitations', i.e. the facility with which communication between two neurones is now possible, based on previous experience. These facilitations, Freud argues, are the physical basis of memory, and this idea in turn inaugurates and underwrites the entire panoply of psychical processes, such as thinking, attention, and dreaming.

As Derrida has also noted, the figurative value of Freud's conception of facilitations for his overall theory cannot be too highly stressed. The metaphorical and associative force of the German word, *Bahnung*, cognate of the better known word, *Bahn*, derives from the related meanings of a path or track, and more particularly a railway (*Bahn* or *Eisenbahn*[41]). With this in mind, Freud's letter to Fliess of the 23rd September returns to view. It has been noted previously[42] that the tone of Freud's correspondence with Fliess strikes the reader as surprisingly passionate: 'I write so little to you', he begins, 'only because I am writing so much *for* you'[43] (emphasis mine). The first draft of the *Project* is moreover begun '*in Eisenbahnwagen*' (in the railway carriage) as he returns to Vienna following a stay with the Fliess family. It is fitting that a piece of writing that is itself *en route* from one set of ideas (neurology) to another (psychoanalysis) is itself begun in a railway carriage. Freud's 'train of thought' is developed on a train (*Eisenbahnwagen*) that both enacts the distance between Freud and Fliess, and evokes the communicating pathways between neurones (*Bahnungen*) that effect a passage between physiological and psychical processes.

Derrida's analysis of the *Project* reads Freud anew in order to throw light on his implicit metapsychology. In translating the word *Bahnung* with the French word *frayage*, Derrida maintains the sense of a path or a track (*Bahn*) via the

French phrase '*se frayer un chemin*' (to forge a path), but develops the word in the direction of the violence or force implied in the idea of 'pathbreaking' to account for the effect of (the passage of) Q on the resistant-but-permeable Ψ-neurones. 'Fraying, the tracing of a trail, opens up a conducting path. Which presupposes a certain violence and a certain resistance to the effraction. The path is broken, cracked, fracta, frayed'.[44] Derrida draws attention to the way that Freud introduces a definition of memory only for it to be immediately replaced with a further, subtly different definition that in fact changes the ontological ground of his argument entirely. Freud writes:

> We can then say: Memory is represented *by the facilitations* existing between the Ψ-neurones. [...]

> We can therefore say still more correctly that memory is represented *by the differences in the facilitations* between the Ψ-neurones.[45]

The difference in definitions presented by Freud as a merely incremental elaboration belies a seismic shift that undoes the metaphysics of presence assumed by the first definition. Allowing that the memory installed by facilitations is only operative under a system of differences *between* facilitations renders inoperative the notion of an original inscriptive force of Q and calls into radical question the possibility of a 'first time' (Derrida makes ironical reference elsewhere in his essay to the 'virginity of the receiving substance'). Yet the words that Freud uses around the term *Bahnung* do not necessarily support the violence or effraction implied by the ideas of 'fraying' or 'breaching'. For example, Freud describes facilitations in the same section in terms of an 'absorption' (Ger.: *Absorption*) of Qή by the contact-barriers, and as the 'partial and locally determined lifting' (Ger.: *Aufhebung*) of resistance (to Q). Neither of these terms implies the violence suggested by Derrida's reading. What is also under-emphasised in Derrida's account, I suggest, is the notion of quantities (and ideas) *in transit*.

For Bion, the idea of a thought 'on the way' is an important one. Thoughts without thinkers arrive unbidden on the metaphorical doorstep, like stray animals,[46] seeking a mind or a culture in which they may lodge, if only temporarily. Though he generally uses the idea of transference in its classical definition, there are moments where he seems to expand the concept to indicate a staging-post of the thought *as it travels* through mind, or minds:

> [Transference] is an idea that you have 'on the way' – you transfer it to me as a temporary measure on your way to what you really think or feel. At the same moment the new idea that you have is a temporary one and will be discarded sooner or later. It is another one of those places where you stop on your own particular journey.[47]

Edward Said, in *Beginnings*, cites the psychologist Jean Piaget, who suggests that 'the genesis [of a structure] is never more than a transition from one structure to another, but also a formative transition [*passage formateur*] that leads [*qui conduit*] from a weaker to a stronger [*de plus faible au plus fort*] structure, structure is never more than a system of transformations whose roots remain operative'.[48] The *passage formateur* in the *Project* leads from neurological ideas (the neurone and Q/Qἠ) to the point where the *Project* can be discontinued in favour of a wholly new science, psychoanalysis, stripped entirely of its neurological scaffolding.

The idea of the scaffold appears in *Transformations* in a discussion of the argument between Bishop Berkeley and Isaac Newton. Berkeley satirised Isaac Newton's evocation of mysterious, non-empirical entities called 'fluxions' to provide the logical underpinnings of his theory of calculus. He wrote that Newton

> used fluxions, like the scaffold of a building, as things to be laid aside or got rid of as soon as finite lines were found proportional to them. But then these finite exponents are found by the help of fluxions. Whatever therefore is got by such exponents and proportions is to be ascribed to fluxions: which must therefore be previously understood. And what are these fluxions? […] They are neither finite quantities, nor quantities infinitely small, nor yet nothing. May we not call them the ghosts of departed quantities?[49]

Like Newton, Freud develops an array of hypothetical entities – his Φ-, Ψ- and ω-neurones – which must each be 'previously understood' in order for him to advance his argument. Freud is by no means unaware of the 'unfortunate tinge of arbitrariness' that seems to surround each new step in his reasoning, though he presses on at each moment of difficulty 'follow[ing] a Darwinian line of thought' that provides a functional, teleological warrant to continue at each stage.

Freud's discussion of facilitations and contact-barriers in the *Project* suggests that his theoretical constructions are of a piece with his compositional difficulties. Having noted that 'Every Ψ-neurone must in general be presumed to have several paths of connection with other neurones – that is, several contact-barriers',[50] he pauses to consider that anyone 'engaged scientifically in the construction of hypotheses will only begin to take his theories seriously if they can be fitted into our knowledge from more than one direction', unconsciously evoking an analogous relationship between his Ψ-neurones and his hypotheses. Seeking to avoid the 'arbitrariness of a *constructio ad hoc*', he then proceeds to shore up his theory of two classes of neurones with an ingenious circular argument to the effect that he has not invented his two classes of neurones so much as 'found them already in existence', in the form of an earlier hypothesis (concerning external and endogenous sources of stimuli) which was itself the original basis of his distinction of Φ- and Ψ-neurones.

Freud further suggests that the Ψ system might be structured as a 'sympathetic ganglion' that bridges internal and external sources of stimulus. The psychoanalyst and neuropsychologist Mark Solms has described this as a system designed to 'associatively link endogenous needs (expressed as drives) with the external objects that satisfied them'[51] expressed by 'the formula 'I feel like this about that''.[52] In so doing, Freud invokes a secondary, internal interface between external and internal sources of stimuli modelled on the original distinction that has carried his discussion to this point, in effect placing *en abyme* the structure of his argument thus far.

Freud's sympathetic ganglion is one of a number of points in the *Project for a Scientific Psychology* where a carefully developed argument builds to the emergence of a new idea that renders some of the preceding points redundant. By locating the interface between external and endogenous stimuli deep within the heart of the Ψ-neurone (recast as a sympathetic ganglion), Freud begins to move further away from a neurological account towards the psychology that is his stated objective. The planks of his neurological scaffolding remain in place, however, and serve as a platform for further development.

The sympathetic ganglion and the ψ-neurone can be seen as distant forebears of alpha-function, which first appears in *Learning from Experience* as a placeholder term 'intentionally devoid of meaning' during Bion's discussion of the activities that enable the subject to process experience. By the time of *Elements of Psychoanalysis*, Bion has arrived at a working definition of alpha-function as 'that function by which sense impressions are transformed into elements capable of storage for use in dream and other thoughts'.[53] Like Freud, Bion is wrestling with the difficulty of beginning to write about something that is only really 'thought' in the act of writing itself; in both cases, their enquiries proceed through the creation of one or more 'imaginary facts', as Bion writes in *The Italian Seminars*: 'I shall start by having a speculative imagination, something that is not a fact, an imaginary fact'.[54] The *Project* contains a great number of imaginary facts that nevertheless provide important ways for Freud to begin to talk about the elements required for a scientific psychology – memory, learning, attention, thought, and dream – and a number of passages anticipate an object-relations model and coincide with Bionian ideas to a remarkable degree.[55]

'A main characteristic of nervous tissue,' Freud writes, 'is memory: that is, quite generally, a capacity for being permanently altered by single occurrences'; learning 'on the basis of memory' comes very close to Bion's theorisation of 'learning from experience' in recognising the need to account for the cumulative and progressive structuration of 'mind' (to be understood ambiguously in terms of both a physical and psychic reality) that does something *with* experience other than the primary process (or 'primary nervous system'[56]) reflex of discharge. Freud's description here of an iterative process of conduction and differentiation also seems to anticipate alpha-function, which is not innate, but learned and internalised from early and ongoing encounters with another mind.

For Bion, the mother's capacity to receive and respond empathetically to infantile distress, and her ability to convey a helpful, alternative reality to the child – a state of mind he terms *reverie* – leads to the establishment of the child's own mind and ability to contain and process his own experience. In a suggestive passage, the *Project* seems to anticipate object relations theory as well as the communicative aspect of projective identification. Motor discharge of tension cannot, in itself, adequately achieve the 'unburdening' of endogenous stimuli that keep coming from the inside of the organism, just as the infant is at first unable to generate either the change in its external environment (for example, procuring food) or a change in his or her frame of mind (feeling reassured and less fearful), that would bring about a cessation of the internal feelings of discomfort. Rather, Freud suggests, it requires '*extraneous help*, when the attention of an experienced person is drawn to the child's state by discharge along the path of internal change. In this way this path of discharge acquires a secondary function of the highest importance, that of *communication*'.[57] The result of this external help, aside from the discharge of endogenous Q and the satisfaction of the need, is that 'a facilitation is then formed' that serves to teach the system to know what to do in case the need should arise again. In Freud's own words, it is the '*the process of conduction itself*' – that is to say, the experience of thought – 'that creates differentiation of neural pathways and consequently an improved conductive capacity for subsequent conduction'.[58] This account of learning seems to approximate that which in Bion's model of thinking is the development of the mind through the 'mother's alpha-function'.[59] The point is made succinctly by Freud: 'it is in relation to a fellow human-being that a human-being learns to cognise'.[60]

Bion, like Freud, also locates thinking as a response to the *discrepancy* between the conditions served up by external reality and the internal investment (translated by Strachey as 'cathexis') in an idea related to need and desire. 'I shall limit the term 'thought'', Bion writes in 'A Theory of Thinking', 'to the mating of a preconception with a frustration'.[61] Consider now Freud, who speaks of a Ψ process of 'judging [...] evoked by the dissimilarity between the wishful cathexis of a memory and a perceptual cathexis [...]. Their non-coincidence gives the impetus for the activity of thought, which is terminated once more with their coincidence'.[62] Although the terminology is different, I suggest that both Bion and Freud conceive of a similar process.

There are further points at which Freud's conjectures seem to anticipate both Bion and Klein. Freud's contention that 'what we call *things* are residues which evade being judged'[63] evokes Bion's description of beta-elements to a remarkable degree, even to the extent of intimating that they result from the evasion (or failure) of psychical processing (alpha-function, in Bion's terminology), a point implicit in Bion's nomenclature (beta-elements are genetically more primitive than alpha-elements, and yet they are called *beta*, logically coming after alpha-elements, having failed to be transformed by alpha-function[64]). Bion, too, conceives of beta-elements as somehow more concrete and 'thing-like' in quality, as well as less 'ephemeral' than thoughts.[65] Freud's evocation of 'secretory' (or 'key') neurones, mentioned in passing in the *Project*, also seems to anticipate his later formulation of a death drive, specifically in its more Kleinian conception (understood as a primary and inherent destructiveness witnessed by anxiety and unpleasure). These secretory neurones, he suggests, do not discharge Qή into the muscles (via motor activity), but rather stimulate the system unpleasantly from within. 'Unpleasure,' he writes, 'is *released* from the interior of the body and freshly conveyed up',[66] creating an inexhaustible supply and circulation of aggravating Qή within the body that presses continually for discharge.

The *Project* closes with a section that dwells, with a certain irony, on the problem of 'error' in the process of thought. Freud is not unaware that his own line of reasoning, using a single neurone as the basis for a description of the entire complex of a thought-process, may itself introduce error into the basis of his argument: 'This defect in thought originates from the endeavour, *which, indeed, we are copying here,* to substitute a single neurone for the complex – which is necessitated precisely by the immense complexity. *These are mistakes in judgement or faults in the premises*'.[67] In an intriguing and seemingly performative aposiopesis, he abruptly breaks off his discussion following a discussion of the emergence of thoughts into consciousness: 'Nevertheless, [thoughts] usually emerge [into consciousness] (1) if the smooth passage [of quantity] has reached an end or has come up against an obstacle, and (2) if it has aroused an idea which, for other reasons, calls up indications of quality – that is, consciousness. At this point the discussion may be broken off'.[68]

Freud outlines a number of different kinds of thinking, including practical thinking, 'cognitive' thinking, and judgement. Practical thinking, the original basis for all types of thinking, is that which tends towards the discharge of Q and modification of the external world in order to meet the 'exigencies of life'. By contrast, cognitive thinking is of a more theoretical or contemplative kind, less related to the immediate need to do something about the quantities of stimulus exerted on a system. One of the advantages of cognitive thought, for Freud, is that it enables thinking to be done ahead of time, before a practical need arises: 'If the thought-process lasts too long, its product will have become useless in the meantime. For that reason we *'think ahead'*'.[69] In its way, the *Project* does just that: it is an example of a prior thinking that, in this case, precedes the entire body of psychoanalysis, but which nevertheless stands Freud in good stead for the more narrowly 'psychical turn' that his ideas will take. It is reminiscent of Georg Lichtenberg's insight that 'what we have to discover for ourselves leaves behind in our mind a pathway that can also be used on another occasion'.[70] The pre-thinking that has been done by 1895 sets 'in train' the whole panoply of psychoanalytic ideas that will find expression in *The Interpretation of Dreams*, the *Three Essays*, and even *Beyond the Pleasure Principle*; and establishes a pathway that nevertheless moves the initial thought on from one place to another: 'What was originally a laboriously established thought-connection afterwards becomes, owing to simultaneous full cathexis, a powerful facilitation. The only question about it is whether it is always effected along the pathway that was first discovered or whether a more direct connection may be followed'.[71]

By the end of the *Project for a Scientific Psychology*, Q and thoughts (not the *thinking* of the thought but the thought itself: the 'thought without a thinker') have become virtually interchangeable: Q is described as '*in flow*';[72] and thoughts leave behind a 'thought-facilitation' as the outcome of the passage of Q and Qή through the neuronal system. In conclusion, I argue that the 'excessively intense idea' that animates the *Project for a Scientific Psychology* may be productively considered as a 'thought without a thinker', seeking the apparatus that will enable it to be thought. This creative 'project' is echoed internally within the text through the figures of Q and Qή, the two varieties of stimulus from external and internal sources. Together, they come close to representing that which Bion will term O[73]: namely, the ultimate reality – or stimulus, to use Freud's language – to which we are subject, and which cannot be apprehended (as with Q/Qή) except in small quantities (large irruptions of Q are synonymous, for Freud, with pain[74]) and through alpha-function or the sympathetic ganglion. In *A Beam of Intense Darkness*, James Grotstein has described thoughts without a thinker as 'unthought thoughts [that] emerge from the two arms of O (inherent pre-conceptions and sensory data of emotional significance)',[75] which might be otherwise described as endogenous and exogenous stimuli. Examined as a *creative* piece of writing that aims to bring Freud's embryonic idea to term, the *Project for a Scientific Psychology* can be seen to enact in its writing the creative process itself.

Notes

1 Bion, *Complete Works*, 5:14 (*Elements of Psychoanalysis*, 3).
2 Said, *Beginnings: Intention and Method*, 3.
3 Bion Talamo, 'Bion: A Freudian Innovator'.
4 Lacan, *Écrits: The First Complete Edition in English*.
5 Bion, *Complete Works*, 4:272–73 (*Learning from Experience*, 4–5).
6 Freud, *Standard Edition*, 1:281–397. Subsequent references to the *Project for a Scientific Psychology* (noted as *Project*) are to this edition.
7 *Project*, 347.
8 Civitarese, *The Violence of Emotions: Bion and Post-Bionian Psychoanalysis*, 14.
9 *Project*, 295.
10 Solms and Saling, *A Moment of Transition: Two Neuroscientific Articles by Sigmund Freud*, xii.
11 Laplanche, *New Foundations for Psychoanalysis*.
12 Freud's word 'nachträglich' has been translated as 'après-coup' by Laplanche. In English it has been rendered variously as 'deferred action' or 'afterwardsness'. See, for example, discussion by Rosine Perelberg in *Time, Space and Phantasy*, 2008, 2n1.
13 Freud, *Standard Edition*, vol. 19.
14 Derrida, 'Freud and the Scene of Writing', 75.
15 For a discussion of the different and disputed translations of *Bahnung*, see, for instance: Cassin, *Dictionary of Untranslatables: A Philosophical Lexicon*, 610–11.
16 The following quotations from Freud's letters to Fliess all taken from Freud, *Standard Edition*, vol. 1.
17 *Project*, 283.
18 Denoting the three neuronal classes phi-psi-omega, characterised by permeability, impermeability and (registering) perception, respectively.
19 *Project*, 284.

20 *Project*, 285.
21 *Project*, 283.
22 Bion, *Complete Works*, 6:154 (*Second Thoughts*, 110).
23 The *Ouvroir de Littérature Potentielle*, or 'workshop for potential literature'.
24 Perec, *Les Mots Croisés*, 11. My translation: 'La fabrication d'un mot croisé se compose de deux operations tout à fait differentes et, à la limite, parfaitement indépendantes l'une de l'autre: la première est la construction de la grille, la seconde la récherche des definitions'.
25 Perec, 11. My translation: 'une tâche fastidieuse, minutieuse, maniaque'.
26 Perec, 13. My translation: 'sans y penser'.
27 Bion, *Complete Works*, 5:34 (*Elements of Psychoanalysis*, 35).
28 http://www.larousse.fr/dictionnaires/francais/potence/62991?q=potence#62280 [accessed December 2020].
29 See Figure 1.
30 John Keats' poem, 'On First Looking into Chapman's Homer', includes the lines:
    Then felt I like some watcher of the skies
    When a new planet swims into his ken
31 Bion, *Complete Works*, 10:177 (*Taming Wild Thoughts*, 29).
32 Described by James Strachey in his introduction to the *Project* as Q's 'mysterious companion [...]. Both [Q and Qή] undoubtedly stand for 'quantity'. But why this difference between them? [...] There is no question that the difference is a real one, though Freud nowhere explicitly announces it or explains it' (*Project*: 289).
33 *Project*, 295.
34 The idea of bootstrapping is taken from climbing: pulling oneself up 'by one's boot-straps' describes the process of using one's bootlaces to establish a foothold.
35 *Project*, 287.
36 Bion, *Complete Works*, 4:263 (*Learning from Experience*, Intro 3).
37 *Project*, 177.
38 *Project*, 297.
39 *Project*, 287.
40 *Project*, 299.
41 A German etymological dictionary suggests that the connotation of 'railway' emerges from around 1840: http://www.dwds.de/?view=1&qu=bahnen [accessed December 2020].
42 For example, in Shirley Nelson Garner's essay in Hunter, *Seduction and Theory: Readings of Gender, Representation, and Rhetoric*.
43 My translation of the original: 'Ich schreibe so wenig an Dich, nur weil ich soviel für Dich schreibe'. Freud, *Aus Den Anfängen Der Psychoanalyse, Briefe an Wilhelm Fließ, Abhandlungen Und Notizen Aus Den Jahren 1887-1902*. Indeed, Fliess' role in the composition of the *Project* cannot be overlooked, suggesting, as it does, an exemplary instance of the container-contained relationship described by Bion and explored in detail in the chapter about B.S. Johnson.
44 Derrida, 'Freud and the Scene of Writing', 77.
45 *Project*, 300. Italics mine.
46 Bion, *Complete Works*, 10:175 (*Taming Wild Thoughts*, 27).
47 Bion, *Complete Works*, 9:126 (*The Italian Seminars*, 28).
48 Said, *Beginnings: Intention and Method*, 192.
49 Berkeley, *The Analyst*; quoted in Bion, *Complete Works*, 5:267 (*Transformations*, 157).
50 *Project*: 301.
51 Solms, *The Feeling Brain: Selected Papers on Neuropsychoanalysis*, 149.
52 Solms, 169.
53 Bion, *Complete Works*, 5:9 (*Elements of Psychoanalysis*, 4).
54 Bion, *Complete Works*, 9:142 (*The Italian Seminars*, 47).
55 A point made briefly by Chris Mawson (Bion, *Complete Works*. 4:256).
56 *Project*, 296.

57 *Project*, 318.
58 *Project*: 298–9. Italics mine.
59 Bion, *Complete Works*, 4:303 (*Learning from Experience*, 36).
60 *Project*, 331.
61 Bion, *Complete Works*, 6:154 (*Second Thoughts*, 111).
62 *Project*, 328.
63 *Project*, 334.
64 See discussion on this point by Grotstein, 2007, 62, and in this volume, chapter five.
65 Bion, *Complete Works*, 10:177 (*Taming Wild Thoughts*, 29).
66 *Project*, 320.
67 *Project*, 384. First italics mine.
68 *Project*, 375–6.
69 *Project*, 383.
70 Lichtenberg, *The Waste Books*, 37.
71 *Project*, 385.
72 *Project*, 375.
73 Bion's term O will be discussed in greater detail in chapters five and eight. Briefly, it is Bion's shorthand for 'ultimate reality' or the noumenon, following Kant.
74 *Project*, 307.
75 Grotstein, *A Beam of Intense Darkness: Wilfred Bion's Legacy to Psychoanalysis*, 73–74.

3 Pompey's thought-worm: Stevie Smith's *Novel on Yellow Paper*

If a thought without a thinker comes along, it may be what is a 'stray thought', or it could be a thought with the owner's name and address upon it, or it could be a 'wild thought'. The problem, should such a thought come along, is what to do with it.[1]

Stevie Smith may be best known for her poetry, but she also published three novels. The first of these, *Novel on Yellow Paper*, came out in 1936, after a publisher told her that he would consider printing her poetry, but only if she first wrote a novel. *Novel on Yellow Paper* is a first-person narration by Pompey Casmilus, a young woman who works as a private secretary. Near the beginning, she writes:

The thought that comes to me now, that I am riding this horse, that puts his ears back and dances across the shadows, and glances with hatred and panic at the white gate posts, is the thought of all that I wish to say in this book, is the thought that works at me like a worm, like an intestinal worm that pulls and drags its alexandrine length along those five hundred yards of trouble.[2]

In what follows I would like to develop the narrator's suggestion that the book is the result of a *thought*, and more specifically to consider Pompey's striking characterisation of the thought as something that 'works at [her] like a worm', an 'intestinal worm' that models thought both as a parasite and as that which creates or holds open the space of the intestine. The figure of the intestinal worm is remarkably resonant with Bion's suggestive analogy between thinking and digestion. In *Learning from Experience*, he describes beta-elements as 'undigested facts', contrasting them with alpha-elements that 'have been digested by alpha-function and thus made available for thought'.[3] It also recalls Bion's statement that 'thinking is a development forced on the psyche by the pressure of thoughts – not the other way round'.[4] I suggest that the intestinal worm is the thought without a thinker, structured as a parasite that is both inside and outside the mind. The book's ostensibly antisemitic themes are also reconsidered via the trope of parasitism. The figure of the parasite additionally

DOI: 10.4324/9781003006619-3

informs a reading of the book's subtitle and Pompey's ironic refrain, 'Work it out for yourself', and the suicidal intention that it seems to suggest. As Pompey chides her readers for their mindlessness, she also calls on the mind of the reader to supply the alpha-function that she was herself denied through the early death of her mother.

I also attempt a Bionian analysis of Stevie Smith's complex and characteristic handling of tone. Extending Bion's use of the Grid for the analysis of literature, I suggest that both Stevie Smith and Bion exemplify the use of 'column 2 formulations' that resist the emergence of catastrophic change. While Bion considered the Grid 'a feeble attempt to produce an instrument',[5] finally unsatisfactory for his use as a clinician, his use of it in *Transformations* (to comment on Bishop Berkeley's comments to Isaac Newton) achieves a surprisingly sensitive textual analysis that confounds the apparent austerity of his approach.

Early in the narrative, Pompey issues a warning to her readers: 'This is a foot-off-the-ground novel that came by the left hand'.[6] While the image has, perhaps, a sexual connotation, which Pompey does not deny – 'But oh how I have enjoyed sex I do enjoy myself so much I cannot pass it over'[7] – it also characterises Pompey's 'waggishness', her frivolous and apparently unserious approach to life. Her beaus reiterate the point: she is *ungründlich* (from German: 'not thorough'), according to Karl;[8] for Freddy, she is *indécise* (from French: 'irresolute, indecisive').[9] It is also a description of her writing style, which comes to Pompey, as indeed it came to Stevie Smith, in a continuous stream-of-consciousness monologue.[10] The correspondences between the character of Pompey Casmilus and Stevie Smith are abundant, and thinly veiled: like Pompey, Stevie Smith worked as a secretary while writing poetry, lived in suburbia with a beloved aunt, lost her mother to an early death and her father to his *Wanderlust*; and both Stevie Smith and Pompey claim ownership of the text (*Novel on Yellow Paper* is both Stevie Smith's and Pompey's novel). The manuscript of *Novel on Yellow Paper* was, in fact, typed on yellow paper (according to Spalding, the title was originally a placeholder name after Smith's original suggestion, 'Pompey Casmilus', was turned down[11]). Several features of the text draw the reader's attention to the book's metafictional qualities, including the question of writing under a pseudonym. The opening lines of the novel replace the traditional invocation of the muse with an address to Casmilus, revealing that Pompey's surname is itself a *nom de plume*:

> Casmilus, whose great name I steal,
>
> Whose name a greater doth conceal[12]

The 'greater name' of Casmilus is Hermes, the Greek god of boundaries and border crossings, able to travel to and from the underworld. Pompey's name is at some remove from her birth name, Patience, just as 'Stevie' was for the writer christened Florence Margaret (significantly, it is with the image of a tigress called *Flo* that the novel will close). In an amusing twist, some critics assumed that Stevie Smith was a pseudonym of Virginia Woolf. One reviewer even went so far as to write to Woolf personally to tell her: 'You are Stevie Smith. No doubt of it. And *Yellow Paper* is far and away your best book'.[13]

Pompey, who works for Sir Phoebus Ullswater, uses her writing to mitigate the 'orgy of boredom to which [her] soul is committed',[14] writing on yellow paper in order to avoid sending the pages of her novel to her employer's clients by accident. Like Kismet, the easily distractible horse from Cornwall with whose image the novel opens, that 'dances across the shadows, and glances with hatred and panic', Pompey's distinctive voice glances over the whirlwind of her social life and friendships, introducing characters who are dropped moments later, promising confidences that never materialise. For the reader unaccustomed to her foot-off-the-ground style, Pompey warns, there is nothing to do except abandon the book from the outset.[15] The book, she says, is 'the talking voice that runs on', a collection of her thoughts that 'come and go and sometimes they do not quite come and I do not pursue them to embarrass them with formality to pursue them into a harsh captivity'.[16] Pompey agrees (as did Stevie Smith) to punctuate the book for ease of reading, though she finds it 'very extremely difficult'.[17]

Characterising her thoughts as wild animals that should not be pursued 'into a harsh captivity' brings her into a remarkable resonance with Bion's description of the 'thought without a thinker'. In *Taming Wild Thoughts*, the 'wild' or 'stray' thought puts one in mind, perhaps, of a cat, more or less suitable for domestication:

> If a thought without a thinker comes along, it may be what is a 'stray thought', or it could be a thought with the owner's name and address upon it, or it could be a 'wild thought'. The problem, should such a thought come along, is what to do with it. Of course, if it is wild, you might try to domesticate it.[18]

The thought of all that Pompey wishes to say in this book is a rather different animal: not a cat, but a worm, in parasitic relationship to its intestinal host. As others (e.g. Najarian[19] and Stevenson[20]) have noted, much in Stevie Smith's work turns out to be densely allusive to the canon. In this instance, it is Alexander Pope who provides the doubly ironic intertext from his 1711 *Essay on Criticism*: 'A needless alexandrine ends the song/ That like a wounded snake, drags its slow length along'.[21] Pope's implication is that the alexandrine – twelve-syllable poetic meter – is a ponderous form favoured by the pretentious writer: a 'wounded snake' for Pope (a veiled suggestion, perhaps, of failed potency), an intestinal worm for Smith, and a Franco-Anglo poetic *worm*[22] that supplements what is comic in Pope's snake through the bathetic figure of the worm. Less deadly, the worm is nevertheless capable of working at Pompey from the inside, 'pulling and dragging' its way through her intestine: the body of the worm the intestine's uncanny mimesis, the parasite vouchsafing its host. Like a worm, perhaps, Stevie Smith's original draft of

Novel on Yellow Paper was a singular and linear text that was, according to her biographer, begun by her 'writing six thousand words in one night' and completing the rest within ten weeks.[23] The segmentation of the worm – in the form of extensive punctuation absent in the initial draft – came later, at her publisher's insistence. The alexandrine is also the form used by Racine in *Phèdre*, which becomes an important reference in Pompey's developing theme of the nobly chosen suicide.

But it is the figure of the worm as a *thought*, as that from which the entirety of the novel springs, that is especially striking, and resonant with Bion's idea of the 'thought without a thinker'. For Bion, the determination of thinking is 'simplified if 'thoughts' are regarded as epistemologically prior to thinking and that thinking has to be developed as a method or apparatus for dealing with 'thoughts''. He describes the way that the thought – that psychical entity that steps in where some anticipated *thing* has proved not to be – places a pressure on the personality to develop a mind: 'an apparatus has to be produced to make it possible to think the already existing thought'.[24] Bion is acutely attentive to the role that models play both in his own work and in the minds of his patients. Attention to the implicit model enables the analyst to answer the question: what does a given individual *do* (or purport to do, in omnipotent phantasy) with their thoughts? He goes on: ''Thinking' can be regarded as the name given to a model or abstraction derived from a realisation; with an actual patient the problem is to determine what he represents by the term thinking'.

Pompey's image of the thought-worm proposes one such answer (and moreover explicitly relates thinking to writing). The thought or thoughts that are constitutive of *Novel on Yellow Paper* are figured paradoxically as something originating both from within and without: the alien parasite is nevertheless deeply internally installed. The worm is also an intestinal double that both mimics and defines the shape of the intestine. Without its worm, there is no intestinal space: the worm can be seen as a stenting device holding open the otherwise negative, potential space of the intestine. Steven Connor suggests that Bion's formulation of the thought without a thinker describes a pre-Cartesian ego defined negatively around the existence of thoughts: 'Before the achievement of the state of *cogito ergo sum*, there is a stage in which it would be possible to say *cogitationes sunt, ergo non sum*: there are thoughts, therefore I am not'.[25]

Pompey's thought-worm brings to mind another worm-like creature described by Freud in *Beyond the Pleasure Principle*, the infusorian (or 'animalcule'). Recounting a scientific study that claimed to demonstrate the potential immortality of the infusorian, he noted that the infusorian's death seemed to come not from any trend within the organism's vital processes, but from a failure in the creature's environment. Demonstration of the infusorian's immortality would, however, prove to be prematurely concluded: subsequent studies cast doubt on the original experiment, in which the nutrient fluid that surrounded the infusoria was replaced at each new generation. When this did not happen, and the infusoria were left to swim in fluid contaminated by their own waste products, they, too, died. Freud's curious tale of the infusorian is one of those revealing, apparently incidental moments so characteristic of Freud's writing, where the apparent trend of his theoretical statements up to that point shifts, and turns. Having won back his hypothesis that all life routes toward death, he disavows the preceding excursion into infusorian territory: 'At this point the question may well arise in our minds whether any object whatever is served by trying to solve the problem of natural death from a study of the protozoa'. Yet in an aside, he also suggests that the death of the infusorian provides a template for human mortality:

> An infusorian, therefore, if it is left to itself, dies a natural death owing to its incomplete voidance of the products of its own metabolism. (It may be that the same incapacity is the ultimate cause of the death of all higher animals as well.)[26]

Death is the result of the 'incomplete voidance of the products of [one's] own metabolism'. Pompey's thought-worm produces the novel, but eliminating it from her system risks taking the intestine (that is, by analogy, her mind) along with it, threatening a 'mindlessness' to which the narrator would prefer suicide. While *Novel*'s subtitle seems to signal that Pompey may be on the verge of taking her own life, it is also a protest against a kind of mindless, 'prefabricated' thinking. As a private secretary she is required to do other people's thinking, to ventriloquise[27] other people's thoughts, signing the Baronet's letters in his name, or composing a fictitious report about the Amazon for the Baronet's mother, for which she draws inspiration from the games of her childhood, even as it must efface or exhaust her own capacity for thinking. Doing all the thinking for other people, she tells the reader, makes her very tired, more tired than anyone else in the world.[28] As a secretary she is never in a position to comment on matters in her own capacity; she reflects that she cannot even make the 'grand remark' of responding to enquiries after Sir Phoebus' health: it is not her place to do so. And there is a bigger irony in this: the writer that she is does not have the licence, or ability (as she fears) to tell too much of the truth, and it makes her a 'desperate character'.[29]

Working for a magazine publisher, she also depicts the vacuous content of the women's weeklies: sanctimonious relationship advice, homilies of married life, facile advice on interior décor, all characterised by a kind of airy thoughtlessness and a 'a certain type of vulgarity, allied with stupidity'[30] that she despises. Her narration is punctuated by pages of her unattributed favourite quotations, which she sarcastically suggests may serve the reader as ready-made conversation at 'high-class parties', as they serve her in her role as secretary, where she uses them to pad and ornament her employer's speeches.

Elsewhere she describes her contrarian relationship to religion. Though not finally a believer, the mental engagement entailed by the high church tradition appeals to her: she detests the simplification of doctrine to appeal to 'bone lazy' people unwilling to 'use their brains'. For Pompey, 'stupidity is a sin'.[31] The 'working-out' that she invites the reader to do for her- or himself runs in parallel with the 'working-through' of the thought through Pompey's mind. Thus the role of her readers in 'working it out' may be to lend the use of their mind to do some of the work both of receiving and working further on her thoughts.[32] The gesture of asking the reader to supply some of the 'work' recalls Sterne in *Tristram Shandy*:

> Writing, when properly managed (as you may be sure I think mine is) is but a different name for conversation. As no one, who knows what he is about in good company, would venture to talk all; – so no author, who understands the just boundaries of decorum and good-breeding, would presume to think all: the truest respect which you can pay to the reader's understanding, is to halve the matter amicably, and leave him something to imagine, in his turn, as well as yourself.[33]

All of this contrasts sharply with earlier scenes in which it is Pompey herself who seems unable to think, either through a kind of 'thoughtlessness' (in the conventional sense of the term) or an inability to think in the face of strong emotions. Two of the novel's 'Jewish' scenes exemplify this. Near the beginning of the novel, Pompey recalls a party she attended. Looking around the room, she is suddenly elated to realise that she is the 'only goy' – that is, non-Jewish person – at the party. 'Hurrah to be a goy!' she exclaims, 'A clever goy is cleverer than a clever Jew'.[34] The offensiveness of this statement is the more remarkable for its inclusion in a novel in which the narrator is closely identifiable (and *was* identified) with the author herself. In her biography, Frances Spalding notes that Stevie Smith's apparent antisemitism lost her a number of Jewish friends,[35] and Kristin Bluemel writes, 'Is it as bad as it seems?' How could [Stevie Smith] have begun her career in 1936 with this apparent celebration of racial or ethnic superiority?'[36] Bluemel, who considers the antisemitic aspects in all three of Smith's novels, attempts to recuperate her reputation by arguing that Smith intentionally presented a complacent public with unpalatable truths about the insidious commonplace of anti-Jewish feeling. She notes Smith's use of the Yiddish word 'goy', Jewish slang for the gentile, that positions Pompey as an 'insider'[37] of Jewish culture even as she is contemptuous of it. Pompey is a 'hanger-on' in Jewish society, and the antisemitic trope of the Jew-as-parasite (to which we shall return) offers an ironic identification. Her vision of Germany's prospective cruelty to the Jews is also remarkably prescient. While at one point we hear Pompey thinking romantically of 'sleeping, [...] happily dreaming Germany', the thought gives way to darker imaginings: 'But the dream changes, and how is it to-day, how is it to-day in this year of 1936, how is it to-day?'[38] During a holiday in Germany, she encounters the growing tide of anti-Jewish feeling and recognises the impending danger: 'Ugh that hateful feeling I had over there, and how it was a whole race was gone run mad', she declares, perceiving a 'feeling of cruelty in Germany, and the sort of vicious cruelty that isn't battle-cruelty, but doing people to death in lavatories'.[39]

There is, however, another scene that I want to consider in detail. This time, Pompey is with her Jewish friend, Rosa, whose friend Lottie challenges Pompey to 'dress with more *chic*'. 'So,' broods Pompey, as she allows herself to be stood in front of a long mirror, while Rosa's friend playfully – and patronisingly – adorns Pompey with a hat, a sequinned coat, and fur around her neck, and Rosa shoots pleading looks to Pompey not to object for the sake of Rosa's friendship with Lottie.[40] Within a scene of growing tension – Lottie's arrogance, Pompey's affront at being thus 'played' at dress-up, and Rosa's pleading look – Stevie Smith uses pauses to subtle effect. Micro-moments of narrative pause alert the reader to the fault lines of Pompey's personality, and her stated potential to become 'a tiger' – cruel and unsparing – when confronted by certain kinds of vulgarity.[41] The scene continues, and we observe the suspended image of the three woman: Pompey laughing silently the while, Lottie busying herself with clothes and accessories, Rosa anticipating the coming explosion. The narrative suspension between Pompey's silent laughter and the line that follows signals the interruption, not only of Pompey's good humour, but of Pompey herself, for the narrative resumes in the third person ('there [...] was Pompey'), alerting us to a moment of dissociation that will become even more marked in the passage that follows. Pompey's fury invokes the classical antisemitic trope of the Jew as Christ-killer, noting the resulting tableau of the three women 'in front of a long thin mirror, with a Rosa and a Lottie beside, as if it was Christ crucified between thieves'. The scene continues, taken up with impersonal details of the room and the dispassionate account of her reflection in the mirror, the dissociative performance of her anger and humiliation seeming to happen in slow-motion ('there was the dark face of Pompey, [...] a fringe falling [...], one hand outstretched'), and finally a moment that is literally *unthinkable* giving way to a trivial thought about her gloves:

> And there was something that I didn't like, *that I couldn't think, and then I thought*: It's the gloves are wrong.[42]

Suddenly throwing the gloves to the floor, she pours tea into the drinking goblet reserved for use by Lottie's pampered dog. Tilting it slowly, Pompey proceeds to let the tea fall 'drop by drop' on to 'careful Lottie's carpet', concluding with a retort modelled on the Beatitudes: 'Blessed are they that shall not be offended'.

It is a remarkable, disturbing scene, never referred to again, and even more offensive, I suggest, than the earlier 'Hurrah to be a goy!' scene; surprisingly, it does not seem to have attracted significant critical attention. Its specifically antisemitic aspects – the references to the Crucifixion and the New Testament – are more 'considered' insults than the imbecility of getting 'shot right up' at the realisation of being the only non-Jewish person at the party. Where Pompey only entertains that thought within the confines of her head, here we encounter the *passage à l'acte* from anger to revenge. A further anecdote develops the theme of the parasite. In her inventory of her acquaintances, she describes a Jewish couple, 'Cyril the Sponge' and his partner, Prunella, in terms that again evoke the antisemitic stereotype of parasitism, ironic given Pompey's own parasitic existence (and her absolute awareness of it). Like Cyril the Sponge, Pompey is the frequent recipient of lavish weekend hospitality that she is unable to return, a 'lucky girl who [gets] entertained pretty freely one way and another'.[43] She is undoubtedly aware of the bargain she makes in accepting other people's hospitality, and which she nevertheless misses no opportunity to criticise. With Prunella, there are yet further points of identification and allusion: Pompey suggests that as an unmarried woman Prunella is an 'emotional careerist' liable to attempt suicide when things go wrong. Prunella's name (presumably reminding Pompey of prunes) also affords her an oblique reference to the intestinal theme (via the idea of constipation), with an allusion both to Jonathan Swift[44] and the Jewish intellectual, Max Nordau.[45]

In the tea-spilling scene, it is something *unthinkable* that precipitates her extraordinary, calculated response to Lottie's effrontery: 'And there was something that I didn't like, that I couldn't think, and then I thought: It's the gloves are wrong'. From a psychoanalytic point of view, the succession of elements is precisely observed: first the bad feeling, the failure of alpha-function, then a different kind of thinking that aims 'to rid the psyche of accretions of stimuli',[46] by projecting the bad feeling into an unrelated object. The abrupt shifts in tone, fragmented phrases ('like I was'), and the light, rattling repetition of the connective 'and… and I…' belie Pompey's breezy *gladness* – 'Oh how glad I am I am not Lottie Beit, and how glad I am I am not Rosa' – though the oscillation of 'I am I am not' suggests an ambivalent identification with both Lottie and Rosa nonetheless. Later, on her travels to Germany, she regrets her behaviour, attempting to assuage the fear that by her thoughts alone she may have done real harm: 'I felt real wicked the way I had felt about the Jews myself. As if that thought alone might swell the mass of cruelty working up against them'.[47]

Her feared omnipotence – that her thoughts alone might really enact damage – is in marked contrast to the descriptions of her physical frailty and nervous disposition. Reflecting on her childhood, Pompey alerts the reader to a history of, of all things, *intestinal* crisis in the form of peritonitis at age five, along with a traumatic birth (she is born with a broken arm).[48] We encounter the party girl ('Pompey No Weakness'[49]) debilitated by late nights with Harriet, and feeling 'real unearthly' after a long journey. Aside from these moments of debilitation there are also places where her narrative seems to punctuate around something – some *thing*, some memory – that is itself too traumatic to be represented within the narrative, despite the 'running on' style so distinctive both to Stevie Smith and to Pompey. Telling the reader of her late nights with her friend, Harriet, she describes a typical routine of staying up too late, becoming overtired, and (because Harriet hasn't room to put Pompey up for the night) finally and with great weariness having to leave. The exhaustion – and exertion – is more than Pompey can bear, evoking a fragility and collapse beyond her immediate tiredness: 'So the last minute has come and we can neither of us bear another minute not to be in bed. But I think that Harriet could always bear it but I no I cannot bear it because I cannot bear it'. Immediately after this section, there is a pause, a break in the narrative, and the intrusion of a new, hallucinatory voice: '*Have you ever had a shock?* said the funny doctor'.[50] The sudden abruption of Pompey's voice alerts the reader to some previous experience, not yet explained but suddenly present in the narrative interruption, that has been too much for her to bear, a breakdown of some kind. Only later on do we learn that she is recalling her nervous collapse in the aftermath of her relationship with a boyfriend, Freddy.

Though attributed to flu, it is the loss of her 'sweet boy Freddy' that pre-cipitates her mental and physical collapse. On some previous occasion walking out 'too far' (and recalling the line in Smith's most famous poem, 'Not Waving But Drowning', of being 'much too far out all my life'[51]), she has a hallucinatory 'vision of the fiend' among the litter of newspapers and wrapping paper, re-turning 'profoundly disturbed' to her hotel. The pause between the two scenes suspends not only the narrative but Pompey's subjectivity: her indefatigable presence, the 'talking voice that runs on', suspended across the moment that follows an extremity of mental exhaustion, the moment that precedes the aftermath of her 'shock'. I suggest that the pause is itself the place of trauma, of that which is unrepresentable and unthinkable by Pompey. A similar impression occurs in a later scene in which her feelings of distress shift abruptly into a passionate lamentation ('Oh Jesus Christ') that ends with a distracted statement of severe and pitiless realism: 'this then is what this then is what'.[52]

Pompey offers her readers lengthy and detailed descriptions of her 'ivory towers' – places of mental refuge away from the 'fetid and debilitating' at-mosphere of London. There is a haystack in a sunny field made just for her – 'the right haystack, the right moment, and the right solitariness' – with a ladder to climb and then knock away because 'she doesn't care if she never wakes up again' from – and here she is insistent – a specifically *dreamless* sleep.[53] Her desire to avoid dreaming is repeated later, when she equates the 'night space' with horror ('*Ah night space and horror, keep my dream from me*'[54]). To her ivory tower she adds another mental enclave, the one reserved for the thought of suicide, a theme that announces itself obliquely from the very first page, when Pompey begins her narrative not with salutation but with farewell:

> Beginning this book [...] I should like then to say: Good-bye to all my friends, my beautiful and lovely friends.
>
> And for why?
>
> Read on, Reader, read on and work it out for yourself.[55]

She describes the thought of suicide as a bulwark against trauma, and recounts her early traumatic experience of being sent away from home during a period of childhood illness. But worse, for Pompey, is the cynicism that comes when she realises that suffering will not end her unhappiness: after days of crying she is appalled to realise that she remains, unhappily, alive. What affects her even more is the realisation that the maid who doted on her did so 'not at all [on the basis of] a deep feeling, but as one might pet, pat and cuddle a puppy'.[56] This 'deceitfulness of outward similarity', of appearances that deceive, so terrifies her that she begins to cultivate the thought of death as an escape. It is likewise fear that she feels in relation to her mother, whose suffering from heart disease leaves Pompey 'so furious and so powerless'.[57] Thus suicide becomes, for Pompey, a 'rich and spacious thought', the safeguard of human pride, and a 'wise thing that every intelligent, sensitive child'[58] should be introduced to from an early age.

For Pompey, personal pride is vouchsafed by the ability to take one's own life in the face of what is unbearable. The motif of the freely chosen death appears both in her telling of Tolstoy's story (that Pompey knows in its German translation), *Der Lebende Leichnam* ('The Living Corpse'), and in *Phèdre*, in which Racine's eponymous heroine prefers suicide to disgrace. Her mother's suffering, and hers, forced to endure her own helplessness, is recalled in the novel's painful and pathetic closing image of injured pride and self-determination. It is the story of a tigress, Flo, who, in a fit, falls backwards in a pool at the zoo. After being 'subjected to the indignity of artificial respiration', the 'mighty and unhappy creature' is brought unhappily back to life for a few moments and set back unsteadily on her feet, before finally dying of some 'unnameable [...] outrage'.[59]

Between suicide and trauma Pompey picks out a third way that is embodied in her attitude of the '*toute entière* visitor', for whom the rhythm of *visiting* – doing the rounds of social engagements, spending time with her friends and then leaving again – enables her to appreciate her friends without having to endure the too-close contact of permanent relationship. She is grateful for the visit, grateful to be able to leave, and furthermore grateful to know that she will visit again.[60] The 'rhythm of visiting' in her blood recalls the *fort-da* scene described by Freud in *Beyond the Pleasure Principle*. He observes his grandson, at the age of one and a half, playing repeatedly at a game that involves throwing a wooden reel into his cot, 'uttering at the same time his expressive o-o-o-o', which he takes to be the German word *fort* ('gone'). The game continues: 'He then pulled the reel out of the cot again by the string and hailed its reappearance with a joyful *da* ('there')'. Freud interprets the child's game in terms of its specifically psychical work of recuperating the lost and jettisoned object:

> The interpretation of the game then became obvious. It was related to the child's great cultural achievement – the instinctual renunciation [...] which he had made in allowing his mother to go away without protesting.[61]

Visiting allows Pompey to negotiate relationship by vacillating between the *fort* and the *da*, the coming and going, enabling a paradoxical experience of equilibrium based on oscillation. Indeed, Freud remarks on the 'vacillating rhythm'[62] that marks the battle of the life and death instincts. But the flickering connection with the object also evokes the traumaticity of contact: of something to be taken in small doses because the full blast of relationship might overwhelm her resources. It is something that she has already experienced, after all, with the illness and death of her mother. She laments her inability to have done anything to help her mother as she was dying. All she could do, she says, was 'go on being there steadily and without a break until the end': a sustained and traumatising contact.[63]

Pompey's inability to sustain contact also leads to the end of her engagement to Freddy. Of all her suitors, he is the most lightly sketched, but he represents the stability and conventionality of suburban life that Pompey can only observe from the outside. Even as a fellow resident of the imagined London suburb of Bottle Green, she perceives herself to be an outsider, nostalgic for her own neighbourhood but with 'no means of getting into the inside-of it'. With Freddy by her side, she has been able to experience having 'visited in Bottle Green'.[64] It is the breaking-off of Pompey's engagement that precipitates the crisis that her narrative intimates: the physical crisis of her influenza, her 'vision of the fiend' while she is ill, and the passages about visiting, marriage and suicide, in which she declares a preference for the rhythm of friendship – in which one may come and go – that is 'antipathetic to marriage'.[65] Nevertheless, Pompey experiences love's loss as a 'tearing inside' and the destruction of an unconscious link:

> And between two people without knowing it a love may grow up, and a link may form, and no one knows or guesses. And so it has been. I did not know. But when it is over, then it is tearing inside, it is 'tearing in the belly' one would wish oneself dead and unborn. And one does little things and goes to see friends and does one's work and fusses with this and that and feels in one's heart the drift and dribble of penultimate things, and thinks: To-morrow I shall be dead.[66]

The profoundly visceral quality of Pompey's pain suggests that, by leaving her, Freddy takes a part of Pompey with him. Again, it is something intestinal, a 'tearing in the belly' that recalls the worm that 'pulls and drags' its way through her. Connor[67] notes that it is Bion who suggests that 'nobody is able to generate the capacity to think endogenously for themselves'; rather, thinking develops from the *linking* of minds, prototypically in relationship with the mother whose capacity to think lends another mind to think the thoughts and feelings that are as yet too overwhelming for the child to bear. Indeed, Bion describes passion as 'evidence that two minds are linked'.[68] In recalling her anguish of her mother's slow and agonising death from heart disease, Pompey evokes, with great precision, the reciprocal failure and loss of intimate, sustaining relationship that is, in part, experienced as a confusion of function. It is Pompey's mother who cannot breathe, who is tended to day and night and given cylinders of oxygen. But within her description there is also the personal anguish of the child unable to be sustained by its own mother: 'If you cannot breathe how can you breathe the oxygen?'[69] she asks. It is the thought without the thinker, the failure of the organ that would make thinking and feeling possible.

Pompey's liminality, her status as a '*toute entière* visitor', is also developed in her discussion of the church. We learn that Pompey, at around the time of her mother's death, wanted to get 'inside-of' Christianity, but found herself unable to generate the affect that would make it possible for her to do so.[70] Repeatedly Pompey finds herself 'hankering after the inside-of position but getting just this near to it and no nearer'. It is not that she is unfeeling – her love for Freddy and her aunt, her capacity for fury, and the sorrow she felt at her mother's suffering – offer eloquent testament to her capacity for emotion. She nevertheless recognises in herself some inability to accede to a certain kind of affirmation, an inability to be 'altogether completely serious', despite trying very hard to be. She identifies herself with the 'spirit that denies': 'Sometimes I used to get downright morbid, chaps, I used to sit and cry, thinking there I was like Goethe's Mephistopheles, the spirit that denies'.[71]

As ever, Pompey's self-description is undercut by Smith's distinctively facetious tone. It is a characteristic Stevie Smith effect. Sheryl Stevenson[72] has described Smith's tone as 'deliberately non-resonant', a phrase that brings to mind Bion's comments about the kind of patient who speaks with 'no overtones or undertones of meaning'.[73] Of course, Bion is himself a past master of a similar writing style. A prefatory note to *Bion in New York and São Paulo* illustrates something of his idiosyncratic tone:

> I thank all who participated in these discussions with their objections and agreements. Many who read this book will feel that my replies are inadequate and incomplete. That they are inadequate I must admit; that they are incomplete I regard as a virtue especially if it stimulates the reader to complete the answers. I wish the reader as much enjoyment as I had in speaking; if it sends him to sleep may I wish him 'Sweet Dreams and a profitable awakening'.

The question of tone, I suggest, may connect Smith with Bion as writers. Facetiousness, dryness of style, and a certain tempting of the absurd combine curiously to convey a detached and ironic relationship to their discourse. I propose that we can also look to Bion's theoretical statements to describe and analyse literary tone. Though he never attempted literary criticism, he did produce close readings of analytic material, using the Grid to track aspects of tone and the production of meaning.

'The Grid', his paper first produced in 1963 and revised in 1971, introduces the reader to his specialised observational tool designed to analyse the statements made within the psychoanalytic session: both those of the patient and the analyst's interpretations. Taking the form of an 8×9 grid, it combines two axes – a vertical axis tracking the genetic development of thoughts, from beta-elements to algebraic calculi, and a horizontal axis ranging a series of different 'uses' to which statements may be put: as a 'definitory hypothesis', for example, placing two objects in a constant conjunction (column 1); as the notation of something that previously took place (column 3); as a statement that demarcates the site of attention (column 4) or enquiry (column 5), or as an action (column 6). A column 2 formulation, however, is of a different kind. In the 1963 version of 'The Grid', he writes:

> Column 2 is to categorise the 'use' to which a statement – of whatever kind it may be and however untrue in the context – is put with the intention of preventing a statement, however true in the context, that would involve modification in the personality and its outlook. I have arbitrarily used the sign ψ to emphasise the close relationship of this 'use' to phenomena known to analysts as expressions of 'resistance'.[74]

In using the symbol ψ (psi) to denote column 2, he relates the column 2 formulation both to the factor of unconscious resistance and to the development of [a] mind or psyche (for which the ψ symbol is a common psychoanalytic shorthand). Column 2 is also the place of the lie, since 'true thought requires neither formulation nor thinker', but 'the lie is a thought to which a formulation and a thinker are essential',[75] though the complexity of lying will lead Bion to suggest in his revised 1971 paper that column 2 'requires expansion into a 'grid' of its own'.[76] He also places there any material that defers or evades the possibility of encountering one's personal truth, including material 'valuable against the inception of any development in his personality involving catastrophic change'. Chris Mawson provides a helpful gloss: column 2 material 'specif[ies] the acceptance of an answer known at some level to be false, in order to evade the pain of leaving the question open and allowing an evolution, with the possibility of disruptive growth of the mind'.[77] While this may suggest that a column 2 categorisation pertains only to the grossest statements of denial, lying, or bombast, Bion seems to use column 2 more subtly.

While Antonino Ferro[78] has written 'in praise of row C' (the level of 'dream thoughts, dreams and myths'), I suggest that column 2 offers an equally rich seam for thinking about the question of tone. *Transformations* includes the notable occasion, previously mentioned,[79] when Bion uses Grid coordinates to consider Bishop Berkeley's famous retort to Isaac Newton's formulation of the differential calculus. He quotes a section from *The Analyst*[80] to which his analysis will be directed:

> "It must, indeed, be acknowledged that he used fluxions, like the scaffold of a building, as things to be laid aside or got rid of as soon as finite lines were found proportional to them. But then these finite exponents are found by the help of fluxions. Whatever therefore is got by such exponents and proportions is to be ascribed to fluxions: which must therefore be previously understood. And what are these fluxions?

The velocities of evanescent increments. And what are these same evanescent increments? They are neither finite quantities, nor quantities infinitely small, nor yet nothing. May we not call them the ghosts of departed quantities?"[81]

Bion offers the following analysis of Bishop Berkeley's statement, which I cite fully in order to convey its remarkable, disconcerting quality. The coordinates given relate to the Grid;[82] his reference to 'cycles' and to Tβ (denoting the end product of a transformation) are a part of this theory[83] of transformations:

> Berkeley's formulation may be regarded as an F3 contribution. The polemical tone gives it a column 2 category, denying, though he acknowledges the truth of Newton's result, the validity of the method: the ironic tone denies the reality of 'the ghosts of departed quantities'. The pamphlet as a whole is thus an example of an F3 formulation used, in its second cycle, as column 2 to deny both the 'ghosts' component and the H3 component in his and Newton's confrontation. From a psychoanalytic vertex both formulations, Newton's and Berkeley's, can be seen as T β (col. 3) (intended to produce a formulation T β (col. 3) (cycle 2)), or, T β col. 2 (intended to deny emergence of beta-elements).
>
> T Newton β H3 furthers mathematic enquiry: T Newton β col. 2 denies the 'ghosts'. T Berkeley β col. 2 denies, by irony, 'ghosts' and, by polemic, the scientific approach. In both instances the col. 2 dimension is directed against psychological disturbance; why? for fear of the turbulence and its associated 'becoming'.[84]

Discombobulating though the preceding passage may be (and incomprehensible to the uninitiated), Bion does, in effect, perform a detailed textual analysis, which – though explicitly given from a 'psychoanalytic vertex'[85] – nevertheless touches on specifically literary features of the text: tone, the use of irony, and polemic. His analysis also focuses precisely on the line that is the most memorable in Berkeley's account: his image of the 'ghosts of departed quantities'. In this example, a column 2 formulation is indicated by the use of polemic and irony, but it also implicates Berkeley in a relationship predicated on *resistance* to the emergence of something that would unsettle his worldview. In a further example that seems obliquely to recall Stevie Smith's best-known poem, he suggests that (the imposition of) 'desire, memory and understanding' can equally serve the column 2 function by disingenuously substituting 'transformations in K which give a similitude of transformation in O'. Put another way, apparent statements of fact may block passage to deeper truths perceived as catastrophic, such as the emergence of desire: "How I wish I had the chance to swim!" expresses the idea that a particular state of completion (wishing to swim) has been achieved and precludes the unsaturation that would be felt were the individual to *wish* to swim'.[86]

A statement in column 2 can also draw attention to the *function* of column 2, rather than necessarily implicate the speaker or writer in an attitude of disingenuousness or resistance. This, I suggest, is where Bion's and Smith's tone come into play. In his re-reading of Sophocles' *Oedipus The King*, Bion maps the play's characters onto the horizontal axis of the Grid in terms of their mythic function. It is to the unwilling prophet, Tiresias, who 'prefers not to' respond directly to Oedipus' question to know Laius' killer, that the column 2 function falls: his initial refusal to provide prophecy is in the service of Oedipus' ignorance. But Tiresias also represents the attempt to check Oedipus' overweening arrogance, his desire to 'know' something as a fact rather than 'get to know' something through the more challenging process of encountering his internal emotional experience.[87] The provocations of both Stevie Smith's and Bion's characteristic style can be seen to speak to this function: Pompey's gossipy persona may lead a contemporary audience to the discovery of their own prejudice (especially in relation to antisemitism); her insistence that the 'reader work it out for [her- or him-]self' may be finally an invitation not to the suicidal 'secret' (as it initially seems to be) but an opportunity to punctuate the attitude of the complacent reader.

Beneath the surface of Bion's highly stylised and technical analysis of Berkeley, there is deep sensitivity to the emotional evocation of a text that would not conventionally be considered ripe for analysis of either a literary or psychoanalytic kind. His analysis illuminates questions of language *use* and *effect* that are at the same time sensitive both to context and to the response of the reader. This is very different to the style of psychoanalytical literary criticism that would reduce literature to the intentions (conscious and unconscious) of the writer, or perform a 'psychoanalysis' of a character. Freud, despite his warnings in *The Question of Lay Analysis*,[88] nevertheless did 'apply' psychoanalysis extramurally (as in his study of Leonardo) and his forays into literary analysis can be simplistic in their underlying conception of literature. Bion's example – despite its difficulty and abstruseness – is, by contrast, potentially both rigorous and supple in its handling of language, alert to the lightning-quick changes in tone that suggest a new or emerging relationship to the material.

In *Novel on Yellow Paper*, Pompey describes herself as an 'animula, vagula, blandula of the office',[89] invoking Hadrian's deathbed address to his 'little soul' as it departs his body: 'Animula vagula blandula, hospes comesque corporis, quae nunc abibis in loca?'.[90] As the anima (soul or spirit) leaves behind a dead body, so the distracting thought-worm risks taking her 'disintegrating mind' along with it, as it works its way out and into the novel: 'Ah, distracting thought that creeps through the disintegrating mind, unwelcome worm'.[91] Bion's digestive model of thinking also evokes the curious parasitism of the 'thought without a thinker' that is both inside and alien to the mind. Freud's figure of the infusorian that dies if unable to eliminate the products of its metabolism supplements this Bionian model by bringing death into the picture: the over-thinking, under-thinking, ventriloquising Pompey risks eliminating her mind along with her thought, though she would sooner die than submit to the *thoughtlessness* that she despises. Her invitation to 'work it out for yourself' combines with her defence of what is high-brow, complex, and inaccessible (for example, in religious liturgy and ritual) to engage the reader in supplying some of the alpha-function, or mind, that was missing in her experiences with her mother. Following Freud, she seeks to 'follow [her] own path to death',[92] writing the 'rich and spacious thought' of suicide that nevertheless enables her to go on living. Freud suggests that the organism seeks to 'die only in its own fashion', and places the self-preservative instincts in the service of the death drive. Like Hermes, Pompey is suspended in a paradoxical, liminal position: wanting/not wanting to live, thinking/not thinking, visiting/leaving, *fort/da*; wanting to get on the 'inside-of' the church and Bottle Green, but remaining only a visitor. This contrarian aspect is also 'the spirit that denies', the column 2 *mode* that makes of Stevie Smith's character an avatar of the column 2 *function*: hyper-aware and provoking, demanding that the reader work it out, for her- or himself.

Notes

1 Bion, *Complete Works*, 10:175 (*Taming Wild Thoughts*, 27).
2 Smith, *Novel on Yellow Paper, or, Work It out for Yourself*, 210. Subsequent page references are to this edition, noted as *NYP*.
3 Bion, *Complete Works*, 4:275 (*Learning from Experience*, 7).
4 Bion, *Complete Works*, 6:154 (*Second Thoughts*, 111).
5 Bion, *Complete Works*, 7:95 (*Brazilian Lectures: 1973 São Paulo, 1974 Rio de Janeiro/São Paulo*, 98).
6 *NYP*, 38.
7 *NYP*, 121.
8 *NYP*, 244.
9 *NYP*, 43.
10 Spalding, *Stevie Smith: A Critical Biography*, 112.
11 Spalding, 112.
12 *NYP*, 9.
13 Spalding, 115.
14 *NYP*, 16.
15 *NYP*, 38–9.
16 *NYP*, 38.
17 *NYP*, 39.
18 Bion, *Complete Works*, 10:175 (*Taming Wild Thoughts*, 27).
19 Najarian, 'Contributions to Almighty Truth: Stevie Smith's Seditious Romanticism'.
20 Stevenson, 'Stevie Smith's Voices'.
21 Pope, *The Major Works*, 28.
22 The French word for verse (*vers*) is also a homonym with the word for worm (*ver*), creating an additional connection with Pompey's intestinal alexandrine. With thanks to Elissa Marder for this further slide down the slippery worm–slope.
23 Spalding, 112.
24 Bion, *Complete Works*, 4:349 (*Learning from Experience*, 83).
25 Connor, 'Thinking Things', 6.
26 Freud, *Standard Edition*, 18:48.
27 Derived etymologically from the idea of speaking in, or from, the belly: another intestinal situation.

28 *NYP*, 58.
29 *NYP*, 16.
30 *NYP*, 184.
31 *NYP*, 178.
32 Compare this, for instance, with B.S. Johnson's contention that the reader should add nothing to the writer's thought (see chapter four).
33 Sterne, *The Life and Opinions of Tristram Shandy, Gentleman*, 73.
34 *NYP*, 10–11.
35 Spalding, 122.
36 Bluemel, *George Orwell and the Radical Eccentrics: Intermodernism in Literary London*, 29.
37 Bluemel, 30.
38 *NYP*, 49.
39 *NYP*, 103.
40 *NYP*, 61.
41 *NYP*, 184.
42 *NYP*, 62. Italics mine.
43 *NYP*, 20.
44 Swift's satirical poem, *The Lady's Dressing Room*, includes the memorable line: 'Oh! Celia, Celia, Celia shits!'. Swift, *The Poetical Works of Jonathan Swift: Volume 1*, 251.
45 *NYP*, 21.
46 Bion, *Complete Works*, 4:275 (*Learning from Experience*, 7).
47 *NYP*, 107.
48 *NYP*, 73.
49 *NYP*, 59.
50 *NYP*, 70.
51 Lee, *Stevie Smith: A Selection*, 128.
52 *NYP*, 221.
53 *NYP*, 40–41.
54 *NYP*, 83.
55 *NYP*, 9.
56 *NYP*, 156.
57 *NYP*, 157.
58 *NYP*, 155.
59 *NYP*, 251–2.
60 *NYP*, 212.
61 Freud, *Standard Edition*, 18:15.
62 Freud, *Standard Edition*, 18:41.
63 *NYP*, 225.
64 *NYP*, 233.
65 *NYP*, 198.
66 *NYP*, 236.
67 Connor, 'Thinking Things', 9.
68 Bion, *Complete Works*, 5:16 (*Elements of Psychoanalysis*, 13).
69 *NYP*, 225.
70 *NYP*, 173.
71 *NYP*, 181–2.
72 Stevenson, 'Stevie Smith's Voices', 26.
73 Bion, *Complete Works*, 4:283 (*Learning from Experience*, 15).
74 Bion, *Complete Works*, 5:103 (*Taming Wild Thoughts*, 9).
75 Bion, *Complete Works*, 6:309 (*Attention and Interpretation*, 104).
76 Bion, *Complete Works*, 10:8. The Brazilian psychoanalyst, P.C. Sandler, has enthusiastically taken up this task, proposing several alternative 'Grids' (Sandler, *A Clinical Application of Bion's Concepts. Volume 3: Verbal and Visual Approaches to Reality*).

77 Bion, *Complete Works*, 10:105.
78 Ferro, *Psychoanalysis as Therapy and Storytelling.*
79 See also chapter two. I cite the passage at length here again because it aids in understanding Bion's analysis of its *tone* (which is more important to this discussion than the idea of 'scaffolding' previously discussed).
80 Berkeley, *The Analyst.*
81 Bion, *Complete Works*, 5:267 (*Transformations*, 157).
82 See figure 1.
83 A fuller discussion of Bion's theory of transformations appears in chapter eight. Tβ denotes the 'end product' of a transformation, and is not to be confused with beta-elements/β-elements: Bion, *Complete Works*, 5:135 (*Transformations*, 10).
84 Bion, *Complete Works*, 5:268 (*Transformations*, 158).
85 Bion's more precise rendering of the conventional phrase 'point of view'. See, for example: Bion, *Complete Works*, 7:44 (*Transformations*, 10).
86 Bion, *Complete Works*, 6:265 (*Attention and Interpretation*, 52–53).
87 Bion, *Complete Works*, 6:131 (*Second Thoughts*, 86).
88 Freud, *Standard Edition*, vol. 20.
89 *NYP*, 204.
90 Loeb Classical Library https://www.loebclassics.com/view/hadrian-poems/1934/pb_LCL434.445.xml [accessed December 2020]. Attributed to the Emperor Hadrian. The Loeb suggests the following translation: 'Dear fleeting sweeting, little soul /My body's comrade and its guest /What region now must be thy goal?'
91 *NYP*, 210.
92 Freud, *Standard Edition*, 18:39.

4 Restoring the lost container: B.S. Johnson's *The Unfortunates*

> Container and contained are susceptible of conjunction and permeation by emotion. Thus conjoined or permeated or both they change in a manner usually designed as growth.[1]

After many years of relative obscurity, the work of the British novelist B.S. Johnson has been brought to a new audience following the publication of a volume of his collected short fiction, plays, and prose (*Well Done God! Selected Prose and Drama of B.S. Johnson*); and the re-publication of four of his seven novels,[2] for which an extensive and thoughtful biography by Jonathan Coe,[3] published in 2004, prepared the way. *The Unfortunates*,[4] Johnson's memorable 'book-in-a-box' and his fourth novel, was republished in 1999, some three decades after its original publication.

The Unfortunates is remarkable for its physical form. It comprises 27 loose sections (or 'chapters') collected, rather than bound, within a box. Aside from two sections indicated to be read 'First' and 'Last', the remaining sections 'are intended to be read in random order'.[5] As with all of Johnson's novels, the form of the novel was designed as a way of 'solving particular writing problems': in this case, according to Johnson himself, to deal with the 'randomness of the material'.[6] Johnson's experiment in form was not entirely new: the French writer, Marc Saporta, had previously published his *Composition no. 1,* presented in its entirety as loose single pages within a box (there is evidence that Johnson became aware of *Composition no. 1* while he was writing *The Unfortunates*[7]).

The Unfortunates presents a novelistic account of events that took place in Bryan Johnson's life. I hesitate to describe it as a 'fictional account', because Johnson was generally vehemently opposed (though a little inconsistently) to the writing of fiction and the telling of 'stories'. Indeed, he is perhaps best known for his controversial and arguably self-limiting mantra: 'telling stories is telling lies'.[8] He was, above all, committed to truth-telling in his novels, a form he considered suitable for the telling of both fiction and non-fiction. *The Unfortunates* exemplifies Johnson's use of a form more usually associated with fiction to recount an experience that was, undoubtedly, his own. It recalls and captures Johnson's visit, in real life, and while working as a sports journalist, to cover a football match in Nottingham. The trip brings back memories of his

DOI: 10.4324/9781003006619-4

friendship with Tony Tillinghast, 'Tony' in the novel, a fellow student who died very young of cancer. Jonathan Coe describes their friendship:

> While still an undergraduate at King's College London, Johnson had been editor of the student magazine *Lucifer*, and had once made a trip to Nottingham to make friendly contact with the editorial board of that university's magazine. On this trip he had been introduced to a Nottingham undergraduate called Tony Tillinghast, and the two became close friends. The friendship was spiky and combative: Tony was a serious, assiduous scholar, bent on an academic career; Johnson professed to despise academia, claiming that the work of literary critics and historians was only worthwhile if it helped writers to produce better books. Taking up this challenge, Tony had read *Travelling People* in manuscript, chapter by chapter as Johnson wrote it, scribbling copious annotations in the margin. The novel had been dedicated to him and his wife June. And then, in late 1962, Tony had been diagnosed with cancer. Two years later he was dead, at the age of just twenty-nine.[9]

In what follows I propose that what has been overlooked in previous Johnson criticism is the bearing that the nature of Tony and Bryan's friendship – in effect, one of mentor and 'mentee' – has on the formal solution taken by Johnson in creating a 'book' loosely assembled within a box. Previous readings of *The Unfortunates* have tended to focus on the loose sections – and the way in which they function as a metaphor for the experience of randomness, disorder, and chaos – than on the box itself. This reading is hardly surprising given that Johnson himself understood the work in these terms. Nevertheless, I argue that a Bionian conception of the container–contained relationship and the part played by 'another mind' in the development of thinking draw out the many places in the text where issues of thinking and mind are predominant. Johnson's narrator searches repeatedly for an image that will best figure the mind:

the mind as a   think of an image[10]

As the mind (and body) of Tony disintegrates, Johnson loses his friend's containing mind which has played such an important role in his writing. I propose that *The Unfortunates* is Johnson's attempt to restore the lost container of Tony's mind, not only through the box, but through writing. I will also consider how *The Unfortunates* is essentially a book *about* writing, and look at the ways in which B.S. Johnson and Bion share a central orientation to truth in their work.

The opening lines of the first section draw our attention to something known but not realised as the narrator arrives at the train station: 'But I know this city!   ' [sic]. Here, and throughout *The Unfortunates*, phrases and words are riven by textual spaces that seem to indicate a gap or suspension in the narrator's mind, sometimes inviting the reader to make up the word that is missing, but more frequently signalling what is too painful – perhaps unthinkable – for the narrator to contemplate. The technique recalls the ellipses that separate (and connect) the textual thoughts in Johnson's earlier work, *Trawl*, an auto-biographical account prompted by a three-week voyage on a fishing trawler. Where there are (literal) points of connection in *Trawl*, here there are narrative gaps: places where, as the reader learns later, 'the mind has fuses'.[11]

The narrator's recognition of the town he once knew plunges him immediately into the memory of Tony in the depths of his illness: 'his cheeks sallowed and collapsed round the insinuated bones, the gums shrivelled, was it, or shrunken', an uncanny *memento mori*. As a sports reporter, Johnson got used to being sent to cover football matches at a moment's notice, barely registering the details of the assignment, and with few pre-conceived ideas of the task at hand. In 'A Theory of Thinking', Bion describes the 'pre-conception' as an 'empty thought' seeking to mate with a 'realisation'[12] or what he will later describe as the process of 'saturation'.[13] This idea seems to be echoed in Johnson's use of the typographical symbols that accompany each section of the text. The 'Publisher's Note' that appears in all of Johnson's recent re-publications reminds us that he was personally and minutely involved in the details of typesetting. 'First' is identified by an outlined circle, thus: ○, suggesting, perhaps, the empty, but delineated space, which the novel will aim to fill or saturate as the text progresses (that the symbol that accompanies the last section is a solid black circle seems to support this reading). With Bion in mind, it also evokes the figure of O, Bion's shorthand for unknowable reality, for the pure (and unmediated, unassimilable) blast of truth. In *A Memoir of the Future*, a dreamlike voice traces a frenzied account of O, which leads 'from nothing to consciousness to sleep to dream to waking thoughts to dream thoughts to nothingness to O = zero, from O = zero to O which is O = oh! to O which is a picture which is a picture of a hole or greedy mouth or vagina'.[14] Using Bion's terms, Johnson's opening declaration ('But I know this place!') signals the mating of a pre-conception with a realisation, enabling a potential for emotional growth.

In a text that provides a minimum of narrative framing, the first section nevertheless signals a number of themes and narrative threads. Tony's illness is the first of these, and his physical disintegration is drawn vividly and unsparingly. Further images of decay are dispersed throughout the novel, in accounts of the local bars that the narrator visits during the course of his day. Describing the ill-preserved décor of a pub that claims to be one of the oldest in England, he looks for the 'signs of venerableness' that would allow him to see and admire the pub's antiquity. But the pub has been crudely preserved in various ways, and he is disappointed.[15]

Unable to venerate the past, he is left 'with only association'; his memories – alone – must do the work of mourning. The elegiac mode suggested by the narrator's first memory of Tony is shown to be complicated or forestalled in some way; the work of mourning, that Peter Sacks[16] argues is the function of the elegy, not yet achieved. Jahan Ramazani's account of the 'modern elegy' – enacting a melancholic, unachieved mourning – is closer to what I believe to be at work in *The Unfortunates*, though I suggest that Ramazani's remark about the twentieth-century phenomenon of 'self-elegy' may be closer still, being 'often more *compensatory* than elegies proper'.[17] I propose that what prevents the narrator's capacity and desire for 'veneration' is the loss of the shared mind that the narrator associates with Tony. In 'First', we encounter a lengthy and striking description of Tony's mind, and indeed the use of it made by the narrator: a mind for detail likened to the 'documents in the Public Records Office', a mind 'efficient, tidy [...], not as mine is, random', and one from which the narrator 'learnt, selected and elected to hear what I needed'.[18]

The comparison of Tony's mind with the narrator's ends with the question of how the narrator, now bereft, can 'place his [Tony's] order, his disintegration'. Although the narrator refers to Tony's 'fine mind', his own order and disintegration are also at stake. It is a question of how to make sense of the appalling randomness with which a young and promising life was cut short. But it is also a question that speaks to the narrator's difficulty in having to complete this hardest of tasks, in the absence of Tony's mind, to supplement the narrator's inadequacies. What he is struggling to achieve, the text implies, is to re-find and make use of what he had previously 'learnt, selected and elected to hear': in other words, to find within his own mind the framework of thinking that Tony's mind had afforded him.

The description of their relationship recalls Bion's account of the container-contained relationship. In *Learning from Experience*, Bion outlines a developmental theory of thinking predicated on the availability of another person's mind (templated on the mother's *reverie*) to receive and transform the anxiety of experiences that are initially fragmentary, meaningless and unassimilable. Starting from Melanie Klein's description of projective identification, he 'abstract[s] for use as a model the idea of a container into which an object is projected and the object that can be projected into the container, [...] designated by the term contained'.[19] The containing mind that models thinking for the other comes to be installed, through introjection, as a reliable template for psychical function, or that which Bion calls alpha-function.

The narrator's (and B.S. Johnson's) friendship with Tony suggests a relationship of the kind that Bion describes. Their initial collaboration arises out of a challenge made by the narrator. Tony, the more assiduous student and critical thinker, values criticism as 'a discipline of the highest kind in itself'. The narrator replies that criticism is only useful if it results in better writing, and puts their different conceptions of criticism to a test: he will show Tony the drafts of his novel as he is writing it, and see whether Tony's criticism can make him a better writer.[20] The piece of writing that they thus set out together to improve will become the narrator's first published novel (in B.S. Johnson's life, the book that will be published as *Travelling People* in 1963), and Tony and the narrator collaborate in 'discussing, improving, refining, deleting'; Tony 'reading and correcting'; the narrator noting that 'after he had read it I was more confident in what I had done, that it had passed the scrutiny of someone whose opinion I respected'.[21]

As his friend and writing mentor, Tony enacts the role of the container that enables the narrator to project both his writing, and his anxieties about writing, on- and into a reliable and sensitive recipient. The numerous vignettes of their relationship centre repeatedly on episodes related to his writing, with the narrator remarking that he took from Tony 'only what [he] needed', as well as noting Tony's 'generosity of mind', his capacity to alert the narrator to things that he should have known about, and to rein in his excesses.[22] Tony's undergraduate dissertation and later PhD thesis centred on James Boswell, Samuel Johnson's famous biographer. As Boswell writes [Samuel] Johnson, so B.S. Johnson's narrator will come to write Tony, making a promise to him on his deathbed that he will tell the world about their friendship, that he'll 'get it all down, mate'.[23] Their relationship recalls Sherlock Holmes' comment to Watson (another literary example of one person writing another), in Conan Doyle's *A Scandal in Bohemia*: 'I am lost without my Boswell'.[24] After Tony's death, the narrator is asked to write his epitaph, and suggests a line by Brecht: 'he made suggestions, and we accepted them'.[25]

Emphasising the importance of Tony's containing role shows certain aspects of Johnson's elegy (or self-elegy) in a more sympathetic light. The seriousness of Tony's condition only becomes clear to the narrator when he is unable to attend the launch party for the narrator's first novel due to his illness,[26] an apparently trivial prism. Reading *The Unfortunates* in terms of the lost container-contained relationship (and the specific role that Tony played in bringing the narrator's book to publication) makes sense of what otherwise seems an unduly solipsistic response. As Tony's health deteriorates, his capacity to receive the narrator's work diminishes. He recalls an occasion when Tony's role as critical friend fails, something he can only now see and understand at the distance of many years. On the way home from seeing him, he tries to explain to his girlfriend that Tony's comments this time were not 'really constructive'; that he was no longer truly interested in the narrator's work: 'I was disappointed, but I can see now that it was reasonable that the book would seem irrelevant to him, everything must have, in his condition'.[27]

Despite his importance to the narrator, Tony is at moments an ambivalent figure subject to the narrator's feelings of hostility and rivalry. He recalls surprise – and possibly, quiet satisfaction – in noting spelling mistakes and other errors in Tony's dissertation.[28] Tony's academic bent, his striving to complete his PhD and win a research post, contrasts with the narrator's desire to pursue creative writing above all else. As age-peers, there is something in Johnson's account that suggests that Tony is sometimes experienced not as the mother-container but as a more phallic, intruding interlocutor against whose streams of words the narrator has to defend himself: 'there were times when he talked so much that I had to shut off part of my mind, he talked me into that much insensitivity'.[29] Tony's 'fine mind', the 'sort of mind [...] that could marshal an argument methodically',[30] also generates an excess, and the proliferation of unassimilable particles of thought that recall Bion's description of beta-elements:

And so on and so forth, that was a phrase Tony used too much, for suggesting continua of thought or information or knowledge, in conversation. And so on and so forth, to end almost every sentence, on one occasion, I remember, it annoyed me, the repetition, and I only just forbore from telling him about it, then, at one of those times I had to shut my mind off.[31]

Bion describes the container-contained relationship as a symbiotic one in which both parties – paradigmatically, the mother and the infant – benefit from the encounter: 'in terms of a model the mother derives benefit and achieves mental growth from the experience: the infant likewise abstracts benefit and achieves growth'.[32] The container-contained relationship comes to be characterised by its mutuality and the reciprocal growth of a containing function that supports both parties. The narrator's ambivalence is compounded by his own inability to reciprocate the containing function that Tony enacts for him. In a scene from a day out together, he fails to protect Tony from himself after a drink in the pub: on this occasion it is Tony who is the learner (driver) needing guidance and a second pair of eyes. Another driver backs into his path, but Tony does not see the other driver and keeps going. Unable to reach the brake, the narrator half-remembers that he may have managed to press the horn. The other driver stopped in time, but the narrator cannot even be sure whether it was he who saved the day.[33] On yet another occasion we find him uncomfortably attempting to comply with June's suggestion that he spend time with Tony in Brighton in order to cheer him up, 'take him out of himself'. Riffing on that peculiar, resonant phrase, the narrator wonders how 'a common expression can become so like a philosophical statement'.[34] The strangeness of its formulation brings home the metaphorical force – and impossibility – of June's request. Taking Tony 'out of himself' implies that Tony's mind and his 'now alien body' can be divided from each other, his mind a part-object that can be relocated away from the site of cancerous growth. The narrator recognises the futility of the task, laughing bitterly that he was unable to curb the cancer, to give Tony the one thing that might have helped him.

Cancer is an important motif in Johnson's work. It appears in at least two of his other novels, in *Christy Malry's Own Double Entry* and *House Mother Normal*, where the reader learns that cancer is dormant inside the cruel 'house mother' of an old people's home, lying in wait to undermine her sadistic triumph over her charges as well as her authority within the text. The character of Christie Malry is similarly undone by a case of the 'lumps' that proves terminal, and Johnson's mother, whose death is the occasion of his final novel, *See the Old Lady Decently*, was also dying of cancer during the writing of *The Unfortunates*. Cancer, never directly named in *The Unfortunates*, is a persistent figure of the 'random, arbitrary, gratuitous'.[35] It is the silent, cellular bad object that erodes Tony's body; the force of chaos and randomness that destroys Tony's ambitions, undoing the patient hard work through which he sought to build a career and a home. It is a figure of unstoppable, proliferative growth – the 'too much' of Tony's discourse from which the narrator has occasionally to protect himself, and the creeping confusion of the narrator's own thoughts. Tony's tumour is described as 'explosive, runaway, zealous, monstrous', a force that is perversely strong even as his body weakens; it cannot be destroyed save by killing 'the good as well as the bad cells'. When doctors cut him open to remove the tumour, they find that 'its feelers or fingers or tentacles had grasped right round the collarbone', and that the most they can do is to use radiotherapy to 'stop its growth, at least'.[36]

Bion describes mental growth as the development of the container that 'develops by accretion to produce a series of sleeves that are conjoined'.[37] His thesis in *Learning from Experience* aims precisely to account for the ability of the mind to grow progressively in its capacity through the development of the container-contained relationship, or, to use Bion's notation, $♀♂$. Interestingly, he places cancer in an analogous relationship to the mind when he writes about death in his third autobiography:

> death is not a matter of practical consequence to anyone, but it is the animate, continuing-to-live object that has to bury or otherwise dispose of the dead object. If your eye offends you pluck it out: if your cancer offends you cut it out: if your mind makes you uncomfortable... what then?[38]

There is something in Johnson's account of Tony's illness that suggests that his cancer effects a grim parody of Tony's qualities: it is as strong as his mind, as prolific as his words. The proliferation of new cells offers a perverse mimesis of the mind's processes, the alpha-elements and dream-thoughts that generate a profusion of images, words, oneiric flashes seeking narrative sequence, and the container-contained relationship in the mind that grows through successive 'matings' of a pre-conception with a realisation.

Bion describes a pathological variant of the container-contained relation-ship, the 'minus' container-contained, or $-(♀♂)$, in which envy and rivalry predominate to effect the 'denudation' or stripping of the apparatus for thinking, a kind of 'eating-away' of the mind by itself. $-(♀♂)$ is 'an internal object without an exterior [...] an alimentary canal without a body [...] it is the resultant of an envious stripping or denudation of all good and is itself destined to continue the process of stripping [...] as existing, in its origin, between two personalities'.[39] In *The Unfortunates*, it is the figure of cancer that undoes meaning and seems to reverse the function of the mind, making un-derstanding impossible. It is, moreover, an internal undoing, an intimate parasite. The narrator laments his inability to understand that 'this thing could just come from nowhere, from inside himself'. He can neither understand, nor stop trying to understand, even as he admits his own capacity to 'accept that all is nothing, that sense does not exist'.[40]

The cancer that erodes Tony's body and mind is also identified with the disintegrative forces that impede the narrator's ability to think. Throughout the novel we are offered glimpses of the narrator's difficulties with thinking as well as observations of 'how the mind works, remembers these things, not others'.[41] The narrator's mind 'clutters itself up with so much rubbish';[42] like Tony, he 'want[s] to impose some order on this overgrowth'[43] amid a confusion and profusion of details and lists: memories that 'will not fall into place';[44] images of 'rejectamenta'[45] and debris. He reflects 'yes how the mind arranges itself, tries to sort things into orders, is perturbed if things are not sorted, are not in the right order, nags away',[46] and he struggles to find an adequate response to Tony's cancer, its blind destructiveness and the way it defeats the narrator's attempts to impose meaning where meaning fails: 'so why this, if it is so meaningless, anything means something only if you impose meaning on it, which is in itself a meaningless thing, the imposition'.[47] The gaps and swerves in the text (quite aside from the breaks imposed by the unbound sections) also speak of moments of disorientation, of cliché unable to evoke an emotional experience:

> These melodramatic idiotic moments in which life is completely These stale thoughts, this stale[48]

For Johnson the question of meaning-making poses a further difficulty that is born of the exacting demands that he makes of his readers. In *Well Done God!*, he rejects the notion of a critical or imaginative reader who brings his or her own ideas to the literary object:

> For readers it is often said that they will go on reading the novel because it enables them, unlike film or television, to exercise their imaginations, that that is one of its chief attractions for them, that they may imagine the characters and so on for themselves. Not with my novels; […] I want my ideas to be expressed so precisely that the very minimum of room for interpretation is left. Indeed, I would go further and say that to the extent that a reader can impose his own imagination on my words, then that piece of writing is a failure. I want him to see my vision, not something conjured out of his own imagination. How is he supposed to grow unless he will admit others' ideas? If he wants to impose his imagination, let him write his own books. That may be thought to be anti-reader; but think a little further, and what I am really doing is challenging the reader to prove his own existence as palpably as I am proving mine by the act of writing.[49]

As Johnson himself published literary reviews, it is a remarkably contrarian and arguably defensive position. He seems to suggest that the reader *qua* reader should under no account add, make or impose any meaning not intended by the writer, gesturing to an ethics of 'separate spheres' in which the reader and the writer remain within the bounds of their roles. Johnson limits himself, too, to an ethics of truth-telling that disbars him from writing fiction (though in this he proves inconsistent: *Christie Malry* is unmistakeably fictional – the absurdism of its plot and Johnson's metafictional references moreover keep this point uppermost in the reader's mind). Rather than encouraging the reader (the actual reader, or the reader that exists in B.S. Johnson's mind) to assist in the shared work of making meaning, he is suspicious of what the reader may bring to (or take away from) his work. I suggest that Johnson's conception of the writer's relationship to his audience comes close to Bion's formulation of $-(\female\male)$.

It is also important to foreground the extent to which *The Unfortunates* is predominantly a book *about* writing, and the experience of writing. Both the novel's innovative form and its powerful themes of death and loss can overshadow this. There are at least three writing projects within the text. The first of these is the report of the football match that the narrator must file by five o'clock that day. This is hack-writing to a deadline: writing not to 'tell the truth' but to fill a 500-word-shaped hole within tomorrow's newspaper. Within the time of the novel, there is also the writing of the narrator's first book and the role played by Tony in guiding the work to its successful publication, making the narrator (and Johnson) a published author. Finally, there is *The Unfortunates* itself, the making good of the narrator's promise to Tony on his deathbed that he'll 'get it all down, mate'.

The narrator is sent to watch a football match between City and United. At the match he pours scorn on the 'well-paid pseuds who write their reports from prepared telling phrases',[50] while nevertheless taking pride in his ability as a professional writer to 'write to these tight deadlines, and to these precise lengths',[51] allowing the quality of the writing to be secondary. His professional assignment requires him to write not the truth but to provide an exciting, sensationalist account, though 'it would help if there were anything worth writing about. [...] Bollocks to that, bollocks to this stinking match'. The narration depicts the scene of 'live' writing, the match report as it emerges, interrupted first by the narrator's thoughts, and a second time by the spoken punctuation when he files the report by telephone to the newspaper office. It also appears in an edited, 'published' version, shorn, as the narrator feared, of its more erudite phrases, inside *The Unfortunate*'s box: a dramatisation, perhaps, of the stripping effect (or $-(\female\male)$ in Bion's terms) of what he imagines to be the hostility and rivalry of his editors. He wonders whether 'this bloody reporting language [may] affect, destroy even, my own interest in language', how the deadline forces him to use 'the words which first come into my head, which is not good, relying on the chance of real words which may come in only the two hours of a match',[52] his report deadline another kind of container in which words are placed, pseudo-words, readymade, alongside the 'chance of real words'. Bion describes this kind of deathly, readymade language, characterised by the overused phrase, 'yes I know', as 'a sort of modern version of the unconscious, a kind of way of doing without an unconscious by having such an apparatus of mental bricks and mortar'[53] that makes it possible to do without thinking at all. Pope's 'needless alexandrine'[54] also makes an appearance, this time in a self-consciously erudite reference to a player called Alexander:

Devoid of real incident, the match dragged its slow length, no, yes, there's Alexander, earlier, when he hit the bar. Alexander, dragging his slow length along from right back, [...] like a wounded snake has to be worked in somewhere, no, it'll never work, too contrived, scrub it.[55]

The question of how to write truth without contrivance is seen in two depictions of rain, offering a call-and-response (or the other way round, depending on the order in which they are read) to the writer's dilemma:

Images for rain are common, I cannot think of one, I do not need to think of one, really, for what purpose?[56]

It begins to rain, rain like an extension of the air, wet air, not falling in drops, in material terms, that is, in drops one would call drops, but a fine air mist of wetness, of rain, that makes me blink, that just depresses me one stage further, that does not soak, or give me cause to feel abandoned. Does it?[57]

The differing passages offer two characteristic voices of B.S. Johnson: the one withering, high-handed, pouring scorn on the very attempt to write yet another image for rain, the too-easy metaphorisation of disappointment through the image of rain on a grey day in a Midlands town; the other passage self-conscious and close-written, the *vernissage*, by degrees, of a consciously hesitant image of 'rain like an extension of the air' that nevertheless achieves a subtle and honest description ('that does not soak, or give me cause to feel abandoned'). In Bionian terms we might venture that the first example registers a preconception of rain as well as Johnson's resistance to the psychical work that would place it at risk of becoming a column 2 formulation[58] – the realm of the lie – while the second version enacts the successful mating of the pre-conception with its realisation: ironically, the saturation (of meaning) of rain by Johnson's finely wrought description of 'rain like an extension of the air'.

It is not, then, surprising that the narrator's account of the news of Tony's death is characteristically unsentimental, the fact of his death mentioned seemingly in passing: 'for he had died that evening'.[59] It appears in the novel's shortest section by far, occupying less than half a printed page; the most important 'fact' of the novel no more than a subordinate clause on a 'throwaway' page, a literally *detached* account. And like death itself, the notice of Tony's passing is no respecter of narrative propriety, for the section comes when it comes – maybe halfway through reading, maybe immediately after the first section. It cannot be ideally placed within a literary-chronological re-ordering of *The Unfortunates*; no surprise or mystery attaches to it. In another section Johnson provides a memorable image of smoke rising from the crematorium as the narrator walks away from Tony's funeral. Ascending in a straight column, 'as far as smoke can ever be said to move in a straight line', it moves into and disperses 'into the haze, the sky, it was too neat, but it was, it was'.[60] It is, I suggest, a fitting final image of Tony: the lost container disintegrated, dispersing into air.

Previous commentators have followed Johnson in placing greater emphasis on the loose sections than on the box itself. Johnson described 'a certain point' when the mass of ideas that preceded each novel would coalesce, '[come] to have a shape, a form that I recognise as a novel'.[61] His account of this process comes very close to the selected fact described by Poincaré and taken up by Bion:

> If a new result is to have any value, it must unite elements long since known, but till then scattered and seemingly foreign to each other, and suddenly introduce order where the appearance of disorder reigned. Then it enables us to see at a glance each of these elements in the place it occupies in the whole. Not only is the new fact valuable on its own account, but it alone gives a value to the old facts it unites. Our mind is frail as our senses are; it would lose itself in the complexity of the world if that complexity were not harmonious; like the short-sighted, it would only see the details, and would be obliged to forget each of these details before examining the next, because it would be incapable of taking in the whole. The only facts worthy of our attention are those which introduce order into this complexity and so make it accessible to us.[62]

Johnson writes: 'this crucial interaction between the material and myself has always been reduced to a single point in time: obviously a very exciting moment for me, and a moment of great relief, too, that I am able to write another novel'.[63] In the case of *The Unfortunates*, however, this 'moment of relief' seems to require a supplement (the box), since the material at hand – questions of untimely death, a promising life stricken by cancer – does not allow of resolution: the cancer does its work inexorably, bringing disintegration rather than resolution. In his formulation of the container-contained relationship, Bion drew inspiration from his fellow psychoanalyst, Elliott Jaques, who described the 'integrative reticulum' that must be in place in order for creative work to be possible. The integrative reticulum is a psychical object that holds together the fragments of a project, a new thought, or an experience of growth:

> the mental schema of the completed object and the means of creating it, organised in such a manner that the gaps both in the mental picture of the object and in the methods of creating it are established. Consciously, it is a combination of any or all of concepts, theories, hypotheses and working notions or hunches. Unconsciously, it is a constellation of ideas-in-feeling, memories-in-feeling, phantasies and internal objects – brought together and synthesised to the extent necessary to direct behaviour, even if not sufficiently to become conscious.[64]

What is important, in other words, is that the artist can conceive of the project as a whole, however shadowy, and allow a conception of the completed object to organise the work itself. In the case of *The Unfortunates*, the integrative reticulum that Jaques describes is given concrete form, and the narrator's thoughts, memories and encounters are placed within the box with a minimum of other structure. Johnson's narrator marvels precisely at the mind's capacity to contain, hold, and in some measure be both affected and unaffected by all 'these things': 'How the mind can take these things in, calmly, discuss them, hold them, and still be affected, terrified by them! The mind'.[65]

But the integrative reticulum that Bion calls on in his formulation of the container-contained relationship can also fall apart. In Jonathan Coe's introduction to the 1999 republication of *The Unfortunates*, he recounts Johnson's instructions to readers of the original Hungarian edition. Due to publishing costs, the novel was printed as a bound book, entirely contrary to Johnson's wishes. He was nevertheless able to append a prefatory note in which he suggested how readers might recreate the intended effect. The edition included a page of symbols at the back of the book, referencing the symbols at the head of each section. These could, he suggested, be cut out, 'place[d] [...] in a suitable receptacle', in order to determine, tombola-style, the next section to read. But this solution could not recover the 'physical feel, disintegrative, frail, of the novel in its original format'.[66]

Johnson also wrote that 'the whole novel reflected the randomness of the material: it was itself a physical tangible metaphor for randomness and the nature of cancer'; that it provided a better 'solution to the problem of conveying the mind's randomness than the imposed order of a bound book',[67] and this view is taken up by commentators such as Nicolas Tredell, Patrick Parrinder, and Philip Tew, even where, in the case of Parrinder, it is thought to be 'not a very successful device', since 'there is no way of re-ordering the twenty-seven sections so as to introduce a previously hidden element of surprise'.[68] My contention is that to argue that *The Unfortunates* fails for lack of 'surprise' would be missing the point: while Tony's cancer shocks, it does not surprise – it does what cancer does; it reminds us that we all die in the end.

Other commentators, including Greg Buchanan, Kaye Mitchell, and Glyn White, recognise that the box device is not only a way to foreground the theme of randomness, but they also neglect to consider the box in detail. White notes how 'randomness as an experience for the reader immediately gives way to specificity'[69] and suggests that 'ultimately, there is more to gain from the format than the partial experience of randomness'. He also comes closest to describing the experience of reading *The Unfortunates* with the text progressively 'whittle[d] away'[70] with each completed section. Buchanan pursues another interesting line of analysis, noting how the reader's involvement in having to 'put the book together' effects a denaturalisation of the book format that echoes the processes of illness, leaving Tony, for example, needing mechanically to perform previously automatic bodily functions (such as moistening his lips after his saliva glands are destroyed by treatment). He also notes Julia Jordan's suggestion that 'each sentence contains its own first – and sometimes second and third – draft'.[71] This is especially clear in the match report section, where we see phrases alternately selected and rejected, but it is elsewhere at work where anecdotes are taken up and reworked within or between sections. Where this technique seems to aim at an increasingly subtle approximation of the narrator's emotional truth, it stands in marked contrast to the thin and stereotyped depictions of the narrator's former girlfriend, Wendy, who appears in the text as a cipher for feminine betrayal. In *A Memoir of the Future*, Bion has recourse to a metaphor of cancer to describe the way that thoughts can be 'undigested': he notes the way that a character's 'small sarcasm at [her husband's] susceptibility to a pretty face began to harden, to remain undigested. Envy lay waiting, single-celled, to become malignant'.[72]

Mitchell suggests a phenomenological approach to *The Unfortunates* in which the act of reading 'concretis[es] the text, making it into the work that it is',[73] each reading assigning a temporary ordering. But she finds that the text produces 'an *impression* of randomness' that is ultimately 'disingenuous', citing Judith Mackrell, who finds that there is not more 'than a superficial experience of indeterminacy'.[74] She also describes the box as a 'coffin' that returns the question of *The Unfortunates*' elegiac intent into view. Contemporaneous criticism (described by Tredell and Parrinder) apparently agreed that the novel failed as an elegiac piece, since it evidently focused more on the narrator than on Tony. Buchanan cites Julian Jebb who suggests that the characters of the novel 'seem more like visitors to a consciousness than individuals encountered, observed and described',[75] though Tredell argues that the 'elevation of the elegist over the elegised is not peculiar to *The Unfortunates*: it is inherent in the very form of the elegy'.[76] Jebb's analysis is congruent with my suggestion that *The Unfortunates* may be better understood as an attempt to restore an internal object: the work of mourning the recreation of a container, enacted performatively by the box device, but also in the process of writing.

This is undoubtedly an ambivalent process, a way both to 'be done with' the painful material of the past as well as to integrate it. Johnson described his writing as a kind of exorcism, suggesting that he was in some way haunted by the things in his mind. What haunts the narrator, in Bionian terms, are images of the dying Tony identified with the disintegration of the containing mind that is, in fact, a part of the narrator. For Johnson, writing enacts the psychical evacuation of mental pain; he describes writing as a kind of exorcism, 'to remove from myself, from my mind, the burden of having to bear some pain [...]: in order that it may be over there, in a book, and not in here in my mind'.[77]

Yet *The Unfortunates* also gestures positively towards the possibility of 'grow [ing] towards' bigger and more complex writing projects. The narrator recalls how he and Tony discussed his next idea – for a novel as yet larger than his capacity to achieve it:

> I was not big enough to write it, yet, that the idea was bigger than I was and I would not have the techniques to handle it, would have to grow towards it. [...] I am still not big enough for that one.[78]

This mysterious other book – the book still unachieved – is the book awaiting the growth of the narrator, the book for which he (and his mind) will have to be 'big enough'. The work of restoring the lost container that is effected by *The Unfortunates* can also make it grow. Bion suggests that love is involved in growth, and that the mind that grows through love also becomes able to receive love.[79] Johnson's ambivalence towards his readers and to criticism (useful, for Johnson, only if it helps to build better writers) is nevertheless accompanied by the fleeting recognition that there is a role for an *other* in the apprehension of art. He cites Rilke: 'Works of art are of an infinite loneliness and with nothing to be so little reached as with criticism. Only love can grasp and hold and fairly judge them'.[80]

Johnson's solipsism has been noted by many of his critics, and it is reflected in both his creative work and his commentary. His earlier novel, *Trawl*, both begins and closes with I ('I, always with I ... one always starts with I.. and ends with I'[81]). The final page of *The Unfortunates* suggests that the narrator continues to oscillate between Johnson's characteristic self-orientation (only ironically might we redescribe this as 'single mindedness') and the possibility of offering up his personal experience to a wider audience; true understanding, for Johnson, must avoid generalisation; truth is in its essence solipsistic: 'In general, generalisation is to lie, to tell lies'.[82]

In *Cogitations*, Bion returns the word, publication, to a more literal reading – *public-ation*: the making public of a private truth. He suggests that the process of truth-telling, which he relates to a broad definition of scientific method, is not completed until it can be made available to 'common sense', a term he uses not in the conventional way but to indicate the possibility of correlation between different people, or between different 'senses' within an individual. For Bion, truth cannot finally be only personal. He writes that 'the physical act of writing and carrying through all the other acts, up to and including public-ation, constitutes being a man of action *for the writer*':[83] in other words, the 'social component' of writing is not incidental. Between the passage above and the final words of the novel Johnson leaves a quarter-page of blank space, suggesting the time of a decision, or indecision, the question of whether to end the novel with a variant on his usual mantra ('telling stories is telling lies'), or to venture toward 'public-ation'. Eventually, the narrator continues:

> Not how he died, not what he died of, even less why he died, are of concern, to me, only the fact that he did die, he is dead, is important, the loss to me, to us

The last word – 'us' – left pendant and unpunctuated ends *The Unfortunates* on a cautiously hopeful note, suggesting that the narrator can now accede to 'public-ation', with the restoration of relationship, of being 'two-minds-to-write': the narrator re-integrating the part of his mind that is Tony's true legacy.

Notes

1 Bion, *Complete Works*, 4:356 *(Learning from Experience*, 90).
2 Johnson, *Albert Angelo, Trawl, House Mother Normal* and *Christie Malry's Own Double Entry*, all London: Picador (2013).
3 Coe, *Like a Fiery Elephant: The Story of B.S. Johnson*.
4 Johnson, *The Unfortunates*. As a collection of loose sections, *The Unfortunates* poses a certain challenge to referencing conventions. I follow other commentators in using the opening one to three words of each section (as seems appropriate in each case), followed by a page reference. Johnson provided an alternative device – a different symbol at the top of each section – but these are difficult to reproduce typographically.
5 'Note' printed inside the box itself.
6 Johnson, *Well Done God!*, 19–25.
7 Coe, 231.
8 Johnson, *Well Done God!*, 389.
9 Coe, 21.
10 The estate, 5.
11 Then they, 5.
12 Bion, *Complete Works*, 6:154 *(Second Thoughts*, 111).
13 Bion, *Complete Works*, 5:25 *(Elements of Psychoanalysis*, 25).
14 Bion, *Complete Works*, 12:44 *(A Memoir of the Future*, 36).
15 Away from, 2.
16 Sacks, *The English Elegy: Studies in the Genre from Spenser to Yeats.*
17 Ramazani, *Poetry of Mourning: The Modern Elegy from Hardy to Heaney*, 30. Italics mine.
18 First, 3–4.
19 Bion, *Complete Works*, 4:356 *(Learning from Experience*, 90).
20 The opera, 1–2.
21 Again the house, 1.
22 Then he, 4.
23 So he, 5.
24 Conan Doyle, *The Penguin Complete Sherlock Holmes*, 150.
25 Last, 3.
26 Then they, 1.
27 Sometime that, 3.
28 The estate, 6.
29 Then he, 2.
30 That was, 3.
31 Again the house, 2.
32 Bion, *Complete Works*, 4:357 *(Learning from Experience*, 91).
33 Southwell, 3.
34 Sometime, 1.
35 Just as it seemed, 3.
36 Just as it seemed, 6–8.
37 Bion, *Complete Works*, 4:358 *(Learning from Experience*, 92).
38 Bion, *Complete Works*, 2:26 *(All My Sins Remembered*, 27).
39 Bion, *Complete Works*, 4:363 *(Learning from Experience*, 97).
40 For recuperation, 2.
41 Again the, 4.
42 Cast parapet, 2.
43 Then he, 1.
44 The estate, 8.
45 His dog, 4.
46 Southwell, 1.
47 Away from, 3.

48 His dog, 4.
49 Johnson, *Well Done God!*, 28.
50 Time!, 5.
51 Away from, 1.
52 The pitch, 5–7.
53 Bion, *Complete Works*, 9:39 (*The Tavistock Seminars*, 36).
54 See chapter three.
55 The pitch, 6.
56 Away from, 1.
57 Time!, 3.
58 See chapter three for a fuller discussion of the column 2 formulation.
59 June rang, 1.
60 We were, 1.
61 Johnson, *Well Done God!*, 23–24.
62 Poincaré, *Science and Method*; quoted in Bion, *Complete Works*, 4:339 (*Learning from Experience*, 72).
63 Johnson, *Well Done God!*, 23–24.
64 Jaques, 'Disturbances in the Capacity to Work', 360.
65 Cast parapet, 2.
66 Introduction, xii.
67 Johnson, *Well Done God!*, 25–26.
68 Parrinder, 'The Novels of B.S. Johnson', 54.
69 White, *Reading the Graphic Surface: The Presence of the Book in Prose Fiction*, 115.
70 White, 116.
71 Jordan and Ryle, *B.S. Johnson and Post-War Literature: Possibilities of the Avant Garde*, 55.
72 Bion, *Complete Works*, 12:19 (*A Memoir of the Future*, 10).
73 Tew and White, *Re-Reading B.S. Johnson*, 52.
74 Tew and White, 55.
75 Jordan and Ryle, *B.S. Johnson and Post-War Literature: Possibilities of the Avant Garde*, 55.
76 Tredell, *Fighting Fictions: The Novels of B.S. Johnson*, 111.
77 Johnson, *Well Done God!*, 18–19.
78 I had, 5–6.
79 Bion, *Complete Works*, 4:301 (*Learning from Experience*, 33).
80 Johnson, *Well Done God!*, 397.
81 Johnson, *Trawl*, 183.
82 Last, 6.
83 Bion, *Complete Works*, 11:164 (*Cogitations*, 169).

5 With and without Bion: supplementing an uncanny reading of Mary Butts

We do not know where the mental boundaries are, nor do we know where the impulses commence.[1]

Mary Butts' short story (first published in 1932), 'With and Without Buttons', recounts the strange tale of two sisters who, deciding to play a spooky trick on their fervently rationalist neighbour, find themselves subject to a 'genuine' haunting beyond their control.[2] A box of gloves 'with and without buttons' in a shared attic becomes the locus of uncanny happenings as single gloves belonging to a previous tenant appear in both the sisters' and their neighbour's home. A strange story told strangely, 'With and Without Buttons' foregrounds a number of curious emphases – buttons, beginnings, and the invocation of an uncanny natural force that pervades the precarious boundaries between house and house, house and nature, and between the sisters themselves and their neighbour, Trenchard, whose masculine scepticism provokes the story's unfolding.

In what follows I develop a reading of 'With and Without Buttons' using a number of Bion's ideas to address the strange features of Butts' text. In doing so I proceed from and acknowledge the suggestive use of Bion's work made by Jacqueline Rose[3] to think about another work by Mary Butts, *The Death of Felicity Taverner*, though the specific contention of her essay (relating Bion's figure of the 'bizarre object' to disquieting literary moments marked by psychotic mechanisms) is pursued in the next chapter rather than here. Mary Butts is a wayward writer whose inclusion in the Modernist canon, as Nathalie Blondel observes,[4] has perhaps been held back by the unevenness and eccentricity of her work.[5] Best known for her 'Taverner Novels' (*Armed with Madness*, published in 1918, and *The Death of Felicity Taverner*, in 1928), Butts' style is both unmistakeable and maddening: there are glimpses of crystalline prose alongside awkward narrative handling, and her writing is steeped in the affected, complacent world-view of the privileged English upper class. Her passionate credulity for the occult (most prominent in *Armed with Madness*, which turns around an imagined discovery of the Holy Grail) takes her into murkier territory than the work of her contemporaries, such as T.S. Eliot or Rainer Maria Rilke, for whom the evocation of pre- and ultra-human forces

DOI: 10.4324/9781003006619-5

provides ballast and recuperation against a world laid low by man's destruction. Where *Armed With Madness* strays into melodrama, the 'dirty' (and mal-odorous) little trick and ghost story at the centre of 'With and Without Buttons' is undergirded by a greater natural reality of something Butts names 'Tide', percolating the fragile human-made boundaries of house and garden.

Freud's essay, *The Uncanny*, frames a psychoanalytic insight into the gen-eration of the particular and peculiar unease created by uncanny literary effects. While 'With and Without Buttons' unquestionably partakes of the literary uncanny, I argue that the story merits a supplementary Bionian reading to make fullest sense of the story's uncanny aspects. I argue that his description of beta-elements, the protomental system and the caesura, and his theory of O and transformations can enable a more detailed reading of Butts' strange tale.

The story begins with a curious maxim that places it from the outset in an ironical relationship to truth: 'It is not only true, it is comforting, to say the incredulity is often no more than superstition turned inside out'. Butts' opening line suggests that truth will have but an incidental value in 'With and Without Buttons', but that there will be truth in the tale, all the same. For a story in which gloves will play such a central role, the figure of the reversible surface giving on each side to incompatible viewpoints is a curious one, drawing attention to the boundary fabric that performs a perverse (and *reverse*) intimacy of opposing sides, while nevertheless enacting or staging their dis-continuity. The double surface of the glove, with a capacity both to enclose the hand within and the object without, is the medium of contact while at the same time disavowing or precluding the possibility of an intimate contact, skin-to-skin. The glove is a second skin and a way of touching the world, as well as an ironic figure of potential erotic contact (we will come later to the story's erotic and sensual themes).

This first line also seems to signal the reversibility of perspective, the way that meaning can give way to its opposite. Bion described the 'binocular vision'[6] required of the analyst to see both the conscious and unconscious aspects of communication and drew attention to the interdependence of meaning:

> One of the weaknesses of articulate speech is shown in the use of a term like 'omnipotence' to describe a situation that in fact cannot be described at all accurately with a language that is of one kind only. 'Omnipotence' must always also mean 'helplessness'; there can be no single word that describes one thing without also describing its reciprocal.[7]

As its first line suggests, Butts' story will rely on a reversible perspective in which two apparently opposed ways of thinking (rationalism and superstition) exist simultaneously and form part of a total phenomenon. The theme is echoed in the situation of the two sisters (the non-narrating sister chiefly an amplification or double of the narrator) who live in one half of a formerly unitary house since divided, and now only connected through the attic. It is Trenchard, their very near neighbour, who provides the provocation for the story that unfolds: he irritates the sisters by suggesting that religion is a mere psychological trick: 'It was only because Trenchard said at lunch that the mass was a dramatised wish-fulfilment that what came after ever happened'. Butts evokes the language of psychoanalysis ('dramatised wish-fulfilment', 'reaction exercises') to frame 'With and Without Buttons' as a riposte to that which she calls the 'faith of disbelief [that is] as inaccurate as its excess', which she did, in fact, identify with Freud and psychoanalysis. Butts' biographer, Nathalie Blondel, notes that she read Freud 'from the 1910s' (the earliest translations of Freud's work into English appeared from 1909[8]), but rejected his ostensible commitment to rationalism and official repudiation of supernatural phenomena.[9] Although we do not know whether Butts read Freud's 1919 essay, *The Uncanny*, I suggest that the two texts stand in ironically companionate relationship to each other: Butts' story seeming to exemplify the effects of a specifically literary uncanny described by Freud, within a tale dedicated to overcoming the excessively rationalist sensibility that takes Freudian ideas as its bulwark.

Locating the 'beginning' of the story is no easy matter. The opening lines convey the anticipation of a story to be told while making clear that the matter – still troubling – is nevertheless in the past. Denouncing their churchgoing, the sisters' neighbour Trenchard provokes the narrator and her sister to defend the cast of mind that imbues ritual with 'real' significance, and they seek to find a way to 'suggest him into an experience'. They fix on a plan of placing gloves, taken from a box of 'old-lady' gloves they have found in the attic, around Trenchard's home, and then feeding him a spooky story:

> We'll put them there and get asked round for the evening and start when we see one, and that's where our village story begins. All that he has to get out of us is there *is* a story [...]

'Starting' has, of course, a double meaning in this context: the sisters will feign shock ('start') in order to begin their trick. With this decided, the sisters start to plot the details of their game, along with the story they will tell Trenchard to convince him of supernatural doings. As would-be story-makers and story-tellers ('before we begin we'll *do* something'), they nevertheless allow that the story-*work* (chiefly upon Trenchard's mind, suggested into an experience) will not be achieved under their aegis: 'This is what we planned, understanding that, like a work of art, once it had started, its development could be left to look after itself'.

And so it goes: the story 'begins' before they have a chance to do so themselves. Visiting Trenchard one evening, they learn that he has already discovered not one but two odd gloves lying around. Only the second of these is the one planted by the narrator's sister; the original glove is a mystery. With this unexpected development, the narrator's sister is forced to extemporise a ghost story; the improvised story will nevertheless coincide in every detail with the subsequent 'story' given to the narrator by a local: that the houses of both Trenchard and the sisters were formerly inhabited by one Miss Blacken, an old maid ('nice about her hands'), and her brother. The narrator, not realising that her sister is making up the story, takes umbrage at her for *beginning* too soon:

> 'Why didn't you tell me you had begun? Why didn't you coach me?' Then she said:

> 'To tell you the truth, I hadn't meant to begin.'

The story's strange beginnings multiply. The narrator suggests that 'it was as though – and we had known this to be possible before – it had already started itself'. When further gloves appear, it is Trenchard who remarks on beginnings:

> 'Hullo,' he said, 'there's another. It's beginning. That makes four.'

> It was then that it had begun. If you could call *that* beginning.

'With and Without Buttons' presents the reader with so many beginnings and motive impulses (the intention to trick Trenchard, the ruse of mysterious objects, Trenchard's desire to hear a story, and an improvised story lent unexpected weight by corroborative local story-telling), and yet these remain collectively insufficient to account for the story that actually unfolds, taking the story-telling sisters by surprise. As such, Butts' short tale seems to offer a commentary on the art of story-telling itself, drawing attention to the properly uncanny power of words and ideas to 'suggest [people] into an experience'.

The theatre critic Peter Brooks[10] has suggested that 'a word does not start as a word – it is an end product which begins as an impulse, stimulated by attitude and behaviour which dictates the need for expression'; one can wonder whether the specific *words* of the story evoke or communicate a prior or primitive impulse that only emerges in narration. Without seeking to ground the story in a story-outside-the-story (recalling Derrida, *il n'y a pas de hors-texte*), Bion's theory of the protomental system offers a way to trace and detect the emotional, psycho-somatic/soma-psychotic datum that exists within the text. It is therefore with that strangely insistent word, 'buttons', that I pursue not a 'real beginning' but the text's semantic penumbra. The figure of the buttons appears at the end of a long list of prospective aids to the haunting planned by the two sisters: 'last year's leaves, delicate damp articulations; coloured pebbles, dead flies, scraps of torn paper with half a word decipherable.... A mixture of these or a selection?' The narrator pushes her sister on to greater enumeration: 'dead bees, feathers, drops of candle-grease? Old kid gloves? With and Without Buttons. That will do'.

The phrase 'With and Without Buttons' (thus capitalised) arrives fully formed, appearing throughout with a persistent and baroque emphasis. David Matless[11] calls attention to the narrator's variation on the phrase ('Some have all the buttons and some have none and some have some') as a 'rune'. Butts' buttons are ubiquitous, proliferative and maddening: every scene in which a ghostly glove appears is ornamented with a button-based detail, though no pattern or meaning in the number or appearance of buttons can be readily discerned. They nevertheless contribute to the story's strange effects: the buttons seem to haunt the story despite appearing as an incidental detail. Whoever or whatever the 'ghost' may be in 'With and Without Buttons', it is not as concerned with the buttons as the characters seem to be (barring one late occasion, in which buttons are found in a bowl of food). In a journal entry from 1930,[12] Mary Butts tried to account for the ghostly effects created by M.R. James, the writer whose stories she much admired (and to whom she intended to dedicate her story): 'It occurred to me that the horrid details by which James gets his effects are *incidental*'.

I argue that an adequate reading of 'With and Without Buttons' must take the buttons specifically into account. While Freud's essay *The Uncanny* offers a starting point for analysis, it does not offer a way to make sense of all of the strange features of Butts' story. 'With and Without Buttons' is nevertheless in many respects an exemplary instance of the literary uncanny, with its combination of haunting, doubles, and automatisms. It is therefore worth stepping through a Freudian analysis, not least because of the way the story addresses itself so pointedly to a style of rationalism that takes Freudian arguments as its basis. Much of what is at stake in the German original of *The Uncanny* is the concept of home and homeliness, *Heimlichkeit*: the uncanny is what is literally unhomely, *unheimlich*. Tracing the dictionary definition of *Heimlichkeit* to the point where it begins to shade into its opposite, *Unheimlichkeit*, Freud notes a quotation by Schelling that suggests that feelings of uncanniness arise when the privacy of what is *heimlich* is exposed: 'everything is *unheimlich* that ought to have remained secret and hidden but has come to light'.[13]

In 'Buttons', the home is a divided place – a house literally divided to make two dwellings: the sisters on one side, Trenchard on the other – with the shoe-box containing old gloves that will serve for the haunting in the loft 'by the door into his place when these houses were one'. There exists from the outset a cosy arrangement of neighbourly intimacy (the neighbours are frequently in each other's homes, or venturing through 'the gap in the hedge' that divides a shared orchard), though it is a shared infestation that provides the initial motive for a meeting: 'A nest of wasps had divided their attention between us, and we had met after sunset to return their calls with cyanide and squibs'. There is something darkly menacing in the image of the swarming wasps that do not respect neighbourly boundaries. They offer a clue to the instability of the border between the sisters and their neighbour; they are suggestive, perhaps, of an erotic aspect to the hazing and fragmentation of neighbourly boundaries: unlike bees, wasps proliferate 'unproductively', and they entail no sacrifice in deploying their sting. There is also something ugly about the use of cyanide and squibs (small explosives) to stay their propagation. The figure of the wasps crowding the boundaries of the divided house draws attention to something shifting, unstable and the more potent for being minutely fragmented: they require a brutal response since it is impossible to contain them with precision.

The creeping animism of the gloves (themselves a metaphor for the mysterious hand that leaves them around, the 'invisible hand' of the ghost story) recalls Freud's category of 'dismembered limbs, a severed head, a hand cut off at the wrist, feet which dance by themselves'.[14] This remarkable list nevertheless receives only glancing discussion by Freud; he suggests they are all to be understood chiefly as tokens of castration, an analysis he has already connected to the figure of the eye in 'The Sand Man'. For Freud, the detachability of body parts simply symbolises the missing or castrated penis, and the fear attendant on that unconscious idea. In 'With and Without Buttons', this argument does not seem compelling. The character of Trenchard plays foil to the sisters' desires, and it is their decision to 'suggest him into an experience' that sets the events of the story in train. The traces of an erotic aspect to the relationship between the sisters (more specifically the narrator) and their neighbour are readily discernible.

Freud notes 'the theme of the 'double'' as another 'uncanny harbinger', seeing in it the relic of the 'surmounted stage' of primary narcissism, or the development of the super-ego.[15] The narrator's sister functions as one such double; she seems to function chiefly as a convenient expositional interlocutor while never coming into focus as a character separate from the narrator. Certainly, the narrator's references to her sister have a facetious quality throughout, declaring on one occasion that she 'can rarely attain to [her] sister's breadth of mind'; on another, commenting ironically (since *she* is the sole narrator) that she 'recognised a master's direction' in her sister's plotting. They are together in every scene except two: the occasion when the narrator goes into the village to make enquiries of their house's former resident, and later on, in the brief but disturbing scene where the narrator and Trenchard are alone together (the sister is sent away to fetch perfume). The presence of the sister-double, I suggest, detracts the reader from the story's *potential* erotic theme that would otherwise centre more squarely on the relationship between the narrator and Trenchard.

'I am seeing him now, more vividly than I like', declares the narrator early on. There is vividness, too, in the name itself. 'Trenchard' suggests the nature of the challenge that he presents to the sisters' worldview: the entrenchment of rationalism, something hard and unyielding, the sturdy outerwear of the trench-coat; and, perhaps, the experience of trench warfare. The story hints at Trenchard's involvement in the East African campaign, which ended in 1917, as he recognises the smell of 'bad skins' from his time in Africa. The image of Trenchard and the sisters lined up on either side of a divide also evokes the peculiar intimacy with the enemy entailed in trench warfare. The sisters are infuriated by Trenchard's refusal to believe in supernatural forces, whether God or ghosts, and by his desire to 'sweat for our conversion; to shame us into agreement' with his rationalist views. The confrontation that sets in motion the sisters' desire to play a trick on Trenchard is notable for the menacing evocation of his anger that is also suggestive of sexual arousal ('[I] saw his healthy skin start to sweat and a stare come into his eyes. That should have warned me').

The story foregrounds a dense and heady sensuality in the environment, taking place 'one hot, sweet, blue-drawn summer, in a Kentish orchard'. The orchard ripe with fruit and 'night hunting cries and scents of things that grow and ripen' convey an earthly fecundity, explicitly female, that the barriers of the house and dividing hedge can do little to stay: 'With every door and every window open, the old house was no more than a frame, a set of screens to display night, midsummer, perfume, the threaded stillness, the stars strung together, their spears glancing, penetrating an earth breathing silently, a female power asleep'. Female, reproductive power is nevertheless contrasted with 'sex'. The narrator declares with breezy arrogance that getting Trenchard to 'make love' to them would be a simple enough (and possibly incestuous) task: 'We could have made him make love, to either or both of us, any day of the week'. What really motivates the sisters' stratagem, rather, is desire for the 'power [that] women sometimes want to have over men, the pure, not erotic power, whose point is that it shall have nothing to do with sex'.

The dichotomy between 'sex' – particularly the mannered flirtations and liberal mores of a bohemian upper class – and a 'purer' eroticism associated, perhaps, with female fertility, places the related question of pleasure between uneasy opposites: sex is unreal and without value in its frothy, 'society' guise (the sisters try to look 'like Paris' by way of compliment to Trenchard), or violent, visceral, and of a piece with the forces of nature that permeate their encounter. The narrator's description of the provocation they seek to bring about in Trenchard also has a recognisably sexual connotation ('if he doesn't rise the first night'). Indeed, the sisters' decision to base their spooking on gloves (rather than the many other objects they consider) is strengthened by their feminine association; they are 'the sort of things a man never has in his house'.

The box of kid-leather gloves that they find in the loft formerly belonged to Miss Blacken, the 'regular old maid [...] if maid she'd ever been', whose story hints darkly – and inconclusively – at an obscene secret centred on a lost petticoat (identified obliquely with the 'nasty slummy rag' that appears on their first visit to the loft, and with the smothering cloth of the final scene), night-time wanderings, and her care of her hands, suggesting a feminine delicacy at odds with her repellent figure, or hinting at masturbation ('dirty things done in a delicate way'). From the local who offers information about Miss Blacken and her brother one might infer an incestuous relationship with her brother: 'Not that you could be saying regular old man for him, for he wasn't either, if you take my meaning, Miss'. But there is no final revelation about Miss Blacken (or her brother) – no hint of prostitution, incest, secret affair, no actually *sexual* aspect at all, and it is perhaps precisely this unachieved or absent sexual life that lends horror to her story.

For all their sexual confidence, it is the sisters, as unmarried women, who are most closely identified with the spectral presence of Miss Blacken, and with the *pudeur* that the gloves of an old maid 'nice about her hands' evoke. The gloves occupy a strange place both as intimate and public apparel: delicate, form-fitting items, literally a second-skin both enabling and deferring the potentially sexual aspect of physical contact between the narrator (and her sister-double) and Trenchard. Seen from this perspective, the gloves suggest the symbolism of the hymen or a sheath, of that which establishes or resists sexual contact and the desire to touch. In the later scenes before the party, the gloves take on a more life-like, tumescent aspect: one appears up the back of the narrator's dress, 'open like a hand' that 'collapse[s] a little' when Trenchard touches it. The final glove is 'yellow-orange kid-skin, still and fat', with 'the wrist and the fingers open and swollen'.

The gloves (and the buttons) also give way to a stickier ending that evokes a more carnal encounter and suggests, perhaps, a more specifically female physicality. The 'filthy nonsense' that causes Trenchard's exclamation while he is dressing for the party is the discovery of a 'patch of grey jelly' (on the 'stiff' linen of his shirt) that prompts the sisters to feel 'as if there were slugs about, the things of which we are most afraid; and that we must keep our long dresses tight about us'. The gloves and the rag in the loft develop a mysteriously repellent aroma, the smell of 'bad skins' that Trenchard recognises, and a bottle of perfume owned by the narrator's sister is found suddenly to have acquired 'the sweetness, like a lady-like animal, of old kid gloves'. The scene that takes place just before this is particularly striking. With her sister sent away to fetch perfume, the narrator is alone with Trenchard for the first and only time in the story. Though of a piece with the breathless melodrama of the closing pages, it has in isolation a strikingly dissociative, oneiric quality that suggests a sexual scene or a scene of trauma:

> She ran away, and I stood still, aware of my shoulder-blades and the back of my neck, and all of my body that I couldn't *see*. Doors would not open easily. I heard him swearing and stumbling, the clang of a bucket tripped over and kicked away in the yard.

The fragmentary, staccato quality of the writing conveys to startling effect the narrator's awareness of her physicality (and of all her body that she 'couldn't *see*', her *heimlich* parts) that immediately precedes Trenchard's stumbling flight into the courtyard. The two moments of the scene (her awareness of her body, the fleeing man) invite a reading of a phantasied or attempted rape, but leave open the question of whose violation is at stake. I suggest that the final scene of the story, in which Trenchard is discovered overcome, apparently smothered, by a dirty piece of cloth (that is perhaps Miss Blacken's lost petticoat), develops the theme of an overwhelming, female sexuality that subjects the neighbour to a phantasied oral violation: 'Some of it was in his mouth. We pulled it out. His tongue and mouth were stained'. Having been rescued from underneath the petticoat, Trenchard gives his own account, with the final words of the story emphasising his trauma's *olfactory* aspect:

> the next thing I knew it had wrapped itself round my head and I couldn't get it off. I tore at it and tried to get out. Then I couldn't bear it any more. It was winding itself tight. Then I must have passed out. But, oh God, it was the smell of it…

A narrow reading of the gloves along the lines that Freud suggests in *The Uncanny* would obscure the themes of intimacy, contact, and female sexuality. I contend that what is uncanny about the gloves is not that they are detachable or that they suggest a severed limb (or penis), but that they enact a 'tele-touching' at once remote and intimate. They preserve a boundary of decorum (protecting lady-like hands from the contamination of sexual touch) associated with the *pudeur* of Miss Blacken, which is lent an obscene tinge that may be grounded finally in nothing more than the obstinate, unfortunate, or indeed wholly accidental preservation of her virginity into old age. There is nothing new in calling attention to Freud's blind spot in respect of female sexuality, to which his famously 'failed' case study of Dora attests.[16] Freud is also at pains throughout *The Uncanny* to play down the thesis, described by Jentsch, that ascribes 'the essential factor in the production of the feeling of uncanniness to intellectual uncertainty',[17] though like a revenant itself it persists in returning to Freud's consideration. 'With and Without Buttons' foregrounds intellectual uncertainty from the outset, with the narrator making clear that Trenchard's capacity to *think* is permanently disturbed by the affair: 'Now he cannot think what he used to think, and he does not know what else there is that he might think'.

Additionally, the many references to an impersonal force that drives the story ('It was trying to get out anyhow') can equally suggest the existence of a *thought* rather than the existence of a *ghost* (the ghost of a thought, perhaps). The flicker of Trenchard's anger that erupts when the narrator tells him to 'stop boring [them] with his wish-fulfilments' gives rise likewise to a thought that will drive the development of the narrative: 'It did warn us, but it wound us up also'. The trope of 'winding up' a mysterious figure ('it') recurs on two later occasions: at a moment when the sisters realise that they are no longer the authors of their own story ('I know what it is we've done,' said my sister, 'we've wound it up') and during Trenchard's closing description of the smothering cloth ('It was winding itself tight'). Deciding to wait overnight for the details of their 'good idea' to give Trenchard a nightmare, the narrator's sister declares that she 'can feel one about'.

In the fifth of his Tavistock seminars, Bion is asked to relate two terms of his own invention – the protomental (or proto-mental) system or 'apparatus', and the beta-element. His answer is instructive, but it is worth taking a moment to situate both of these concepts in turn. Of the two, his formulation of beta-elements is better known, but in fact the protomental system is the earlier term. It appears in Bion's first book, *Experiences in Groups*, as 'a level in which physical and mental are undifferentiated'[18] and the matrix from which the group behaviours that he describes as the 'basic assumptions' emerge. Despite the always suggestive word 'matrix', Bion's conception of the protomental system is of a system or level of mind (or more accurately, some precursor of mind, 'proto-' mind) rather than a space or place (such as a womb). Bion's conception of the protomental system nevertheless bears comparison with Julia Kristeva's later concept of the 'chora',[19] although as it pre-dates his association with Melanie Klein it does not, as one might expect, reference the relationship to the maternal body, even as it alludes to intra-uterine life. It is, rather, a level of 'mind' on the border of somatic and psychical processes, which can nevertheless manifest a state of distress 'in physical forms as in psychological'.[20] While Bion's formulation of a protomental system passes largely into disuse after *Experiences in Groups*, he continues to seek to articulate aspects of mind that cannot adequately be located through the classical distinction between the conscious and unconscious. In later years, he borrows the term 'caesura' to describe moments that mark the passage or re-activation of somatic and psychical material in(to) new levels of mind. What we describe as a thought, he suggests, has a pre-history that may be rooted in 'somatic' or 'embryological' modes of 'thinking':

> The embryologist speaks about 'optic pits' and 'auditory pits'. Is it possible for us, as psycho-analysts, to think that there may still be vestiges in the human being which would suggest a survival in the human mind, analogous to that in the human body, of evidence in the field of optics that once there were optic pits, or in the field of hearing that once there were auditory pits? Is there any part of the human mind which still betrays signs of an 'embryological' intuition, either visual or auditory?[21]

The 'impressive caesura of birth' described by Freud and cited by Bion[22] is only one of innumerable 'caesuras' that mark moments where the experience of one system penetrates into another, where something is realised, a thought takes shape, or a life-decision (such as marriage) is enacted. Returning to the question posed in the *Brazilian Lectures*, he evokes a frontier between mind and body that may sometimes be recognised in poetic expression:

> But there are things that do seem to me to suggest this combination between the body and the mind. Why do the old anatomists call part of the brain the 'rhinencephalon'? Why a nose brain? Why is a patient always complaining of a rhinitis? Psycho-somatic? Soma-psychotic? Take your choice. 'Pure and eloquent blood spoke in her cheeks, and so distinctly wrought, that one might almost say, her body thought' [Donne, 'The Second Anniversary'].[23]

He suggests that the rhinencephalon, or 'nose brain', may be one of several precursor modes of intelligence (the optic pits, the alimentary canal), which, though largely supplanted by the function of the cranial brain, nevertheless remain in vestigial form. 'Smell', he suggests elsewhere, 'can be one of the long-range methods of communication'.[24] The question of smell also appears in *The Uncanny*, but it goes unremarked in Freud's account of a short story where he had himself been (exceptionally, if we are to believe him) affected by a sense of the uncanny: 'I read a story about a young married couple who move into a furnished house in which there is a curiously shaped table with carvings of crocodiles on it. Towards evening an intolerable and very specific smell begins to pervade the house'.[25]

Nicholas Royle has identified the story as 'Inexplicable' by L.G. Moberly[26] and traced a number of uncanny smells in this and other stories, arguing that Moberly's concern with the '*recurrence* of smell' suggests 'a link between smell, uncanny repetition and trauma', though he hesitates to speculate on what the nature of that link could be: arguably, smells *linger* rather than recur; they disrupt the notion of beginnings and endings that would ground the possibility of repetition in the *fort-da* mode that Freud will go on to describe in *Beyond the Pleasure Principle*. The smells that pervade 'With and Without Buttons' (flowers, damp skins, scent) succeed in permeating – even perforating – the boundary between skin and skin that is effected by the wearing of gloves. In the closing evocation of the terrible *smell* that is the worst part of Trenchard's experience, Trenchard is perhaps the recipient of something that cannot yet be thought, but that urges communication. It is likewise received at a level that is other than a conscious one: in her journal, Mary Butts described her experience of 'signatures', the term she gave to 'hints, coincidences, prophetic or retrospective of a significant event', in terms of an apprehension of or attention to something for which 'one's brain is not *quite* the right instrument'.[27]

Extracts from *Cogitations* suggest that Bion developed the term 'beta-element' in 1960 (though he describes something recognisably similar as early as August 1959[28]). It appears first in publication in 1962. Bion's account of beta-elements is both complex and shifting, and has invited differing interpretations by commentators. At the simplest level, the category of beta-elements may be described as the stream of sense-impressions that have not been worked on by alpha-function to produce alpha-elements, the most basic elements of thought. Writing in *Learning from Experience*, Bion describes beta-elements as chiefly suitable for 'evacuation', either through the mechanism of projective identification, or by a variety of procedures 'intended to disencumber the personality of accretions of stimuli'.[29] Insofar as they resist their progressive transformation by alpha-function (the processes of mind that enable us to 'learn from experience'), beta-elements persist as 'undigested facts' that neither join the store of our memories nor contribute to the rudiments of thought.

The definition is further complicated by Bion's own early comparisons of beta-elements to the Kantian categories of the noumena and things-in-themselves (a contested category within Kantian scholarship that Kelly Noel-Smith argues Bion misunderstands[30]). It prompts James Grotstein to suggest that beta-elements comprise both 'pre-processed sensory impressions' (pre-processed in the sense of: prior to processing by alpha-function) and the noumenal 'Ideal Forms' implicit in Klein's account of innate or prenatal pre-conceptions (e.g. of the breast) that equip the baby for its initial encounters with the world. Beta-elements have, moreover, an emotional (or proto-emotional) quality, with Grotstein proposing that they are 'O's proto-emotional descendant – that is, the β-element is the emotional sense impression of O: the ghost of O'.[31]

So what does a beta-element look like? The analytic literature is richly equivocal on the topic, since Bion himself describes beta-elements in more or less substantive terms. In one of two essays transcribed from audio in 1977, beta-elements are described as something solidly 'physical', if mysterious:

> The first box I am thinking of is really not suitable for anything so ephemeral as what I usually call a thought, namely, something that is physical; I shall call it a beta-element. I don't know what that means and I don't know what it is, and as it hasn't turned up I am still ignorant. But anyway, there it is, in case that strange creature should exist and should it swim into my ken.[32]

Intriguingly, the phenomenon that Bion describes may approximate something that Mary Butts described as a part of her spiritualist cosmology. In Roslyn Reso Foy's account of 'With and Without Buttons', she associates the smell as a part of what Butts identifies as 'Elementals': 'an ancient belief in the animal-thing, seen, heard and smelt, but impervious to touch and infecting like a poison'.[33] Butts compares such elementals to Ariel and Caliban, spirits that evoke in humans the 'fear that there is animal life outside the animals he knows, less than human life and more, and infinitely malignant'. In 'With and Without Buttons', the skins of the gloves become elementals revealing the supernatural life outside the 'skins, furs, shells and feathers of our earth' [...].[34]

Where Butts' 'elementals' reveal 'supernatural life' animating organic objects, beta-elements manifest psychical debris. Elsewhere Bion suggests that beta-elements can also be *words*, but words used for hallucination rather than the representation or abstraction of reality. Writing in *Attention and Interpretation*, he contends that 'the word representing a thought is not the same as the identical word when it is representing an hallucination'.[35] Bléandonu makes the connection with beta-elements directly: 'As the concept of hallucination has a long and loaded history of meaning, Bion prefers to use the term 'beta-element'. This enables him to relate the 'hallucination' encountered in clinical practice to the 'thing-in-itself' of philosophical speculation'.[36]

The buttons invite an analysis along these lines. Heralded in the title, and thrust egregiously into every scene, they nevertheless add little functionally to a story that starts with the placing of gloves (whether they have one or several buttons, or none) and continues through a series of such events to a dénouement that finally features neither gloves nor buttons. While the buttons briefly take centre-stage in one of the final happenings (their appearance on top of a bowl of strawberries), they play a less significant role than the events that follow, in which the buttons give way entirely to gloves that seem to swell and shrivel, patches of 'grey jelly', the smell of 'dead skins', and smothering rags. What is chiefly uncanny in the figure of the buttons is the narrator's and the sisters' (and even Trenchard's) insistence on enumerating the buttons in each new scene of 'haunting'. No pattern or meaning can be readily identified in the sequence of these numbers: none, three buttons missing, two buttons, and so on. They are countable ('some have all the buttons and some have none and some have some'), but as a feature of the story they remain quite *unaccountable*.

That Trenchard himself falls in with the button-counting lends the story an additional uncanny aspect that suggests something too close, more-than-neighbourly, in the sharing of minds between the sisters and Trenchard (in relation to whom the sisters seem to have taken on an almost wifely job-sharing role by the time of the garden party).

The buttons are the most persistent reference among a number of small, particulate or fragmentary objects that are notable throughout the text. The wasps that 'had divided their attention between us' at the beginning of the story are one such figure, as are the items listed as possible 'tangible' aids to haunting, such as leaves, pebbles and scraps of paper. The parade of fragmentary things continues until the narrator's sister alights on gloves and buttons: 'dead bees, feathers, drops of candle-grease? Old kid gloves? With and Without Buttons. That will do'. I propose that these objects are understood best not as incidental detail or literary ornamentation, nor even as sexual symbolism (though the theme of female sexuality and the figure of buttons bears reference to Gertrude Stein's *Tender Buttons*), but as intimations of aspects of feeling and thinking that press upon the story for textual expression. The buttons are *things* – notably tangible, non-abstract – within the frame of the narrative; they are also *words*. They add little to the plot but are an obtrusive, uncanny feature of the text (and the title), inviting further analysis.

A further, overlooked aspect of Bion's formulation of beta-elements is also instructive. In a journal entry from February 1960, he highlights an important aspect of beta-elements: namely, their relation to a sense of an object's 'vitality' or 'deadness'. It takes place within a discussion of infantile development and the destructive attacks made by the infant on its objects:

> In this instance it is necessary to talk about this object which should be non-existent and therefore impossible to discuss. Its importance lies in the fact that the infant, if enraged, has death wishes, and if the object is wished dead, it is dead. It therefore has become non-existent, and its characteristics are different from those of the real, live, existing project; the existing object is alive, real, and benevolent. (*I propose to call the real, alive objects α-elements; the dead, unreal objects I shall call β-elements.*)[37]

The deadness and unreality of beta-elements are of course the more disturbing for nevertheless continuing to *exist*: an aspect of reality can be psychically repudiated (by the child or the adult), but the reality that gives rise to the impressions of those objects will continue to press in on the mind. This model of beta-elements – as the persistence of supposedly 'dead' objects seeking representation – suggests that beta-elements come to *haunt* us, and as such provides an extended way of thinking about the uncanny, and the uncanny effects of 'With and Without Buttons'. The maddening insistence on the buttons becomes more meaningful if they can be taken as narrative – and textual – traces of a repudiated aspect of reality seeking expression that is closer to evacuation than to symbolisation. Bion describes beta-elements as 'objects

that can be evacuated or used for a kind of thinking that depends on manipulation of what are felt to be things in themselves as if to substitute such
manipulation for words or ideas'.[38] The reader does not take the buttons to be
hallucinated, but is invited by the narrator to participate in a group experience
in which the story's most egregious feature is shared by all as a kind of empty
code – and equally collectively passed over without comment: the text invites
the reader to be finally as blind to any possible 'meaning' of the buttons as the
characters themselves.

I suggest that 'With and Without Buttons' evokes an emotional, protomental field from which the narrative elements of the story emerge. This is not
to suggest that the emotional atmosphere precedes the story (except within the
terms of the story itself), and it is also not the same as saying that the markers of
an emotional and environmental atmosphere should be read chiefly as metaphors to decorate or dramatise the story, as in the pathetic fallacy (e.g. the
trope of the 'stormy night' suggesting a story of passion). It is not really sa-
tisfying as a 'ghost story' (despite its undoubted uncanny effects), and is finally
uncompelling as an incidental account in the genre of a personal *fait divers*. But
as a self-reflexive staging of a thought and its vicissitudes, it is a remarkable
achievement. The scene where the sisters return to the house at the end of the
evening sets a stage for the tale's unfolding:

> We went home through the orchard in the starlight and sat downstairs in
> the midsummer night between lit candles, inviting in all that composed it,
> night-hunting cries and scents of things that grow and ripen, cooled in the
> star-flow. A world visible, but not in terms of colour.

The scene bears comparison with Bion's transcribed audio-essay ('28 May
1977'). His wife and editor, Francesca, tells us that it was 'recorded by Bion
sitting alone in his study' prior to travelling to Rome. He describes waiting for
a 'thought without a thinker' to come along. An extract gives a flavour of the
essay's charming and curiously languorous atmosphere:

> I have been idling away my time, thinking in this way – a way I could
> describe as being almost thoughtless. If, as a child, I had been caught at it,
> somebody would have said, 'Why on earth don't you find something to
> do?' I would now like to have a look in case I have caught anything in the
> net of my idleness.[39]

Like Bion, the sisters await the idea that will catalyse their determination to
give Trenchard a 'nightmare': they 'can feel one about'. As they go upstairs to
bed, the house is beset by something that Butts names 'tide', as remarkably
evocative as it is formless:

> Through walls and glass, through open doors or shut, a tide poured in, not of
> air or light or dark or scent or sound or heat or coolness. Tide. Without

distinction from north or south or without or within; without flow or ebb, a Becoming; without stir or departure or stay: without radiance or pace. Star-tide. Has not Science had wind of rays poured in from interstellar space?

Whatever else it may be, it is not sea-tide or river-tide: Butts' account of 'tide' suggests something formless but nevertheless substantive, a primeval soup from which something might evolve, and which confounds any possible boundary either man-made or physical ('through open doors or shut'). It evokes a pervasive, irresistible force that takes as its nearest reference the water-tides driven by such cosmological forces as gravity and planetary movements. Had it been intended as a poetic rendering of Bion's concept of O, it would be difficult to better. I suggest that Butts' evocation of 'tide' during the night in which the sisters await the appearance of an 'it' (their 'good idea', a nightmare for Trenchard, a mechanism by which to frighten him, the beginning of a story) is an attempt to register the foundation of an emotional experience (and something as yet prior to a thought) that will unfold into a 'Becoming' (the term is both Butts', and Bion's[40]). To do so I relate two 'eras' in Bion's thinking that address the question of reality in different ways.

The first of these is his hypothesis of the 'thought without a thinker' and that which Sandler has described as his '(onto)genetic view of the development of the thinking apparatus',[41] in terms of Bion's classification of beta-, alpha- and other particles or parts of thought. The second is his description of O and transformations, which does not replace or supersede the first system, but which suggests a theory of observation for the practising psychoanalyst in respect of tracing back and tracking forward the evolution of an originary reality, O, through transformations into and in diverse realms of human activity.

Bion's figure of O first appears in *Transformations* to denote absolute reality: 'what the absolute facts are cannot ever be known, and these I denote by the sign O'. O names that which cannot be experienced directly (other than as an emotional 'catastrophe') but which can be 'stepped-down' or metabolised[42] by transformation into emotional experiences and knowledge wrought in many possible different domains (such as painting, to use Bion's example). Bion frequently quotes Milton's evocation in *Paradise Lost* of something 'won from the void and formless infinite' as a representation of O and its derivatives.[43] If Butts' passage about Tide evokes the O of the sisters, it is also the narrator's transformation of O *in* narration (using Bion's language, O is not transformed *into* narration, but *in narration*). It is the translation of something that is not originally experienced into a form that makes the experience of it possible. Using Bion's earlier analytical tools – the beta- and alpha-elements first described in *Learning from Experience* – we can identify those features of the text that suggest the metabolisation of an idea and the development (i.e. the further evolution) of a thought that the narration is shaped to make it possible to think.

The intangible quality of beta-elements has also led to the simple equation of beta-elements with O. James Grotstein argues that beta-elements should be understood as 'O's phenomenal derivatives'[44] that have failed to be transformed by alpha-function; i.e. that beta-elements do not exist conceptually prior to a notion of alpha-function, and can be defined only on the basis of a failed encounter with alpha-function. It is for this reason, Grotstein suggests, that Bion's naming of beta- (after alpha- in the alphabet) places alpha-elements as prior to beta-, even though beta-elements are genetically the more primitive (and appearing before alpha-elements in the Grid). Grotstein follows Ferro in using the term *balpha* to emphasise the close connection of beta-elements with alpha-function,[45] a formulation that again recalls Bion's allusion to a place *between* beta- and alpha-elements, representing something that exists on the boundary of body and mind. Again, it is 'The Second Anniversary' that provides the example:

> Beta-elements are a way of talking about things which are not thought at all; alpha-elements are a way of talking about elements which, hypothetically, are supposed to be a part of thought. The poet Donne has written, 'the blood spoke in her cheeks … as if her body thought'. This expresses exactly for me that intervening stage which in the Grid is portrayed on paper as a line separating beta-elements from alpha-elements. Note that I am not saying that it is either beta or alpha but the line *separating the two* which is represented by the poet's words.[46]

Using Bionian ideas to supplement a Freudian reading brings the memorable features of 'With and Without Buttons' into clearer focus. Its rich and distinctive atmosphere – replete with buttons, gloves, smells, thoughts intimated but remaining (to borrow a word that Bion uses frequently) 'sub-thalamic',[47] and all that evolves from 'Tide' – plays a substantial role in producing the story's uncanny effects. The story *evokes* (calls forth) a response in the reader that we may describe as 'uncanny', but which emerges less from the story's ghostly happenings than from the unsettled and unsettling – and one might say protomental – background from which the features of the story emerge. Butts' buttons are less spooky in themselves than the sense they convey of another field or level in which the buttons might evolve into future meaning; considered as beta- (or *balpha-*) elements, they are also frightening to the extent that they represent aspects of experience that resist meaning, remaining stubbornly unaccountable in the face of any reading; the gloves likewise do no real harm but draw attention to terrifying ideas that remain unspoken: themes of incest, rape, and female desire.

Notes

1 Bion, *Complete Works*, 11:344 (*Cogitations*, 373).
2 Butts, *With And Without Buttons and Other Stories*.
3 Rose, *On Not Being Able to Sleep: Psychoanalysis and the Modern World*.
4 In her Afterword to Butts, *With And Without Buttons and Other Stories*, 209.
5 E.g. Oliver Conant cited in Foy, *Ritual, Myth, and Mysticism in the Work of Mary Butts: Between Feminism and Modernism*, 112.

6 Bion, *Complete Works*, 7:101 (*Brazilian Lectures: 1973 São Paulo, 1974 Rio de Janeiro/São Paulo*, 105).

7 Bion, *Complete Works*, 11:342 (*Cogitations*, 370).

8 English translations of Freud's work made by A.A. Brill appeared from 1909 onwards. See, for example: 'Dr. A.A. Brill Dies; Psychiatrist, 73'.

9 Blondel, *Mary Butts: Scenes from the Life. A Biography*, 82–83.

10 Brook, *The Empty Space*, 15.

11 Matless, 'A Geography of Ghosts: The Spectral Landscapes of Mary Butts', 345.

12 Butts, *The Journals of Mary Butts*, 339. Italics mine.

13 Freud, *Standard Edition*, 17:225.

14 Freud, *Standard Edition*, 17:244.

15 Freud, *Standard Edition*, 17:234–35.

16 'Fragment of an Analysis of a Case of Hysteria', in Freud, *Standard Edition*, vol. 12.

17 Freud, *Standard Edition*, 17:221.

18 Bion, *Complete Works*, 4:177 (*Experiences in Groups*, 102).

19 McAfee, *Julia Kristeva*, 19.

20 Bion, *Complete Works*, 4:177 (*Experiences in Groups*, 102).

21 Bion, *Complete Works*, 10:38 (*Two Papers*, 42).

22 Bion, *Complete Works*, 10:35 (*Two Papers*, 37).

23 Bion, *Complete Works*, 9:53 (*The Tavistock Seminars*, 54).

24 Bion, *Complete Works*, 9:118 (*The Italian Seminars*,19).

25 Freud, *Standard Edition*, 17:244.

26 Royle, *The Uncanny*, 138.

27 Butts, *The Journals of Mary Butts*, 371–72.

28 Bion, *Complete Works*, 11:66 (*Cogitations*, 63).

29 Bion, *Complete Works*, 4:281 (*Learning from Experience*, 13).

30 Torres and Hinshelwood, *Bion's Sources: The Shaping of His Paradigms*, 129.

31 Grotstein, *A Beam of Intense Darkness: Wilfred Bion's Legacy to Psychoanalysis*, 59.

32 Bion, *Complete Works*, 10:177 (*Taming Wild Thoughts*, 29).

33 Foy, '"Brightness Falls": Magic in the Short Stories of Mary Butts'.

34 Foy, *Ritual, Myth, and Mysticism in the Work of Mary Butts: Between Feminism and Modernism*, 100.

35 Bion, *Complete Works*, 6:234 (*Attention and Interpretation*, 17).

36 Bléandonu, *Wilfred Bion: His Life and Works 1897–1979*, 219.

37 Bion, *Complete Works*, 11:129 (*Cogitations*, 133). Italics mine.

38 Bion, *Complete Works*, 4:274 (*Learning from Experience*, 6).

39 Bion, *Complete Works*, 10:179 (*Taming Wild Thoughts*, 32).

40 'Becoming O', an idea introduced in *Transformations*, is discussed in more detail in chapter eight.

41 Sandler, *The Language of Bion: A Dictionary of Concepts*, 305.

42 The analogy is Grotstein's: 'Thoughts, like glucose, must emerge from a series of intermediate transformations so that the sensory and intuitive impacts of awareness can be slowed down to utilizable elements'. Grotstein, *Do I Dare Disturb the Universe? A Memorial to W.R. Bion*, 15–16.

43 Bion, *Complete Works*, 5:261 (*Transformations*, 151).

44 Grotstein, *A Beam of Intense Darkness: Wilfred Bion's Legacy to Psychoanalysis*, 124.

45 Grotstein, 46.

46 Bion, *Complete Works*, 7:44 (*Brazilian Lectures: 1973 São Paulo, 1974 Rio de Janeiro/São Paulo*, 41).

47 Bion, *Complete Works*, 10:38 (*Two Papers*, 43).

6 Jean Rhys' bizarre telescope: a Bion-emic/-etic reading of *Wide Sargasso Sea*

> There is a screen, a caesura, a resistant material between one particle and the next. [...] Unless some person paints on a piece of glass, like Picasso, so that it can be seen from both sides of the screen – both sides of the resistance.[1]

In *Wide Sargasso Sea*,[2] Jean Rhys reimagines the pre-history of the gothic secret at the heart of *Jane Eyre*: Rochester's previous marriage to Antoinette Mason (Bertha Antoinetta in Charlotte Brontë's 'original') in Jamaica. Writing to Francis Wyndham in 1958, Rhys criticised Brontë's glancing treatment of the 'madwoman in the attic', the 'all wrong Creole scenes' that neglect the 'real cruelty of Mr Rochester'[3] to his young wife, held under lock and key for fifteen years. Rhys' prequel breathes vivid life into Antoinette's spectral presence in *Jane Eyre*, and into the world of the newly emancipated West Indies from where she is brought unwillingly to England. The story of Antoinette Mason (as I will call her, following Rhys' designation) is central to both texts. In *Jane Eyre*, the plot turns around the woman who 'laughs, yells and acts but never speaks', yet who nevertheless functions first to thwart and then enable Rochester's second marriage to Jane. The importance of her role in advancing the dénouement of *Jane Eyre* stands in marked contrast, however, to Brontë's scant development of her as a character and the depiction of her fate under Rochester's charge.

In this chapter I trace the curious figure of the telescope that appears three times in part two of *Wide Sargasso Sea*. The telescope, which sits on a table on the veranda at Granbois, briefly Antoinette and Rochester's marital home, has gone largely unremarked in critical commentary, but can be shown to figure the novel's central themes, including the *othering* and isolation of each of the three communities whose lives are entangled by the islands' colonial history: the black community of former slaves; the white Creoles, the former slave-owning class prior to the abolition of slavery; and the new class of white occupiers who have travelled from Britain to profit from the former plantation-owners' financial ruin. As an instrument of maritime navigation, the telescope is well placed to bring to mind the islands' colonial subjugation by the French and the British and to evoke the shifting mediation of contact with, and distance between, the three communities. The distinctive mechanism of the telescope, extending and retracting

DOI: 10.4324/9781003006619-6

to bring its subject into greater or lesser magnification, also figuratively enacts the shifts both in narrator and narration throughout the novel, most marked in part two. I argue that Bion's theory of the bizarre object can provide a more detailed understanding of the telescope's final outing, in which it seems to enact a moment of recoil and massive projective identification. Jacqueline Rose's suggestive use of the bizarre object to think about texts by Elizabeth Bowen and Mary Butts provided a starting point for the development of this idea.[4] I suggest that the telescope can also be seen as a *caesura*, marking the place where different perspectives collide.

The telescope on the table at Granbois has three outings in part two of *Wide Sargasso Sea*. It first appears early during Antoinette and Rochester's honeymoon, as a detail of the furnishing, during a scene in which their conversation reveals their mutual incomprehension of the other's reality:

'Is it true,' she said, 'that England is like a dream? Because one of my friends who married an Englishman wrote and told me so. She said this place London is like a cold dark dream sometimes. I want to wake up.'

'Well,' I answered annoyed, 'that is precisely how your beautiful island seems to me, quite unreal and like a dream.'

'But how can rivers and mountains and the sea be unreal?'

'And how can millions of people, their houses and their streets be unreal?'

'More easily,' she said, 'much more easily. Yes a big city must be like a dream.'

'No, this is unreal and like a dream,' I thought.

The long veranda was furnished with canvas chairs, two hammocks, and a wooden table on which stood a tripod telescope.[5]

Rhys' description of the veranda is surprisingly practised: a very similar description occurs both in her early short story, 'Mixing Cocktails', in 1927, and then again in her novel, *Voyage in the Dark*, in 1934. In 'Mixing Cocktails', she writes:

On the veranda, upon a wooden table with four stout legs, stood an enormous brass telescope. With it you spied out the steamers passing: the French mail on its way to Guadeloupe, the Canadian, the Royal Mail, which should have been stately and actually was the shabbiest of the lot... Or an exciting stranger![6]

In this passage, the telescope's function (spying the mail steamers) references the West Indies' colonial history, as well as the islands' close historical relationship with Canada. As a domestic object, it offers a window onto the wider world and a chance to see without being seen, a domestic/secret, truly *heimlich*[7] device that offers an *unheimlich*[8] vision of other worlds, by turns exciting or banal (the Royal Mail steamer proves 'the shabbiest of the lot'). Here is the telescope again, in *Voyage in the Dark*:

> Before I came to England I used to try to imagine a night that was quite still. I used to try to imagine it with the crac-cracs going. The veranda long and ghostly – the hammock and three chairs and a table with the telescope on it – and the crac-cracs going all the time.[9]

Rhys' repetition of the various elements of the tableau (not only the telescope, but the hammocks, the wooden table and the veranda) has led Neville Braybrooke[10] to assume that the scene is directly autobiographical. Though possible and perhaps likely, what is most striking is the way in which Rhys will repeatedly deploy the same or similar material across a period of nearly forty years. Kenneth Ramchand 'trace[s] in Miss Rhys' use and re-use of the same material, a progressive distancing in the art of autobiographical fragments and pressures which nevertheless account for the intensity of feeling in all her works'.[11] The depiction of the telescope in *Wide Sargasso Sea* occurs not once but three times, with a subtle change in detail between the first and second appearance giving way to the explosion of the telescope's figurative power on its third and final outing.

On each of the two occasions above, the telescope appears to an unnamed, first-person narrator who is imagining other worlds from the threshold of her domestic environment. By the time of its appearance (or re-appearance) in *Wide Sargasso Sea*, a second person has entered the scene, and a new narrative voice has overlaid Antoinette's initial narration in part one to question the primacy of her reality. Only Rochester has experienced both England and Jamaica; yet he responds defensively to Antoinette's suggestion that England is a 'cold dark dream' from which both she and her 'friend who married an Englishman' want to wake up. Where Antoinette's apprehension is understandable in the light of her inexperience, Rochester's unspoken coda ('No, this is unreal and like a dream') hints at his willingness to sacrifice Antoinette's reality and disavow the evidence of his senses.

The second instance of the telescope takes place directly after Rochester's meeting with Daniel Cosway, the man who claims to be Antoinette's illegitimate half-brother and who purports to offer a friendly 'warning' to Rochester against a backdrop of half-veiled intimations of Antoinette's promiscuity and latent propensity to madness. On his return, the narration notes that 'the telescope was pushed to one side of the table making room for a decanter half full of rum and two glasses on a tarnished silver tray'.[12] It is the beginning of a painful scene between Antoinette and Rochester and the prelude to Rochester's infidelity with the servant girl, Amélie.

It is also the night of *obeah*, in which Antoinette tries first to reason with her husband, grown suspicious and paranoid following Daniel Cosway's interference, and then to win back his love via a potion concocted by her nurse and servant, Christophine. Obeah, the name of the African diaspora spirit cult and its practices, is a motive force in all of the island's three communities, each differently in thrall to its supposed powers and the superstitions that surround it. Antoinette fears Christophine's involvement in obeah ritual[13] but will later plead for her help in the preparation of a potion able to re-ignite Rochester's sexual interest in her. Mason's English friends remark that it is 'evidently useful to keep a Martinique obeah woman on the premises', suggesting that the English newcomers recognise obeah's social influence and intimidatory power. On the night of the fire at Coulibri in which Antoinette's brother, Pierre, is killed, it is the inauspicious vision of Coco the parrot, burning and in flight, that finally frightens the tormenting locals away, though Antoinette's narration slyly notes that 'God who is indeed mysterious, who had made no sign when they burned Pierre as he slept – not a clap of thunder, not a flash of lightning'[14] seems to send forth the unfortunate parrot in direct response to Mason's Christian prayers. Her equivalence of obeah with the techniques of white spiritual supplication and power re-emerges in the later scene where she accuses Rochester of a different kind of obeah – the erosion of her identity that performs another kind of 'soul theft' – at work in his refusal to use her real name: 'Bertha is not my name. You are trying to make me into someone else, calling me by another name. I know, that's obeah too'.[15]

Rochester's 'white' obeah, which will result in Antoinette taking on the uncanny lifelessness of the *zombi*, broken and stupefied by his distrust and infidelity, offers a curious counterpoint to the novel's notable animisms, such as the orchids that 'flourished out of reach or for some reason not to be touched', or the 'needle [...] swearing'[16] as Antoinette labours over her embroidery in the convent. 'All this was long ago,' Antoinette recalls in the first part of the novel, 'when I was still babyish and sure that everything was alive, not only the river or the rain, but chairs, looking-glasses, cups, saucers, everything'.[17] But it is not Antoinette's childhood fantasia that breathes unexpected life into the tabletop telescope on its third and final outing: it speaks to Rochester alone. It occurs during the scene that follows Antoinette's return to Granbois after the events of the obeah night. She bites his arm as he tries to wrest a bottle of rum from her hands:

> My arm was bleeding and painful and I wrapped my handkerchief around it, but it seemed to me that everything round me was hostile. The telescope drew away and said don't touch me.[18]

The startling image of the telescope that recoils and speaks has attracted only brief critical attention. For Judith Raiskin, the telescope illustrates Rochester's 'projection of his fear and alienation onto the people and things around him',[19] but she goes no further in discussing the particular and peculiar figure of the retracting and extensible telescope or to its function as a device that enables 'seeing at a distance'. The projection that Raiskin invokes is the simple displacement of Rochester's own unbearable fear to an external location, but it is also a part of the wider environment in which 'everything round [him] was hostile', the closing-in or totalisation of a paranoiac phantasy. While paranoid projection is undoubtedly at work, understanding the telescope wholly in terms of displacement misses the ambivalence of the object that simultaneously is, and is not, of a piece with the hostile environment and which embodies that hostility not by attack but by recoil. For Liliane Louvel, the 'twice-mentioned' [sic] telescope is an 'antagonistic' object that denies Rochester the clear vision which is its purpose: 'as they multiply illusion, optical devices, supposed to be faithful and objective, magnify or reduce the world, thus blurring judgement'.[20]

Louvel's account of the telescope generalises its role to that of an 'optical device' that is by its nature faulty compared with 'natural' eyesight. In her reading, the telescope can only 'multiply illusion' rather than extend, amplify or elaborate the visual field, and she limits her description of the telescope's mechanisms to magnification and reduction. In fact, it would be more correct to describe the operation of the telescope as one of focalisation, the gathering-in of 'more light than the human eye is able to collect on its own'.[21] I suggest that the telescope should be understood as an object that extends, virtualises, and complicates the character of Rochester. Anthony Vidler, writing in *The Architectural Uncanny*, recalls Sartre's description (in *Being and Nothingness*[22]) in which the body is extended across its tools:

> My body is everywhere: the bomb which destroys *my* house also damages my body in so far as the house was already an indication of my body. This is why my body always extends across the tool which it utilises: it is at the end of the cane on which I lean and against the earth; *it is at the end of the telescope which shows me the stars*; it is on the chair, in the whole house; for it is my adaptation to these tools [...][23]

Sartre's evocation of the body 'at the end of' the telescope suggests a complex and performative virtualisation of bodily boundary that should complicate our reading of the telescope. We do not know who owns it: the telescope is unlikely to 'belong' to Rochester (since he arrived as a newcomer from England with, one might imagine, a minimum of possessions), but it is also not clearly, or no longer, Antoinette's: she inherits the house at Granbois, but (as Rochester makes plain to Christophine) all of her estate has passed into his ownership upon their marriage: 'I assure you that it belongs to me now'.[24] We might imagine that the telescope once belonged to Mason, or even old Cosway, Antoinette's father. It brings to mind (but is not identical to) the larger telescopes on board the ships that have successively brought different communities into harbour: the colonial plantation-owners, enslaved Africans, and the new class of white merchants seeking to make their fortune following the abolition of slavery.

The telescope's implication in colonial conquest suggests a less innocent aspect to the telescope on the veranda at Granbois. While the young narrator in 'Mixing the Cocktails' is motivated by curiosity to spy the arrival of the mail steamers, the history of the telescope attests to a more paranoiac function. Writing in 1609 to his patron, Galileo declares that he has:

> made a telescope, a thing for every maritime and terrestrial affair and an undertaking of inestimable worth. One is able to discover enemy sails and fleets at a greater distance than customary, so that we can discover him [the enemy] two hours or more before he discovers us, and by distinguishing the number and quality of the vessels judge of his force whether to set out to chase him, or to fight, or to run away.[25]

The telescope is thus an instrument that can alternately prefigure, imagine, or forestall a contact with the other; it is both a tool of curiosity and invitation (a way to see at a distance, to bring near what is far away) and a way to maintain distance from what is perceived as 'other' and threatening. Jonathan Crary has related advances in optical technology to the production of distinctive historical subjectivities. He proposes that 'during the first few decades of the nineteenth century a new kind of observer took shape in Europe radically different from the type of observer in the seventeenth and eighteenth centuries', locating optical devices as 'sites of both knowledge and power that operate directly on the body of the individual'.[26] It is therefore surprising that the telescope barely features in his detailed account of significant optical technology, which identifies the paradigmatic optical devices of the seventeenth/eighteenth and nineteenth centuries as the camera obscura and the stereoscope, respectively.

The telescope's role in seafaring and colonial expansion seems a striking omission from Crary's study, not least for the way the telescope contributes to new ways of seeing and relating to subaltern 'others'. Nevertheless his insight that optical technology may be 'related to the production of 'realistic' effects in mass visual culture'[27] can connect the figure of the telescope in *Wide Sargasso Sea* to Angela Smith's contention (in her introduction to the novel) that the novel is *about* perspective, 'pivot[ing] on mirroring and doubling, reiterating the trope of the looking glass'.[28] While Smith contends that this can be understood in terms of the Lacanian mirror stage ('It is almost as if Antoinette is trapped at what Lacan calls the mirror stage of infancy'), I suggest that it is Rochester's self-image, at least as much as Antoinette's, that appears in a refracted – and fractured – mode, recalling Smith's remark that Rochester's perception is 'skewed'. Smith also recalls Edward Said's contention that 'classic realist fiction develops in Europe in the nineteenth century because the 'power to narrate, or to block other narratives from forming and emerging' is a way of asserting cultural superiority'. The telescope's functions of focusing and magnification combine with its historical role in maritime conquest to become a device that figures colonised and subaltern peoples as 'other' – simultaneously remote, exotic, and under surveillance.

Maggie Humm has written of Rhys' 'depiction of telescopes as signifiers of the paternal eye',[29] suggesting a Kristevan analysis of Rochester in which he 'constructs an apartheid between his speech and Antoinette and Christophine's language of songs and body movement'. 'Without his telescope,' Humm continues, 'Rochester fears entanglement in nature', associated with the literally unnavigable spaces of the island (as exemplified in Baptiste's insistence that there is – and has been – 'no road'[30] through the forest). The 'language of songs and body movement' is also connected to Antoinette's sensuality and the disturbing possibilities of sexual life unconstrained by English convention, in which suspicions and traces of miscegenation abound, and where, as Antoinette declares, 'there is never a wedding'.[31] His paranoia activated, Rochester casts an eye – and doubt – on his wife's 'purity' along racial lines:

> Long, sad, dark alien eyes. Creole of pure English descent she may be, but they are not English or European either. And when did I begin to notice all this about my wife? After we left Spanish Town I suppose. Or did I notice it before and refuse to admit what I saw?[32]

Rochester finds Antoinette's eyes 'too large and disconcerting. She never blinks at all it seems to me', suggesting disquiet at the powerful female (and native) gaze to which Rochester finds himself subject. By contrast, it is the male gaze that is figured by the telescope (as well as a kind of telescope, the pocket spyglass) in Freud's essay, *The Uncanny*. Telescopes make an appearance on several occasions throughout Freud's work as a privileged figure of a 'mental apparatus'. In *The Interpretation of Dreams*, the telescope provides by analogy a virtual location for the focalisation of psychical reality:

> On that basis, psychical locality will correspond to a point inside the apparatus at which one of the preliminary stages of an image comes into being. In the microscope and telescope, as we know, these occur in part at ideal points, regions in which no tangible component of the apparatus is situated.[33]

The analogy with the focalisation of the telescopic image is a surprisingly complex one, since the phenomenon described emerges at an 'ideal point, regions in which no tangible component of the apparatus is situated'. Freud's metaphor invokes a virtual location arising necessarily in relation to the telescope that is simultaneously in no way referable to any 'tangible component' of the apparatus itself; its role is to gather and focalise a reality that is only made possible within its confines. In *The Uncanny*, the telescope also appears in Freud's opening etymological analysis of the words *heimlich* and *unheimlich*, where it populates (with no little incidental uncanniness) one of the dictionary examples he draws on to demonstrate the way in which the ostensibly benign quality of *Heimlichkeit* (homeliness) shades into something more sinister and *unheimlich*: 'He had achromatic telescopes constructed *heimlich* and secretly'.[34] Later on, the pocket spyglass that enables Nathaniel's voyeurism in *The Sandman* offers a further detail sustaining Freud's reading of Hoffman's uncanny tale as an allegory of the castration complex. Nathaniel's extending pocket spyglass provides an exquisitely phallic metaphor for uncanny seeing, as well as the basis for his illicit desire for Olympia, the wooden doll that he mistakes for Spalanzani's daughter.

In his analysis of *The Sandman*, Freud identifies the eye with the penis, and it is not too difficult to discern the telescope's phallic qualities: an instrument capable of extension and retraction; an instrument that mediates contact, but also enacts conquest, between a phantasied male body and a feminised, native other. I contend that the recoil of the telescope in *Wide Sargasso Sea* does not figure the patriarchal gaze so much as it witnesses and enacts the collapse and wounding of Rochester's phallic power in the aftermath of Antoinette's attack (the symbolism of her biting his arm is not so far removed from castration). His contact with his wife up to this point has been primarily penile, as is the nature of his insult to her (namely, sleeping with Amélie). For good or ill, the penis-telescope characterises the link between Rochester and Antoinette, and the moment of its recoil is shared by them both. Where a Lacanian analysis might clarify the telescope's shared ownership and the strange identity of their mutual recoil (Rochester *has* the penis-telescope; Antoinette *is* it), it is Bion's idea of the *link* that brings the relational aspect of the telescope into clearer view. The moment of telescopic recoil can be seen both as an attack on the link between Rochester and Antoinette and as an instance of the psychotic mechanism that Bion names the 'bizarre object'.

Bion describes the preconditions of psychosis as 'a preponderance of de-structive impulses so great that even the impulse to love is suffused by them and turned to sadism; a hatred of reality, internal and external, which is extended to all that makes for awareness of it; a dread of imminent annihilation and finally, a premature and precipitate formation of object relations',[35] marked by 'thinness' and 'tenacity'. Certainly, Rochester's account of his first weeks on the island and his decision to marry so quickly resonates with Bion's characterisation of a relationship that is 'premature, precipitate and intensely dependent':

> And when did I begin to notice all this about my wife Antoinette? [...] Not that I had much time to notice anything. I was married a month after I arrived in Jamaica and for nearly three weeks of that time I was in bed with fever.[36]

It is an encounter that is marked both by the 'thinness' of its foundations, as well as by the 'tenacity' with which Rochester will choose to enslave Antoinette in England sooner than countenance Christophine's suggestion of a pragmatic dissolution of their marriage, leaving Antoinette free to take another lover as a divorced woman and remain living in the West Indies.[37]

The bizarre object, which Bion introduces in his early paper 'Differentiation of the Psychotic from the Non-Psychotic Personalities', names a particular mechanism of pathological splitting associated with the failure of alpha-function. In the psychotic personality (or that *part* of the personality that is psychotic), the 'differentiation of the psychotic from the non-psychotic personalities depends on a minute splitting of all that part of the personality that is concerned with awareness of internal and external reality'.[38] The 'bizarre object' is the result of a reversal of alpha-function. It is important to distinguish the bizarre object from the beta-element: the bizarre object arises not from the failure of alpha-function even to begin to process and transform unmediated experience, but from its *reversal*.[39] The image of paper fed through a shredder that is then switched into reverse offers a helpful analogy. What is returned from the reversal of alpha-function is not what it was in the first place: it remains 'half-chewed' and damaged, returning in combination with the traces of personality with which it was originally paired and evacuated. The beta-element, Bion writes, 'differs from the bizarre object in that the bizarre object is beta-element plus ego and superego traces'.[40]

The theory of the bizarre object makes it possible to say that the telescope, in its moment of strange and sudden animation, is not only *like* Rochester: it *is* Rochester. In her commentary on Elizabeth Bowen, Jacqueline Rose[41] writes that the hallmark of the bizarre literary object is that 'things are in the wrong place' when 'the objects of the phenomenal world are granted the capacity to transfer their substance into humans, and […] the reverse'.[42] The telescope figures Rochester in a manner that is more than metaphorical, since it provides not just an identification with his character but a new location for a part of his personality, which in turns brings attention to the dislocation of his mind in this moment of extreme feeling. In the scene described, it also takes on qualities that are not its own, but Rochester's: wounded, paranoid, susceptible to touch, recoiling from attack. It *enacts* his recoil: body-less, it cannot be said as such to embody or incarnate it: the correct word, if it existed in the English language, would rather be one that carried the sense of 'en*thing*' (similar, perhaps, to what Nicholas Royle calls 'enantiodromic animism',[43] an animism that runs in the opposite direction). At the same time it also recoils *from* Rochester ('do not touch me'). The literal retraction of the telescope body suggests a reversal of the extension of Rochester's self even while his mind is subject to a radical, outer-body dislocation from self to thing. The mechanism of Rhys' telescope is remarkably reminiscent of Bion's description of the bizarre object, which is worth quoting in full:

> Each particle is felt to consist of a real object which is encapsulated in a piece of personality that has engulfed it. The nature of this complete particle will depend partly on the character of the real object, say a gramophone, and partly on the character of the particle of personality that engulfs it. If the piece of personality is concerned with sight, the gramophone when played is felt to be watching the patient; if with hearing, then the gramophone when played is felt to be listening to the patient. The object, angered at being engulfed, swells up, so to speak, and suffuses and controls the piece of personality that engulfs it: to that extent the particle of personality has become a thing.[44]

In his paper 'Attacks on Linking', Bion describes a state of mind in which emotion is hated for the way it threatens to establish a *link* between objects, leading to attacks on anything that could have a linking function. Following Klein, the prototype of the link is the 'primitive breast or penis'[45] that enables contact between self and other. The retraction of the penis–telescope that has hitherto stood quietly by evokes the destruction of a link. We learn that Rochester is the product of a patriarchal, emotionally stilted upbringing, where feeling is distrusted: 'How old was I when I learned to hide what I felt? A very small boy. Six, five, even earlier. It was necessary, I was told, and that view I have always accepted'.[46] The perverse logic by which Rochester recognises and yet upholds the colonial and patriarchal system that has worked so much emotional cruelty in him finds a resonant redescription in Bion when he writes: '[the attacks] on the linking function of emotion lead to an overprominence in the psychotic part of the personality of links which appear to be logical, almost mathematical, but never emotionally reasonable. Consequently the links surviving are perverse, cruel and sterile'.[47]

The related questions of perspective, and reality – and *whose* reality is at stake – are central to a reading of *Wide Sargasso Sea*. The novel stands in spectral connection to the 'original', authorised story of Rochester encountered in *Jane Eyre*, and it troubles the primacy of that 'first' encounter by evoking multiple, contiguous realities. The proximity of the differing narrative perspectives of Antoinette and Rochester (as well as the perspectives brought in by characters such as Daniel Cosway, Christophine and Amélie) draws attention to the existence of subtly or markedly different 'realities' that cannot be reconciled. Daniel Cosway's letter to Rochester, in which he seeds the idea that Antoinette may be 'going the same way as her mother'[48] seems to rewrite Antoinette's account of her mother, as well as undermining the reliability of Antoinette's narrative more generally. When Rochester goes to visit, Daniel Cosway sends him away with a suggestion that Rochester is 'not the first to kiss [Antoinette's] pretty face',[49] a sly suggestion that Antoinette is promiscuous, even incestuous: later, in the scene in which Christophine confronts Rochester, Cosway's words are refracted through Rochester's paranoia: '(Give my sister your wife a kiss from me. Love her as I did – oh yes I did.)'[50]

Towards the end of part two, Rhys draws attention to the multiplicity of perspectives through the use of an echo effect in which the reader seems to hear Rochester's mind in addition to his voice, responding to Christophine's accusations:

'But you don't love. All you want is to break her up. And it help you break her up.'

(Break her up)

'She tell me in the middle of all this you start calling her names. Marionette, Some word so.'

'Yes, I remember, I did.'

(Marionette, Antoinette, Marionetta, Antoinetta)

'That word mean doll, eh? Because she don't speak. You want to force her to cry and to speak.'

(Force her to cry and speak)[51]

The scene points to the disintegration of Rochester's mind. We are not shown a Rochester turned 'mad', as we are with Antoinette ('her hair hung uncombed and dull into her eyes [...] inflamed and staring'[52]), yet it is Rochester's narrative that breaks down in part two, and in his narrative that we encounter the most disturbing and complex scenes of the novel.

Bion's description of the *caesura* – to indicate changing states of mind and the emergence of new realities – can help characterise the micrological shifts in perception that seem to take place in Rochester's narrative. Bion extends Freud's use of the word to describe 'the impressive caesura of birth' for use 'as a model to understand far less dramatic occasions which occur over and over again when the patient is challenged to move from one state of mind to another'. He suggests that 'the personality does not develop as it would if it were a piece of elastic being stretched out. It is as if it were something which developed many different skins as an onion does',[53] though in another analogy the caesura is also described as a 'penetration' that is 'effective in either direction' (another role, perhaps, for the telescope): 'It is easy to put it in pictorial terms by saying it is like penetrating into the woman's inside either from inside out, as at birth, or from outside in, as in sexual intercourse'.[54]

The layering of voices (which is also the layering of different aspects of Rochester's mind – his social self, an inner voice, the voices of Christophine and later Antoinette that seem to speak through him) that occurs towards the end of the novel evoke a mind that is moving back and forth between different realities and realisations, a mind flickering across caesuras. Elsewhere, Bion describes the ability of art to create something that can be seen from both the pre- and post-caesural perspectives: 'There is a screen, a caesura, a resistant material between one particle and the next. [...] Unless some person paints on a piece of glass, like Picasso, so that it can be seen from both sides of the screen – both sides of the resistance'.

Antoinette insists that 'there is always the other side, always'.[55] The title of this chapter playfully suggests that a Bionian analysis of the telescope can draw out the *emic* and *etic* dimensions of the novel, and the way that Rhys, like Picasso, writes to both sides of the caesura, enabling more than one perspective to be seen. The terms, '-emic' and '-etic', emerge from the anthropological distinction between ethnography emerging from within (*-emic*) or outside of (*-etic*) a culture. The distinction is difficult to draw in *Wide Sargasso Sea*, where, strictly speaking, no one is indigenous: Antoinette is an outsider (the white Creoles are ironically described as 'white niggers'[56] by their former slaves);

Rochester is clearly an outsider, though the balance of power is currently in his hands; the black and mixed race people represented in the novel are also historical outsiders whose ancestors were taken into slavery during the Middle Passage (Christophine, the novel's most powerful black character, is doubly an outsider, lent a mysterious tinge through her provenance from the nearby French island of Martinique). *Wide Sargasso Sea* stages an encounter between mutually suspicious and hostile communities in which the position of the white Creole (and especially the white Creole woman) is a precarious one. The figure of Antoinette is made to bear the paradoxical brutality of the newly arriving whites who define themselves both in relation to, but distinct and superior from, the white Creole population who are their colonial forebears.

Bion's idea of the link develops Klein's theory of object relations by drawing attention not only to the object of the relationship, but to the link between objects, and the space or field in which the relationship takes place. The Sargasso Sea in Rhys' account is wide and unboundaried: it is, notably, 'the only sea without a land boundary',[57] bordering no coastline; it is 'cold, peaceful and motionless' in Jules Verne's description.[58] As a literary container, it is fittingly a space that belongs to no one, a purely a-relational space to which no person or group can lay final (or prior) claim; a place of dispossession to which all parties are subject, locatable only in terms of the links *between* people or via the mechanisms of colonial and post-colonial seeing. As an instrument of optical magnification, the telescope seems to draw near what is far away, to figure the possibility of relationship even as it keeps people at a distance. It represents several different ways of looking, encompassing curiosity, judgement, paranoia, and voyeurism. The telescope also figures Rochester's capacity to link to Antoinette and seems to describe his paranoiac breakdown and the destruction of the emotional link. In its final scene, it becomes a bizarre object both hostile and persecuted, a wounded phallus, and the locus of Rochester's self-alienation. The Rochester who (re-)appears in *Jane Eyre* is a man of pride and nobility who harbours a terrible secret. Fittingly, Antoinette's revenge, when it comes, will end with Rochester losing his sight, the result of the injury he sustains in trying to save her from the fire that she sets at Thornfield Hall. In the closing, happy scenes of that novel where he is reunited with Jane, Rochester is 'a poor blind man',[59] subject to Jane's female gaze and very limited in what he can see unaided by her 'eyes' ('for I was then his vision'[60]).

Wide Sargasso Sea ends with Antoinette awaking from a dream that seems to foretell a 'future' that we recognise, telescoping the time between the end of Rhys' and Brontë's novels:

> Then I turned round and saw the sky. It was red and all my life was in it. I saw the grandfather clock and Aunt Cora's patchwork, all colours, I saw the orchids and the stephanotis and the jasmine and the tree of life in flames. I saw the chandelier and the red carpet downstairs and the bamboos and the tree ferns, the gold ferns and the silver, and the soft

green velvet of the moss on the garden wall. I saw my doll's house and the books and the picture of the Miller's Daughter.[61]

It is a vision of a life to come that is also populated by images of Antoinette's past: an eye fixed on what is seen at a distance, in relationship to another place and time.

Notes

1 Bion, *Complete Works*, 14:37 (*A Memoir of the Future*, 465).
2 All references to *Wide Sargasso Sea* (noted as WSS) in this chapter are to the 1997 Penguin edition.
3 *WSS*, xiii.
4 Rose, *On Not Being Able to Sleep: Psychoanalysis and the Modern World*.
5 *WSS*, 49.
6 Rainey, *Modernism: An Anthology*, 957.
7 *The Uncanny*, in Freud, *Standard Edition*, vol. 17.
8 Literally 'unhomely', not domestic, but also 'uncanny'.
9 Rainey, 71.
10 Braybrooke, 'The Return of Jean Rhys'.
11 Frickey, *Critical Perspectives on Jean Rhys*, 201.
12 *WSS*, 80.
13 *WSS*, 14.
14 *WSS*, 22.
15 *WSS*, 94.
16 *WSS*, 29.
17 *WSS*, 19.
18 *WSS*, 96.
19 Raiskin, *Snow on the Cane Fields: Women's Writing and Creole Subjectivity*, 135.
20 Louvel, *Poetics of the Iconotext*, 145.
21 https://en.wikipedia.org/wiki/Refracting_telescope [accessed December 2020].
22 Sartre, *Being and Nothingness: An Essay on Phenomenological Ontology*, 349.
23 Vidler, *The Architectural Uncanny: Essays in the Modern Unhomely*, 81. Italics mine.
24 *WSS*, 103.
25 Henry, *Virginia Woolf and the Discourse of Science: The Aesthetics of Astronomy*.
26 Crary, *Techniques of the Observer: On Vision and Modernity in the Nineteenth Century*, 6-7.
27 Crary, 9.
28 *WSS*, xxi.
29 Humm, *Border Traffic: Strategies of Contemporary Women Writers*, 74.
30 *WSS*, 66.
31 *WSS*, 16.
32 *WSS*, 40.
33 Freud, *Standard Edition*, 5:536.
34 Freud, *Standard Edition*, 17:224.
35 Bion, *Complete Works*, 6:86 (*Second Thoughts*, 44).
36 *WSS*, 40.
37 *WSS*, 102.
38 Bion, *Complete Works*, 6:92 (*Second Thoughts*, 43).
39 See the previous chapter for a fuller discussion of this, including James Grotstein's re-visioning of the beta-element as something that has already failed to be transformed by alpha-function.
40 Bion, *Complete Works*, 4:294 (*Learning from Experience*, 25).

41 See also chapter one.
42 Rose, *On Not Being Able to Sleep: Psychoanalysis and the Modern World*, 93.
43 Royle, *Quilt*, 120.
44 Bion, *Complete Works*, 6:96 (*Second Thoughts*, 39–40).
45 Bion, *Complete Works*, 6:138 (*Second Thoughts*, 93).
46 *WSS*, 64.
47 Bion, *Complete Works*, 6:152 (*Second Thoughts*, 109).
48 *WSS*, 61.
49 *WSS*, 80.
50 *WSS*, 102.
51 *WSS*, 99.
52 *WSS*, 91.
53 Bion, *Complete Works*, 10:42 (*Two Papers*, 47).
54 Bion, *Complete Works*, 10:40 (*Two Papers*, 45).
55 *WSS*, 82.
56 *WSS*, 22.
57 https://oceanservice.noaa.gov/facts/sargassosea.html [accessed December 2020].
58 Verne, *Twenty Thousand Leagues under the Seas*, 273.
59 Brontë, *Jane Eyre*, 474.
60 Brontë, 481.
61 *WSS*, 123.

7 Efficient psychosis: notes towards a Bionian Ballardian breakdown

> Out it pours – masses of semi-whispered, disjointed stuff, name after name, some of which I know, some I may be supposed to know, some presumably I cannot be expected to know. [...] It does not require interpretation so much as loud cries of, "Help! Help! I'm drowning, not waving."[1]

J.G. Ballard described *The Atrocity Exhibition*,[2] perhaps the strangest gem in the Ballardian oeuvre, as a series of 'condensed novels' that might, in themselves, form one yet stranger condensed novel comprised of several parts. Published in sections from 1966, and as an integral work in 1970, *The Atrocity Exhibition* remains a remarkable and compelling literary achievement while skirting the limits of readability, both in form and content. The book evokes the mindscape of a series of recurring characters. We seem to watch a central figure (called variously Travis, Talbot, Traven, Tallis, Trabert, Talbert and Travers) as he falls from his former life as a psychiatrist towards and into psychosis. His condition is attended by the impassive clinical observer, Dr Nathan; the shifting characters of Koestler and Vaughan; the conglomerate female figures of Catherine Austin, Karen Novotny and Travis' long-suffering wife, Margaret. Kline, Coma and Xero are shadowy figures who may be products of the central character's hallucination. Beyond these, the text makes frequent reference to a group of celebrities and political figures from the 1960s and 1970s: Marilyn Monroe, Elizabeth Taylor, JFK and Jackie Kennedy, Ronald Reagan, and Ralph Nader, among others.

In what follows, I would like to develop a new reading of *The Atrocity Exhibition* that draws on Bion's theoretical tools. A psychoanalytic reading of Ballard is not new (see, for example, work by Samuel Francis[3]), and Ballard's frequent references to Surrealism and his strong thematisation of perverse sexualities resonate straightforwardly with psychoanalytic themes. Ballard's description of the work as a series of condensed novels also invites analysis in relation to the mechanism of condensation described by Freud in *The Interpretation of Dreams*. Moreover, Dr Nathan's comments on the character's (or characters') predicament are often explicitly, knowingly psychoanalytic. In the chapter-by-chapter commentary that accompanies the main text, Ballard writes laconically that Dr Nathan is the 'safe and sane voice of the sciences. His

DOI: 10.4324/9781003006619-7

commentaries are accurate, and he knows what is going on'.[4] In one instance, Dr Nathan invokes Freud's dream theory almost professorially, noting that 'one must remember that Talbot is here distinguishing between the manifest content of reality and its latent content'.[5]

I propose, however, that it is Bion's – rather than Freud's – work that can most productively address the psychotic aspects, both of content and form, of *The Atrocity Exhibition*. The power and possibilities of the psychotic mind are key concerns for both Bion and Ballard, and they each, in different ways, gesture toward the possibility of a positive or productive conception of psychosis that would be a critical and imaginative reservoir against hegemonic modes of culture. Two 'Bionian' ideas will be useful here: his description of the 'beta-screen' as an agglomerative function of beta-elements, and 'beta-space'. Beta- (or β-) space appears only once in Bion's work, but seems to draw together a number of vivid motifs – surgical, astronomical and nuclear – that resonate with Ballardian imagery to a remarkable degree.

I suggest that Bion and Ballard, at this shared moment of writing in the late 1960s and early 1970s, share something in their thinking of psychosis, broadly understood[6] to extend beyond individual pathology onto questions of culture and writing. The trope of *resonance* provides a way to think about a productive juxtaposition of texts in which the similarities and shared concerns of the two writers result in a mutual amplification. A number of Ballard's motifs in *The Atrocity Exhibition*, such as the emphases on intersecting planes and angles, astronomical space-time, 'world cataclysm',[7] and embryonic development reverberate with themes elaborated by Bion in his clinical journal, *Cogitations*, and in the several collections of transcribed seminars that date from Bion's move to California in 1968: *The Brazilian Lectures* (1973–4), *The Italian Seminars* (1977), *The Tavistock Seminars* (1976–1979) and *Bion in New York and São Paulo* (1977–8). The published transcriptions of these late seminars provide ample demonstration of the strange and provocative images that inhabit Bion's thinking.

The Atrocity Exhibition is formally striking: it consists of a series of paragraphs, each with an inline heading (or 'intertitle') marked in bold type, usually (but not always) derived from the paragraph that follows, which in turn form a densely associative but narratively loose series of fifteen chapters in total. The last three of these stand somewhat apart from the previous twelve chapters; the text also includes an appendix with two surreal textual sketches, 'Princess Margaret's Face Lift' and 'Mae West's Reduction Mammoplasty'. Editions from 1990 onward contain an additional paratextual component of annotations at the end of each chapter, by Ballard himself. What are we to make of this? Jake Huntley has compared *The Atrocity Exhibition*'s format to the structure of scientific papers, calling them blocks of 'hard, gleaming prose'.[8] The overall effect is to evoke a kind of clinical, hyper-rational detachment that is echoed in the character of Dr Nathan, who seems to offer 'reliable', if sardonic, commentary throughout. The paragraph sections also suggest a 'bizarre exhibition catalogue'[9] where the intertitles can be seen to frame or distil the text that follows. In other cases, no

explicit connection can be drawn, though the metaphorical force of the intertitle may be discernible in the content:

> **Dissociation: Who Laughed at Nagasaki?** Travis ran across the broken
> concrete to the perimeter fence. The helicopter plunged towards him,
> engine roaring through the trees, its fans churning up a storm of leaves and
> paper.[10]

The book begins with the single word 'Apocalypse', thus opening into a world
in which disaster is ever-present: imminent, *immanent*, and having already
taken place in the mind – or minds – of Travis (or his avatars: that which
Luckhurst has called the 'T-cell',[11] evoking the figure of a viral replication and
depletion), who occupies a liminal, uncertain status at a psychiatric clinic. In
the opening pages, his wife asks whether her husband was a doctor or a patient. Dr Nathan replies: 'Mrs Travis, I'm not sure the question is valid any
longer'.[12] Moving 'deeper into his own psychosis' in the first chapter, he
provides a shifting, unreliable centre to a book that can be seen as a con-
glomeration of texts rather than as a unified work.[13] Similar in form, most of
the 'chapters' reprise aspects of an inexplicit scenario that involves the central
character; all the chapters call attention to scenes of trauma, atrocity, and war,
whether historical events (the death of John F. Kennedy, for example, or the
Vietnam War) or in the central character's phantasy. Throughout, these themes
are connected to the work of the clinic to which T is attached in a shadowy
capacity: in 'The University of Death', Talbot is a lecturer who shows his
students 'simulated newsreels of auto-crashes and Vietnam atrocities' to illustrate
a 'World War III' scenario, while Dr Nathan watches uneasily in the background. The class is described as being 'consciously complicit' in Talbot's 'long-
anticipated breakdown'; the problem here is a too-vivid awareness rather than a
deficit of consciousness, although it is unclear whether Talbot is himself conscious of his 'growing distress and uncertainty'.[14]

   The chapters in which T appears make possible the minimal construction of a
character in differing phases of a psychosis (breakdown, madness, fleeting moments of recovery) in some relationship to the clinic and Dr Nathan; to a wife,
Margaret; and to one or several lovers. In 'Notes Towards a Mental Breakdown',
Trabert has an office in the psychiatric clinic, as does Travis in (the chapter also
entitled) 'The Atrocity Exhibition'; Talbert is in the last phase of his work there in
'The Great American Nude'. In 'Tolerances of the Human Face', Travers has just
resigned his post. In 'The Assassination Weapon', 'You: Coma: Marilyn Monroe',
and 'You and Me and the Continuum', Travis, Tallis and an unnamed central
character (respectively) is/are fully in the grip of psychosis; in 'The Summer
Cannibals', the sanity of its unnamed central character wavers undecidably. The
later chapters, less connected to the central cast of characters, evoke the detachment of applied sociological research aiming to discern or simulate 'optimum'
atrocities for the purposes of greater social health. The chapter 'Love and Napalm:

Export U.S.A.' describes a study into 'sexual stimulation by newsreel atrocity films':

> Studies were conducted to determine the effects of long-term exposure to TV newsreel films depicting the torture of Viet Cong: (a) male combatants, (b) women auxiliaries, (c) children, (d) wounded. In all cases a marked increase in the intensity of sexual activity was reported, with particular emphasis on perverse oral and ano-genital modes.[15]

Ballard's description of *Atrocity* as a series of 'condensed novels' is profoundly suggestive and invites more than one possible reading. Not least, it suggests the possibility of a long-form story offering the explanatory and contextual links that would make sense of Ballard's densely allusive prose (one might argue that Ballard's later novel, *Crash*, attempts something along those lines, expanding the characters and scenarios from the chapter of the same name in *The Atrocity Exhibition*). Despite his documented interest in psychoanalysis (Ballard originally intended to train as a psychiatrist after medical school[16]), it seems from his own account that it is not the condensation of the dream-work described by Freud that he has in mind. Rather, Ballard regarded his condensed novels as a feat of *distillation* that, by leaving out the linking phrases that are a part of 'forward conventional narrative', could give rise to the proliferation of new ideas:

> I once said those condensed novels, as I called them, are like ordinary novels with the unimportant pieces left out. But it's more than that – when you get the important pieces together, really together, not separated by great masses of 'he said, she said' and opening and shutting of doors, 'following morning' and all this stuff – the great tide of forward conventional narrative – it achieves critical mass as it were, it begins to ignite and you get *more* things being generated. You're getting crossovers and linkages between unexpected and previously totally unrelated things, events, elements of the narration, ideas that in themselves begin to generate new matter.[17]

What is absent in *The Atrocity Exhibition* is a context that could anchor the narrative to stable moorings, even though the depiction of landscape and culture is richly evocative. It is a world of disused and desolate industrial landscapes, faded suburbia, 'derelict roadways'[18] and wrecked cars. Yet while the depiction of location within *The Atrocity Exhibition*, and especially of the suburban housing and motorways surrounding Staines and Shepperton, are detailed and vivid, the relationships of the central character to his environment and to the other characters remain notional and unreal. They are also shifting and unreliable: the character of Karen Novotny dies (on at least three occasions), as does Margaret, the wife; sometime lover Catherine Austin dies along with Dr Nathan and Webster in the first chapter: all three subsequently return. Yet the unexplained or magical shifts in the narrative are somehow incidental to a deeper sense that something is missing or adrift in *The Atrocity Exhibition*: scenes of the greatest ostensible intensity and intimacy – car crashes and sexual scenes (frequently in combination) – nevertheless fail to confer a sense of relationship, of a con*tact* between characters that could elaborate the con*text* (noting that the word, 'text', carries the idea of a weaving or joining together). What Ballard's prose conveys, I suggest, is an absence of the emotional link of the kind described by Bion in 'Attacks on Linking', but in a different way to that described by Steven Connor (in his work on Samuel Beckett): the 'minute fragment[ation]' of experience that Bion associates with the psychotic personality resulting here not in the fragmented monologue of a Beckettian character, but in Ballard's curiously slick but emotionally monotonal textual chunks.

Bion theorises that the psychotic part of the personality attacks 'anything which is felt to have the intention of linking one object with another' due to the existence of an 'internal object [the internalisation of early experiences of relationship] which is opposed to, and destructive of, all links whatsoever'.[19] This manifests itself, in Bion's clinical examples, in the behaviour of the man who stammers and stutters his agreement to Bion's interpretation in such a way that he destroys the collaboration that his agreement implied. The link, Bion explains, is correctly understood to be with the *function* of the part-object rather than with the part-object that concretely represents it: the functions of 'feeding, poisoning, loving, hating', for example, rather than with the part-objects associated with them, such as the breast or the penis. I propose that the attack on linking, taken together with his theory of the beta-screen, can illuminate the tone and form of Ballard's 'condensed novels', and make sense of a text that is powerfully evocative and emotionally flat at the same time.

The beta-screen is first mentioned in *Learning from Experience*, where it appears in a section that follows on from his discussion of the 'contact-barrier' (borrowing from Freud's use of the same term in the *Project for a Scientific Psychology*). It is worth taking a moment here to understand the idea of the contact-barrier, as the beta-screen is, in effect, a *pseudo*-contact-barrier. The contact-barrier is produced by alpha-function, which:

> whether in sleeping or waking transforms the sense-impressions related to an emotional experience into alpha-elements, which cohere as they proliferate to form the contact-barrier. This contact-barrier, thus continuously in process of formation, marks the point of contact and separation between conscious and unconscious elements and originates the distinction between them.[20]

For Bion, the distinction between what is conscious and unconscious is given by a dynamic process (alpha-function) with the boundary itself formed 'on the fly' by those aspects of psychical experience that have been transformed by alpha-function into alpha-elements. James Grotstein describes the contact-barrier as an 'emotional frontier'[21] that changes continually in accordance with the 'nature of the supply of alpha-elements and on the manner of their relationship to each other'. The process described by Bion upends Freud's characterisation of the distinction between consciousness and unconsciousness, since what is unconscious is not 'what has been repressed', but 'what has been transformed by alpha-function': in this way, unconsciousness is an *achievement* of alpha-function, enabling experiences to be relegated to memory or motor recall (e.g. in walking, or driving a car). Indeed, both consciousness and unconsciousness are achievements of alpha-function, which Bion likens to the ability to dream. He describes how 'the patient who cannot dream cannot go to sleep and cannot wake up. Hence the peculiar condition seen clinically when the psychotic patient behaves as if he were in precisely this state'.[22]

Where alpha-function fails, or works only partially and intermittently, there can emerge a pseudo-contact-barrier formed not by alpha-elements but by beta-elements: that is, by those elements that have failed to be transformed by alpha-function, and are thus left untransformed, or, in the case of the 'reversal' of alpha-function, were previously transformed but have now been 'de-' or 'un-' transformed.[23] Beta-elements – the rudimentary and cut-up psychical debris of the mind – flashes of sensory data, expostulations, and notably, *words*, treated as concrete things rather than signifiers in an associative chain – can nevertheless *agglomerate* and *adhere* to form clusters of material that Bion suggests are 'coherent and purposive', mimicking the contact-barrier. In the absence of the contact-barrier's organising principle (alpha-function), there is nevertheless a 'division of sorts, suspended between analyst and patient as it were, but offering no resistance to the passage of elements from the one zone to the other'.[24]

The clinical features of the beta-screen resemble, I suggest, *The Atrocity Exhibition*'s 'jarring montage of jump-cut prose'[25] in which chunks of material – repetitive, vivid imagery, words and ideas shorn of context, and references to pop-cultural icons – are placed in provocative juxtaposition without the links that would enable the production of narrative. The effect of Ballard's prose is dreamlike, hallucinatory; we find a striking likeness in Bion's description of the beta-screen:

> Clinically this screen of beta-elements presents itself to casual observation as indistinguishable from a confused state and in particular from any one of that class of confused states which resemble dreams, namely: 1. An outpouring of disjointed phrases and images which, if the patient were asleep, we would certainly believe to be evidence that the patient was dreaming. 2. A similar outpouring but expressed in a manner that suggests that the patient is feigning dream. 3. A confused outpouring that seems to be evidence of hallucination. 4. Similar to (3) but suggestive of an hallucination of a dream[26]

The beta-screen is designed to 'evoke emotions' in the recipient of the psychotic text. The material produces an 'emotional involvement'[27] in its audience that nevertheless defeats the analyst's capacity to produce interpretations. In *Transformations*, Bion refers to the 'evocative potency' of the beta-screen[28] that, in the implication of the analysand's behaviour, is thought to offer far more interesting and subtle material than anything the analyst is capable of. The beta-screen's strength derives in part from the way that is constructed. While Bion distinguishes analytically between alpha- and beta-elements, he imagines that the reality of the mind presents a far more complex picture, with the 'replacement of a contact-barrier by a beta-screen [...] a living process'[29] that might be likened to an ongoing chemical reactive process in which reversals of alpha-function generate mental debris appropriated for the beta-screen. As with the ozone layer, there can be holes in alpha-function: places in the psyche where the mind breaks down. It is around these sites of erosion and reversal that beta-elements proliferate and agglomerate. There is no 'pure' beta-screen comprised of beta-elements, since by its nature the beta-screen opportunistically takes to itself anything – phrases, ideas, imagery – that, having come undone from the contact-barrier, is available for sequestration: in textual terms, words and images come undone from sites of stable signification and are available for opportunistic re-use in agglomerative, evocative constellations. Hélène Cixous' sensuous account of a kind of writing where 'millions of signs rain down and in their flood they stick to one another, they kiss'[30] may offer an exemplary description of a beta-screen formation. Bion's clinical experience suggests a less ecstatic experience. He recounts occasions when he was aware that his patient was speaking of something 'in a way that makes it clear that he is not meaning or expressing what is ordinarily meant or expressed when the word is used':

> But in the instances I have in mind the difference lies in what seems to be a lack of associations. It is as if the word were a counterpart of the pure note in music, devoid of undertones or overtones; as if, meaning nothing but 'table', it came near to meaning nothing at all.[31]

The Atrocity Exhibition is a disorienting text because the emotional orientation provided by the link is absent. Bion describes three kinds of links that he associates with love, hate, and knowledge (or rather: the functions of those words: loving, hating, and 'getting to know'), for which he uses the shorthand terms L, H, and K, respectively. Bion uses the term 'passion' to describe the nature of linking: 'by passions I mean all that is comprised in L, H, K',[32] and suggests that passion can only be present where two minds (or, put another way, where another mind has been internalised as alpha-function) are linked:

> For senses to be active only one mind is necessary: passion is evidence that two minds are linked and that there cannot possibly be fewer than two minds if passion is present.[33]

The psychotic part of the personality that makes 'attacks on linking' does so precisely in order to destroy the part of the mind, or the mind of the other, that is perceived as hostile and persecutory. It creates a text that is evocative and yet resistant to interpretation, but which can seem to employ a certain guile in the production of a pseudo-formation (the beta-screen) of the contact-barrier. For a text to be 'psychotic', therefore, it does not need to be un-remittingly 'mad': that is to say, entirely incomprehensible or without meaning. The bits and pieces of psychical debris that have evaded alpha-function can be ostensibly sophisticated and articulate, and need not outrage conventional conceptions of syntax and grammar. Something is missing, nevertheless. The emotional link that is absent from the psychotic text generates a dream-like experience that has sequences, but no *consequences*:

> At last I think I see daylight on a point that has baffled me for a long time: what does the psychotic patient think analysis is? [...] [P]artly a mental event in which consequences (as they exist in the world of physical reality) do not exist – there are only sequences. In a dream an act *appears* to have consequences – there are only sequences.[34]

I suggest that the hallucinatory, evocative (but emotionally flat) quality of scenes in *The Atrocity Exhibition*, combined with the formal 'chunking' of text, resembles Bion's characterisation of the beta-screen. Over and over, Ballard develops visually striking – one might say cinematographic – scenes in which exciting things happen or are depicted, but carry no emotional depth. A scene from 'Notes Toward a Mental Breakdown' depicts a film screening that may be a 'real' event, or the representation of the central character's psychosis as he observes (in the preceding paragraph) the naked body of Margaret Trabert:

> Margaret Trabert lay on the blood-shot candlewick of the bedspread, unsure whether to dress now that Trabert had taken the torn flying jacket from his wardrobe. [...] He stood by the window with his back to her, playing with the photographs of the isolation volunteers. He looked down at her naked body, with its unique geometry of touch and feeling, as exposed now as the faces of the test subjects, codes of insoluble nightmares.[35]

Huntley's description of *The Atrocity Exhibition* as jump-cut montage speaks precisely to the 'sequential, yet inconsequential' effect of Ballard's 'hard, gleaming' prose. Ballard splices together vivid images that in themselves have a static, deathly quality: lines of crashed cars, the illumination of arc-lights, test collisions, the abandoned motorcade. It is very different from the textual effects of the 'attack on linking' that Connor describes in describing Beckett's work as pursuing an 'ideal of maximum disarticulation' and the creation of 'jaggedly indigestible' texts.[36] What is disturbing in *The Atrocity Exhibition* is the very *smoothness* of the text, of something that speaks as much of psychopathy as psychosis. In Ballard's own conception, however, leaving out 'the unimportant pieces', of moreover getting 'the important pieces together, really together, not separated by great masses of 'he said, she said' and opening and shutting of doors, 'following morning' and all this stuff' results in '*more* things being generated'. The deletion of the link seems to create a space in which new connections can proliferate. This argument comes close to that which Huntley, citing Gilles Deleuze and Félix Guattari, identifies as *Atrocity*'s 'rhizomic thought': 'The tree imposes the verb 'to be', but the fabric of the rhizome is the conjunction 'and... and... and...' (1991:25). [...] Emergence from several points is precisely how Travis is manifested throughout *The Atrocity Exhibition*, and the lateral spread of the character continuously produces these *clusters of disparate matter*'.[37]

Huntley's schizoanalysis of Ballard is a productive one, though it does not describe the mechanism by which the 'clusters of disparate matter' are produced. It also does not address the question of tone or the emotional experience of reading *The Atrocity Exhibition*. Using Bion's work on the attack on linking and the beta-screen enables a more 'humanistic' account (attentive to the emotional register, given that it is drawn from a clinical setting) that is nevertheless open to a transhuman dimension through the linking of minds. *The Atrocity Exhibition* is a deeply *evocative* text, and a critical reading must take seriously the question of the evocation: what or whose responses does it call out; what resources of the reader or recipient are called on, manipulated or drained in a reading of *The Atrocity Exhibition*? Bion described the attack on linking as an attack not only on the potential connection between analysand and analyst but as an attack on the analyst's mind: these patients are wearying in the extreme because they seem to produce a stream of vivid material that nevertheless defeats the analyst's capacity for interpretation. Ballard the writer cannot, of course, be identified with the psychotic personality (Travis and his avatars) or the psychotic text, despite the success with which these are created. Nevertheless, Ballard does, I suggest, intend an 'emotional experience' for his readers that, as I shall argue, recalls Bion's stated objective in *Learning from Experience*. Both writers, moreover, seem to share an attraction to certain kinds of characteristic imagery.

The Atrocity Exhibition is notable for its evocation of peculiar, frequently technically inflected images that draw on medicine, architecture, engineering, and geology – spinal levels, 'thoracic drops' and neural intervals, concrete landscapes, 'the curvilinear roof of the Festival Hall',[38] porous rock towers and sand-dunes – brought into incongruous connection with obscene scenarios of bodily trauma and a hyper-conceptual sexuality that seeks to generate new acts of intercourse through perverse conjunctions of body with body, body with automobile, body with building:

> Perhaps an obscene version of her body would form a more significant geometry, an anatomy of triggers? In his eye, without thinking, he married her right knee and left breast, ankle and perineum, armpit and buttock.[39]

> The dismembered bodies of Karen Novotny and himself moved across the morning landscape, re-created in a hundred crashing cars, in the perspectives of a thousand concrete embankments, in the sexual postures of a million lovers.[40]

> All these buildings. What did Talbert want to do – sodomise the Festival Hall?[41]

The strange conjunctions that pervade *The Atrocity Exhibition* offer another outcome of the attack on linking: T's progress throughout the chapters can be seen as his persistent attempts to effect a recovery by establishing new acts of linking in phantasy. In his book of the same name, Roger Luckhurst identifies Ballard's phrase, 'the angle between two walls',[42] as a key figure for understanding his work. It is a phrase not without Bionian resonance: in *A Memoir of the Future*, the character of Roland invokes the idea of 'reversed perspective' to describe taking refuge in a corner: 'someone was trying to get me into a corner and club me to death. But thanks to reversed perspective I could cower in a corner where the angles of the walls protected me'.[43] Dr Nathan suggests that 'what Talbert is searching for is the primary act of intercourse, the first apposition of the dimensions of time and space',[44] in which new acts of intercourse can emerge from geometrical abstraction, the 'act of love [become] a vector in an applied geometry'.[45] Bion stages a comparable conceptualisation and defamiliarisation. "We had sex", he writes in *Cogitations*: 'A curious expression that is not known to me'.[46] Similarly, Dr Nathan asks: 'in *what* way is intercourse per vagina more stimulating than with this ashtray, say, or with the angle between two walls?'[47] For Karen Novotny, 'standing in the angle between the walls' proves fatal:

> Her figure interrupted the junction between the walls in the corner on his right. After a few seconds her presence became an unbearable intrusion into the time geometry of the room.[48]

In a daunting undated entry in *Cogitations*, Bion ponders the 'fate of the primal scene' (the witnessing of parental sexual intercourse by the child) in the mind as it is progressively transformed from a sensuous experience (he leaves open the possibility that it exists initially only as a pre-conception) to a higher-order abstraction modelled on geometry:

> The Oedipal chain
> The fate of the primal scene:
>
> 1. There may be an actual sensory experience. This would correspond to the lowest-level hypotheses of empirically verifiable fact.
> 2. The scene assumes the character of a hieroglyph or an ideogram.
> 3. The ideogram becomes (a) formularised, or (b) abstract. If abstracted, then it becomes a figure constructed out of the 'elements' (of Euclidean geometry).
> 4. An intermediate phase derived from another context – the invention of Cartesian coordinates.
> 5. The further abstraction of the scientific deductive system that is Euclidean geometry, to produce the algebraic calculus representing the scientific deductive system that is Euclidean geometry. Thus is established algebraic geometry.
> 6. Further calculi.[49]

For both Bion and Ballard, the sexual question centres not on the circulation of desire, as in the schizoanalytic reading drawn from Deleuze and Guattari, but on the capacity of the mind to think, unthink and rethink sex, and to apprehend the sensuous realisation of sex as it might be reverse-engineered from a prior calculus. Bion's note continues:

> Reverse the direction
> Now the algebraic calculus has to be returned to the lowest-level hypotheses of empirically verifiable data; it can then find its 'realization' in 'space' from which Euclidean geometry supposedly springs. But in fact the calculi that have been produced are many and diverse, including those of non-Euclidean geometry.

Luckhurst discusses Ballard's 'obsessive geometry of walls and ceilings',[50] arguing that Ballard's writing occupies the place of the *hinge*, 'the device which at once joins together and separates two planes or surfaces',[51] and relating this to Derrida's concept of *brisure*, that 'single word for designating difference and articulation'.[52] Ballard, he continues, 'might be said to thematise both the space between and the peculiar oscillation of the permeability and impermeability of borders'.[53]

The figures of oscillation and permeability recall Bion's reworking of the paranoid-schizoid and depressive positions as 'PS ↔ D', which gives birth to mental growth through the discovery of the selected fact. Both Ballard and Bion have recourse to an 'emotional mathematics'[54] that can enable the modulation of reality and the thinking of that which Hari Kunzru describes (in his introduction to *The Atrocity Exhibition*) as 'the junction between incommensurable systems'.[55] T pursues the discovery of a 'modulus' able to be 'multiplied into the landscape of his consciousness',[56] finding it in Karen Novotny, his on/off, real/hallucinated, alive/dead sexual interest:

> This cool-limbed young woman was a modulus; by multiplying her into the space and time of the apartment he would obtain a valid unit of existence.[57]

The psychotic (part of the) personality is also characterised by a failure to establish and sustain alpha-function that Bion describes as a 'primitive catastrophe',[58] being able to do nothing to disencumber itself of the accumulations of stimuli except by the mechanism of projective identification. Yet this mechanism also fails in the absence of a containing mind that can 'receive' and transform the split-off material, resulting in an experience of time and space as unboundaried and infinite. Unprocessed reality, O, is experienced as a phenomenological blast that defeats any attempt at containment. In 'The Assassination Weapon', Dr Nathan declares that 'what the patient is reacting against is, simply, the phenomenology of the universe, the specific and independent existence of separate objects and events'.[59] Bion, who (like Ballard) trained as a medical doctor, likened this to the condition of surgical shock:

> The ensuing state can be most easily expressed by using surgical shock as a model: in this the dilation of the capillaries throughout the body so increases the space in which blood can circulate that the patient may bleed to death in his own tissues. Mental space is so vast compared with any realisation of three-dimensional space that the patient's capacity for emotion is felt to be lost because emotion itself is felt to drain away and be lost in the immensity. What may then appear to the observer as thoughts, visual images and verbalisations must be regarded by him as debris, remnants or scraps of imitated speech and histrionic synthetic emotion, floating in a space so vast that its confines, temporal as well as spatial, are without definition. The events of an analysis, spread out over what to the analyst are many years, are to [the patient] but the fragments of a moment dispersed in space.[60]

In notes unpublished during his lifetime, Bion describes 'beta-space' as the 'mental multi-dimensional space of unthought and unthinkable extent and characteristics'.[61] I propose that beta-space may be seen as a counterpart to the beta-screen formation described in *Learning from Experience*. In the beta-space, psychical elements scatter rather than agglomerate, and the self drains away in an experience analogous to surgical shock. Intimations of always-approaching disaster in *The Atrocity Exhibition* — of 'seismic upheaval'[62] and 'World War III'[63] — take place in a blasted landscape that equally depicts the aftermath of previous catastrophe. The 1967 Apollo 1 disaster, in which three astronauts died in a fire prior to launch,[64] is echoed in references to the assassination of JFK, the 'command module' of Apollo 1 reconceived as the presidential motorcade.[65] The hallucinated figures of Kline, Coma, and Xero may be joined by a possible 'fourth pilot on board the capsule' who may be caught in Margaret Trabert's womb;[66] the phantasy of an additional pilot appears again in a further narrative fragment about a Cold War H-bomber.[67] There are also frequent references to the bombing of Nagasaki and the Vietnam War.

Luckhurst suggests that Ballard's novels take place '*between catastrophes*, in the space after the initial catastrophe and the 'catastrophe' which follows: death'.[68] For Bion and Ballard, both survivors of childhood trauma, exposure to war, and the sudden death of a partner early in marriage, the place of post-catastrophe, or aftermath, is a place in which death has entered the scene, one may feel oneself to have 'died', and yet curiously continue to live. In one of his autobiographies, Bion affirms that he 'died' at the Battle of Amiens: 'Oh yes, I died – on August 8th, 1918'.[69] The creative (and psychotic) mastery of death and disaster is a preoccupation for T, who intends to 'start World III, though not, of course, in the usual sense of the term'[70] and 're-assassinate' JFK. 'But isn't Kennedy already dead?' asks an unattributed voice. 'Not in the sense that you mean', replies Dr Nathan: 'this is an attempt to bring about the 'false' death of the President – false in the sense of coexistent or alternate'.[71]

It is a project that Ballard also takes up in a further chapter. In 'The Assassination of John Fitzgerald Kennedy Considered as a Downhill Motor Race', he follows the example of the surrealist Alfred Jarry[72] to rework and re-implicate the narrative components of the assassination – the role of Oswald, the motorcade, the president's wife, Dealey Plaza and the Book Depository – and 're-dreams' the story in terms of a car race to comic and ironic effect: 'Kennedy got off to a bad start'.[73] The essential features of the assassination – passed on in any retelling – are creatively re-imbedded using the facts and images on public record: 'Photographs of Johnson receiving his prize after winning the race reveal that he had decided to make the flag a memento of his victory'. Writing 'in praise of row C', Antonino Ferro connects Bionian theory with narratology in de-scribing row C (the Grid category of 'dream thoughts, dreams, myths') as 'narrative derivatives' which can be recombined or re-dreamed by the group or the individual to create new stories from the same set of narrative elements:

> One and the same sequence of a[lpha]-elements can be narrated by, for example, a childhood memory; an account of 'external' life; a report of a film, a diaristic genre; an intimate-type genre; or an infinite number of other possible modes.[74]

Writing in the 1960s and 1970s, Bion and Ballard, despite their difference in age, drew on a shared cultural imaginary inflected by their professional con-cerns and personal experiences. As with Ballard, images of space travel, as-tronomy, and atomic disaster proliferate in Bion's seminars and in his private writing. For Bion, the disaster intimated in imagery of atomic war is both a disaster already experienced in the breakdown of the mind's ability to integrate new experience, as well as the disruption experienced by the group in the breakthrough of the new idea.[75]

Bion holds open the possibility that the kind of thinking labelled 'psychotic' might in some instances harbour the 'sane' psychotic who is able to 're-dream' his or her culture in a more creative way. In *Attention and Interpretation*, he names this figure the 'Mystic', the person 'both creative and destructive' who brings the new idea into the group (sometimes called the 'Establishment'[76]), and who sees things in a new way. In the *Brazilian Lectures*, he gives the example of Freud's patient who 'had a phobia which made it impossible for him to wear socks':

> I suggest that the patient did not have a phobia of socks but could see that what Freud thought were socks were a lot of holes knitted together. If this is correct, terms like 'phobia' in classical analysis do not do justice to the facts, and in particular do not do justice to the extreme capacity for observation which is natural to some patients.[77]

The extreme, psychotic disorientation that results in seeing holes instead of socks is reminiscent of imagery in *The Atrocity Exhibition*, with its lists of anatomical detail, images of skin and anatomy blown up to billboard size, and imagery of porous rock associated with the Surrealist painters Ernst and de Chirico:

> A group of workmen on a scaffolding truck were pasting up the last of the displays, a hundred-foot-long panel that appeared to represent a section of a sand-dune. Looking at it more closely, Dr Nathan realised that in fact it was an immensely magnified portion of the skin over the iliac crest. Glancing at the billboards, Dr Nathan recognised other magnified fragments: a segment of lower lip, a right nostril, a portion of female perineum.[78]

T seems to seek to collect precise instances of spatial and temporal configuration along with literal and figurative snapshots of phantasied relationship with female icons such as Marilyn Monroe and Elizabeth Taylor in freeze-frame tableaus of violence and death. Under the intertitle, 'Notes Toward a Mental Breakdown', Travis retreats to his office to escape the sounds of the 'cine-films of induced psychoses' being screened in the lecture hall. Gathering the secret files of his private research interests, a list of incongruent items brings together, *inter alia*, a 'spectro-heliogram of the sun', an architectural drawing of a London hotel, a geological sample, and the time-and-motion photographs by the French scientist Etienne-Jules Marey.[79] Each is an object seen from a very precise professional and technical perspective: astrological measurement, architectural language, or the language of medical diagnostics. Marey's Chronograms, as Dr Nathan explains, are 'multiple-exposure photographs in which the element of time is visible'.[80]

While Ballard's technique seems to repeat the gesture of Cubism, it works not to portray a single object in multiple perspective, but to create a proliferation of incommensurate images that lack a unifying theme. They recall Bion's description of the psychotic patients who present masses of fragmentary material – 'some of which I know, some I may be supposed to know, some presumably I cannot be expected to know' – that seems to confound the analyst's ability to discern a 'selected fact' that would 'unite elements [...] scattered and seemingly foreign to each other'.[81] Ballard ironises conventional two-dimensional representations by having Dr Nathan suggest that the single-frame image enacts a psychotic reversal of the gesture of the chronograms:

> Your husband's brilliant feat was to reverse the process. Using a series of photographs of the most commonplace objects – this office, let us say, a panorama of New York skyscrapers, the naked body of a woman, the face of a catatonic patient – he treated them as if they already were chronograms and *extracted* the element of time.[82]

T's madness consists in reducing 'life' to a static image that has no way of representing growth and development. What he lacks, and seeks, is a qualitative calculus that would enable him to develop a model of relationship not templated on relationships with inorganic or dead others. The enquiry, I suggest, is Bionian:

> How does one *find* the appropriate calculus? Or invent it if it does not exist? Galileo had to get on without the differential calculus in solving the problem of the freely falling body.[83]

Like Travis' reverse chronograms, Bion suggests that analytic interpretation provides only a snapshot of a relationship from which the element of time has been extracted:

> The area which is available for inspection to psychoanalysis is like an expanding universe. As soon as I can understand what it means when I can see a body lying on a couch, the live relationship between me and you, and you and me (either direction) has become a dead relationship between I and it, and it and me, and you and it, and it and you.[84]

Throughout his work, Bion sought to connect the dots between the vagaries of individual pathology and societal behaviours. While recognising the profound disturbance in functioning of his psychotic patients, he saw links between their preoccupations and behaviour with the norms of scientific enquiry. Above all, he took extremely seriously three related 'facts' important for the theory of psychoanalysis: the fact of reality ('O'), the fact of [the existence of the] mind,[85] and the fact of life. Our being alive, he suggested, presents a challenge to scientific practice because it requires that theory take account of relationships between animate beings. The 'weakness [of scientific method] may be closer to the weakness of psychotic thinking than superficial scrutiny would admit', he writes:

> The scientist whose investigations include the stuff of life itself finds himself in a situation that has a parallel in that of the patients I am describing. [...] The inability of even the most advanced human beings to make use of their thoughts, because the capacity to think is rudimentary in all of us, means that the field for investigation, all investigation being ultimately scientific, is limited, by human inadequacy, to those phenomena that have the characteristics of the inanimate. We assume that the psychotic limitation is due to an illness: but that that of the scientist is not.[86]

Bion extends his enquiry into scientific method to questions of communication and reading, and suggests that reading his work must entail an emotional experience for the reader in order for it to be understood. In drafts for *Learning from Experience*, he advises the reader to 'read straight through this book, not to dwell too long on difficulties, and in this way to gain a working knowledge of the book itself'. He continues:

> But the book will have failed for the reader if it does not become an object of study, and the reading of it an emotional experience itself.[87]

This statement is surprising given the tone and form of *Learning from Experience*, which is likely to strike the first-time reader as a peculiarly terse, drily theoretical document. Like Bion, Ballard recognises the difficulty that readers may have with *The Atrocity Exhibition*, and indeed the annotated commentary that appears in later editions offers an accompanied experience of reading that is less forbidding. In the 'Author's note' that appears in the 2001 edition, Ballard offers an instruction to readers:

> Readers who find themselves daunted by the unfamiliar narrative structure of *The Atrocity Exhibition* – far simpler than it seems at first glance – might try a different approach. Rather than start at the beginning of each chapter, as in a conventional novel, simply turn the pages until a paragraph catches your eye. If the ideas or images seem interesting, scan the nearby paragraphs for anything that resonates in an intriguing way.[88]

The figure of resonance that Ballard deploys is suggestive: one resonates with something that activates some aspect of one's self. In *The Atrocity Exhibition*, this is not so much a question of fellow-feeling or shared experience with T or the other characters. In fact, the text is notable in its production of an affect-free, non-resonant landscape. Yet it nevertheless places an enormous demand on the reader to find some way into a narrative that is insistently two-dimensional. *The Atrocity Exhibition*'s difficulty and potential unreadability are a function of an 'evocative potency' that provokes the reader to attempt an emotional experience in relation to a text that activates but also defeats the reader's alpha-function. Bion describes the kind of psychotic patient who insists that the analyst 'should follow every word he says and will constantly inject comments that are intentionally evocative or even provocative'. As with the analyst, the reader is 'to be so treated that he cannot stay awake, and so interrupted that he cannot go to sleep'.[89]

I propose that Ballard and Bion both intend an 'emotional experience' for their readers, and do so through ways of writing that share something with psychotic mechanisms. They also share a preoccupation with the cultural overstimulation of our ability to respond to the mediatised traumas of atrocity and violence. In his 1947 lecture, 'Psychiatry at a Time of Crisis', Bion writes presciently of the effect of daily-repeated exposure to international news and popular entertainment:

We are bombarded with stimuli to which no direct reaction is possible. The newspapers inform us of political problems and decisions that move us emotionally, but to which we can make no direct response. The machinery of the press does little more for us than to ensure that we start and end the day with our daily dose of a sense of frustration and impotence. We contemplate an aeroplane crash in Newfoundland but can do nothing for the victims. We follow the fortunes of our favourite football team but cannot even help by giving up smoking. The vast apparatus of films and cheap fiction feeds phantasies of a world in which moral problems present no intellectual difficulties, and personal relationships assume an irreducible minimum of complexity.[90]

Ballard replies:

Faced with these charged events, we can only stitch together a set of emergency scenarios, just as our sleeping minds extemporise a narrative from the unrelated memories that veer through the cortical night.[91]

Towards the end of his life, Bion seemed to be gesturing towards an appreciation of a psychotic *mode* that confounds therapeutic orthodoxy. He lamented that psychoanalysis was 'so blinded by the concept of 'cure' that it will not consider theories that might be sound but would make people madder, or more fundamentally increase mental instability to a point where sanity was impossible'.[92] This is an undoubtedly challenging statement that on first appearance may outrage our sense of the ethical duties of a doctor, but it is worth considering in more detail. Notwithstanding his clinical experience with extremely disturbed patients, he nevertheless saw in the psychotic mode an aspect of the 'Mystic' or genius that resists the 'Establishment'. He wrote a short story, 'Predictive psycho-analysis and predictive psychopathology: A Fable for Our Time', set in an imagined future after a 'supposed atomic disaster' in which the writer recounts the history of a 'revolutionary discovery' taking place some three hundred years earlier. An everyman called Smith practising 'a rudimentary science called 'psycho-analysis' (sardonically defined as 'made up of two parts: 'psyche' [...] and 'anal'') defies the establishment by keeping an 'open mind' on a psychotic patient ('a woman, thought she was the Virgin and the Duke of Wellington') and comes to the conclusion that 'his candidate was really a new type of immature animal and was not suffering from some malformation of character', demonstrating 'the early embryonic stages of a personality rightly and instinctively, though clumsily, recognised as a menace to the existing order'.[93] Bion suggests that the category of psychosis may be 'too gross, too macroscopic', not unlike the 'sane' person who cannot see the holes for the sock:

If we look at it more closely, in detail, in the way we would have to look at a game of tennis, or a pair of socks, we can see that there may be insane psychotics and sane psychotics. It might be possible to help the insane psychotic to become an efficient psychotic.[94]

How are we to make sense of Bion's gesture towards a conception of 'efficient psychosis'? Though rooted in cultural critique, it is not to be confused with the anti-psychiatry movement associated with R.D. Laing and others. It seems to have something to do with observation and imagination. The efficient psychotic would see *both* the sock and the holes, employing a kind of 'binocular vision' that multiplies the 'vertices' of perception and the possibilities for critical thinking. In so doing they would not foreclose on reality but hold open possibilities of new ways of seeing. Ballard seems to arrive at a similar conclusion:

> On the other hand, being quite serious, the future may be boring. It's possible that my children and yours will live in an eventless world, and that the faculty of imagination will die, or express itself solely in the realm of psychopathology. In *Atrocity Exhibition* I make the point that perhaps psychopathology should be kept alive as a repository, probably the last repository, of the imagination.[95]

A Bionian reading of *The Atrocity Exhibition* draws attention to different levels and aspects of psychotic mechanisms at work within the text. While these undoubtedly include evocations of psychotic dysfunction that bar the development of meaning and affect, tracing what is shared in a Bionian Ballardian imaginary enables a thinking of 'the psychotic' as a mode (in the manner of 'the gothic' or 'the sublime') that describes productive disturbances in thinking.

Notes

1 Bion, *Complete Works,* 11:213 (*Cogitations,* 220–21. Bion may also be (consciously or unconsciously) referencing Stevie Smith's famous poem, published in 1957, 'Not Waving But Drowning' (see also chapter three). This particular 'cogitation' is undated.
2 Ballard, *The Atrocity Exhibition.* London: Fourth Estate, 2014. All page references are to this edition (noted as *TAE*).
3 Francis, *The Psychological Fictions of J.G. Ballard.*
4 *TAE,* 89.
5 *TAE,* 32–33.
6 The OED offers a partial definition of psychosis as 'severe mental illness, characterized by loss of contact with reality (in the form of delusions and hallucinations)'. The UK National Health Service (NHS) website http://www.nhs.uk/conditions/psychosis/Pages/Introduction.aspx [accessed December 2020] describes psychosis as a condition that 'causes people to perceive or interpret things differently from those around them', a strikingly neutral definition of a condition most often experienced (and/or witnessed by others) as a mental health crisis.
7 *TAE,* 1.
8 Baxter, *J.G. Ballard: Contemporary Critical Perspectives,* 24.
9 Luckhurst, *'The Angle Between Two Walls': The Fiction of J.G. Ballard,* 74.
10 *TAE,* 3.

11 Luckhurst, 86. I refer to the central character of *The Atrocity Exhibition* either by the name used in the given chapter from which a quotation is taken, or by the abbreviation, T.
12 *TAE*, 6.
13 The first 15 chapters were originally published individually in 'New Worlds', other magazines and as pamphlets in 1966.
14 *TAE*, 19.
15 *TAE*, 147.
16 Ballard, *Miracles of Life: Shanghai to Shepperton. An Autobiography*, 136.
17 Greenland, *The Entropy Exhibition: Michael Moorcock and the British 'New Wave' in Science Fiction*, 116.
18 *TAE*, 10. Italics in original.
19 Bion, *Complete Works*, 6:152 (*Second Thoughts*, 108).
20 Bion, *Complete Works*, 4:285 (*Learning from Experience*, 17).
21 Grotstein, *A Beam of Intense Darkness: Wilfred Bion's Legacy to Psychoanalysis*, 92.
22 Bion, *Complete Works*, 4:275 (*Learning from Experience*, 7).
23 One way to visualise the reversal of alpha-function is with the image of a paper-shredder when the shredder function is put into reverse: it does not return the previously shredded paper as an untransformed sheet, but in a disturbingly post-shredded form more liable to jam the machine when the shredding function is returned to its normal movement again. (See also chapter six for a discussion of the reversal of alpha-function.)
24 Bion, *Complete Works*, 4:289 (*Learning from Experience*, 22).
25 Baxter, 24.
26 Bion, *Complete Works*, 4:290 (*Learning from Experience*, 22).
27 Bion, *Complete Works*, 4:292 (*Learning from Experience*, 24).
28 Bion, *Complete Works*, 5:275 (*Transformations*, 165).
29 Bion, *Complete Works*, 4:293 (*Learning from Experience*, 24).
30 Cixous, *Stigmata: Escaping Texts*, 141. Also cited in Royle, *Veering*, 200.
31 Bion, *Complete Works*, 11:66 (*Cogitations*, 63).
32 Bion, *Complete Works*, 5:9 (*Elements of Psychoanalysis*, 4).
33 Bion, *Complete Works*, 5:16 (*Elements of Psychoanalysis*, 13).
34 Bion, *Complete Works*, 11:9 (*Cogitations*, 1).
35 *TAE*, 66.
36 Connor, *Beckett, Modernism and the Material Imagination*, 198.
37 Baxter, 29–30. Italics mine.
38 *TAE*, 7.
39 *TAE*, 92.
40 *TAE*, 35.
41 *TAE*, 86.
42 *TAE*, 71.
43 Bion, *Complete Works*, 12:73 (*A Memoir of the Future*, 73).
44 *TAE*, 86
45 *TAE*, 81.
46 Bion, *Complete Works*, 11:308 (*Cogitations*, 321).
47 *TAE*, 95.
48 *TAE*, 60–61.
49 Bion, *Complete Works*, 11:196 (*Cogitations*, 203).
50 *TAE*, 121.
51 Luckhurst, xiii.
52 Derrida, *Of Grammatology [Corrected Edition]*, 65.
53 Luckhurst, xiv–xv.
54 Bion, *Complete Works*, 5:264 (*Transformations*, 154).

55 *TAE*, xviii.

56 *TAE*, 26.

57 *TAE*, 57.

58 Bion, *Complete Works*, 6:133 (*Second Thoughts*, 88).

59 *TAE*, 46.

60 Bion, *Complete Works*, 6:231 (*Attention and Interpretation*, 12–13).

61 Bion, *Complete Works*, 11:301 (*Cogitations*, 313).

62 *TAE*, 1.

63 *TAE*, 6.

64 *TAE*, 65.

65 *TAE*, 74.

66 *TAE*, 66.

67 *TAE*, 133.

68 Luckhurst, 38.

69 Bion, *Complete Works*, 1:296 (*The Long Week-End 1897–1919: Part of a Life*, 265).

70 *TAE*, 7.

71 *TAE*, 47.

72 'The Passion Considered as an Uphill Bicycle Race' in Jarry, *Selected Works of Alfred Jarry*.

73 *TAE*, 171.

74 Ferro, *Psychoanalysis as Therapy and Storytelling*, 28.

75 Bion, *Complete Works*, 6:275 (*Attention and Interpretation*, 64).

76 Bion, *Complete Works*, 6:284 (*Attention and Interpretation*, 74).

77 Bion, *Complete Works*, 7:26 (*Brazilian Lectures: 1973 São Paulo, 1974 Rio de Janeiro/São Paulo*, 21).

78 *TAE*, 11.

79 *TAE*, 1–2.

80 *TAE*, 6.

81 Poincaré, *Science and Method*, 30.

82 *TAE*, 6.

83 Bion, *Complete Works*, 11:204 (*Cogitations*, 211).

84 Bion, *Complete Works*, 7:19 (*Brazilian Lectures: 1973 São Paulo, 1974 Rio de Janeiro/São Paulo*, 14).

85 For example, as in Bion, *Complete Works*, 8:319 (*Bion in New York and São Paulo*, 79).

86 Bion, *Complete Works*, 4:282 (*Learning from Experience*, 14).

87 Bion, *Complete Works*, 11:251 (*Cogitations*, 261).

88 *TAE*, vii.

89 Bion, *Complete Works*, 11:210 (*Cogitations*, 217).

90 Bion, *Complete Works*, 4:52 (*Cogitations*, 345).

91 *TAE*, 145. (Also quoted in Royle, *Veering*, 67.)

92 Bion, *Complete Works*, 11:348 (*Cogitations*, 378).

93 Bion, *Complete Works*, 11:318 (*Cogitations*, 327–32).

94 Bion, *Complete Works*, 7:26 (*Brazilian Lectures: 1973 São Paulo, 1974 Rio de Janeiro/São Paulo*, 21).

95 Frick, 'J.G. Ballard, The Art of Fiction No. 85'.

8   Becoming ray: transformations in Nicholas Royle's *Quilt*

Transformations in O contrast with other transformations in that the former are related to growth in *becoming* and the latter to growth in "knowing about" growth; they resemble each other in that "growth" is common to both.[1]

The poet Rilke wrote that 'the world is nowhere, my love, if not within/ Our life passes in transformation'.[2] Transformation is at the heart of Nicholas Royle's début novel, *Quilt*,[3] which recounts the experience of a father's sudden death and its aftermath. Into this story of unexpected loss and grieving comes the strange figure of the ray, that class of cartilaginous flat fish that includes the 'stingray [...], the electric ray [...], the torpedo, the flat ray, the numbfish, the narky, the fish that numbs or narcotises'.[4] With prodigious enthusiasm, the narrator invites the ray into his life (and his father's house), becoming all-consumed with the details of their care and feeding, while his partner looks on in increasing bewilderment and concern for his sanity. The ray (or rays) open(s) the novel's otherwise personal and domestic narrative to a dimension both mythical and literary. 'Eerie machines for creating and overturning words',[5] the ray story (or *récit*) that begins on the periphery of *Quilt* comes to inhabit the story, the house, and the narrator himself. An exemplary instance of writing that is both creative and critical, *Quilt* combines the narrative of the father's death with the birth of a new theory of ghosts and literature that in some mysterious way proceeds from the rays themselves. It is as much the story of the birth of a new idea as it is a story of death, grief, fish, and madness. The author's afterword develops critical themes given voice within the novel by the son/narrator, and stands both integral and adjacent to *Quilt*, and as a companion to Royle's other literary critical work, including *The Uncanny* and *Veering: A Theory of Literature*.

Transformations, the third of Bion's metapsychologies, attempts to describe the ways in which an impersonal reality, O, is subject to psychical and artistic transformations of various kinds. He describes four: rigid motion transformation, projective transformation, transformation of O in hallucinosis, and transformation in O. *Quilt*, I suggest, veers precariously between a hallucinatory transformation of the son's experience of the father's death, signalling mental ill health and breakdown, and a transformative – even transubstantive – dénouement that might approximate a realisation of Bion's near-mystical concept of 'becoming O'. At the end of *Quilt*,

DOI: 10.4324/9781003006619-8

the reader is invited, along with the son's partner, to make sense of the son's decidedly 'funny turn', a turn that is also literary and theoretical. Finding 'no sign of anything anywhere',[6] the novel closes in mystery but opens to a critical afterword, in which Royle looks to 'inaugurate a new kind of writing and give it a name: *reality literature*'.[7]

A Bionian reading makes it possible to describe, with some precision, the ways in which *Quilt* is a transformative novel. Previous readings, such as those by Arleen Ionescu and Jean-Michel Ganteau, have overlooked the novel's transubstantive ending, and the ways in which the son comes to be identified with the ray. Ionescu has focused instead on the related figures of quilt, cloak or mantle, and suggests that *Quilt* is a 'spectral cover that is belatedly grafted on to Royle's theory of telepathy and the Uncanny'.[8] I suggest that the opposite may be more nearly true: Royle's afterword and theoretical incursions offer critical authority where it may not be needed, since the figure of the ray does the substantive work of the text, which is also a kind of deconstructive un-doing. Ganteau reads the novel as modern elegy, the ending of the novel staging the 'impossibility of survival and the gradual loss of agency'.[9] By contrast, I propose that *Quilt* stages the ways in which the mind responds to loss and pain, and the role of creative response in transformation.

Quilt begins 'in the middle of the night', *in medias res*:

> In the middle of the night the phone rings, over and over, but I don't hear it. First it is the hospital, then the police.[10]

Launching itself into the middle of things, the narration enacts an ironic swerve away from the heart of the 'action', which is, of course, inaction of a very pointed kind: the hospital and police are trying to inform the son that his father has died that night, having fallen out of his hospital bed in unexplained circumstances. But for the son, who is asleep and misses the call, he is not yet dead. They are both dead to the world, son and father.

By beginning the story, the narrator has already unwittingly invited death into the novel's purview; by not hearing the phone in the middle of the night, he postpones the moment of the novel – the story of a father dying – to another day. This is the moment of the 'middle things': what is *in medias res*[11] is the dead centre – a death at the centre – of the novel which, echoing W.B. Yeats (who also provides *Quilt*'s prefatory quotation), 'cannot hold'.[12] It must rather incite or entail a veering or oscillation between times: the times of the before and the after, the 'deep time' of the ray, and time refracted transat-lantically between the son and his partner. Getting his father dressed as he prepares him for his hospital visit (the previous day), the son hears him say 'These things happen from time to time'.[13] The father's stoical phrase on the eve of his death becomes the novel's haunting refrain, emerging time and again to point *Quilt*'s meditation on death and dying. The thing that happens between times – the singular fact of death, between the time of the novel's beginning and ending – is something that cannot be forethought, can only be improvised, *ex tempore*; an event outside of time, something that happens 'from time to time', in a timeframe not one's own.

In *Quilt*, it is the son who outlives the father, the normal way of things. The 'between times' of the novel – that is the end time of the father – is also the time horizon of the son's life. The father's refrain recalls both Freud and Bion: 'there is much more continuity between intra-uterine life and the earliest infancy than the impressive caesura of the act of birth allows us to believe'.[14] After birth, death marks the even more impressive caesura; the continuity of life after death remains harder to imagine than pre-uterine life (notwithstanding the various attempts within religious traditions to reframe death as the beginning of a new kind of life). *Quilt* takes place in this between time: an everyday sort of time that involves the narrator shopping for clothes and wondering 'what does a man do on the day his father dies?';[15] but also in a suspensive gap that the novel bridges with words, or if not with words, with Ω.

Ω, the omega sign, appears throughout *Quilt* between sections, between the telephone in the night that rings unheard and the narrative that takes up the day before. The last letter of the Greek alphabet, omega recalls the biblical appellation of the Father in Revelations: 'I am the Alpha and Omega', the beginning and the end. Signalling the end of times in the Bible, the omega sign that appears two lines in to *Quilt* heralds an end already in play at the beginning of the novel, an ideographic representation of a death not yet accessed in the narrative. It is also a signature textual device, recalling Royle's use of symbols in his earlier, theoretical work, *The Uncanny*. The omega sign may arguably not stand *in* or *for* something else; rather, it may just *stand* as a *stet* or stent that holds open the different times and spaces of the novel, or that institutes a typographic rest, a visually effected pause or writing retreat. The idea of the stent, which the Ω resembles visually, would then be a kind of internal scaffold or canalisation, charged with holding open the space of the novel, or a bracket (attached to a hospital bed) that might have saved the father's life.

Royle's Omega (literally, O-mega, the large or capital O) may also signal the irruption of O, Bion's figure to denote reality; the blast of a pure encounter with that which ineffably *is*: 'What the absolute facts are cannot ever be known, and these I denote by the sign O'.[16] O is a minimalist placeholder for that which is absolutely unknowable except through its transformations. Pictorially evocative, O – derived from the word 'origin' – suggests, too, a primal boundary, container, an open mouth or closed womb, wellspring, the universe, the godhead, the circle of life or infinity, *Ouroboros*. Bion's O is both omega and alpha, but like Ω it is used to signify something that cannot be rendered definitively in words. Like Royle, Bion uses symbols (α, β and ψ among these) where words are inadequate or unhelpful.

The rays, like omega, are already installed prior to the beginning of the story, seemingly outside the 'between times' of the novel. In the prefatory quotation by Yeats, they are obliquely figured as a disinterested chorus: 'certain Shrouds that muttered head to head', originary ghosts anticipating the son's discovery of a 'new theory of ghosts'[17] that places, for Royle's narrator, the ray at the origin of ghostly iconography, from the spooky bed sheets of childish games to the imaginary of the Gothic. A series of aquatic references in the opening pages also foreshadows their first appearance: the father 'an immeasurably beautiful strange ancient fish'[18] whom the son stows at the hospital 'in the entrance way next to a large aquarium', while the son 'struggl[es] like a fish on land to gasp',[19] fighting back tears. When the ray finally makes its entry into *Quilt*, it turns out to have been there all along:

> The ray lurks, impenetrably, around the origins of philosophy.

Retelling the conversation between Meno and Socrates, in which Meno ac- cuses the philosopher of being like the ray that paralyses with its sting, the novel's first *foray* into the ray offers the reader several presumptive statements: the rays are 'thinking's quandary', the 'figure of the already'; 'the paralysing figuration of all knowledge as recollection'.[20] In each of these statements, the rays are placed in a relationship to times present, past and in question (the bafflement of the 'quandary' etymologically raising the query: when? – *quando*?). To understand the story of the ray, the narrator suggests:

> you have to go back into what is called deep time (as if there were any means of doing so). Once upon a slime, before the creation of the Andes, prior to the earliest fossils [...], over 220 million years ago[21]

In a second ray interlude he describes the development of the different kinds of ray (freshwater, marine) that happens between times, from deep time to deep time: 'And all of this, keep in mind, took place in what is called deep time (as if there were any other)'. Deep time, defined by the eighteenth-century geol- ogist James Hutton, describes the geologic time of the universe, a conception of time so abyssal and incommensurate with human experience that the mind 'grow[s] giddy'[22] in contemplation of it. In the days and weeks that follow the father's death, in which the son and his partner set to work clearing the house, there are intimations of time slipping 'out of joint',[23] giving way to dis- turbances in chronology. 'Now that he has died', writes the son, 'I no longer know how long anything takes'.[24] Reflecting on his father's 'love of time',[25] his fascination with clocks and watches and his concern to know the time precisely, the son recalls how he had once imagined his father's last words 'on his deathbed, looking into my eyes and asking: What is the time, please?'.[26]

After the death, before the funeral, the son decides to build a ray pool in his father's dining room, in which four rays, named Taylor, Audrey, Hilary and Mallarmé, are installed. The design and construction of the ray pool are in- vested with a degree of care suggestive of a reparative impetus that identifies the father with the ray:

> I am not going to deny a sense of achievement at having conceived and constructed this ray pool, with its spillway design and lipped feature, at having lined it with the correct quartz sand, after picking over and assessing

it, stone by stone, day after day, at having carefully selected the, I think it's thirteen, individual, perfectly sized rocks, and at having installed the highest-quality filters, pumps, lighting and heating. Everything has been done here that could have been done to ensure an appropriate supply of water and to establish the correct mechanisms for the upkeep and replacing of water, and for the weekly gravel-cleaning and hydro-vac. But any feeling of triumph here is at once also its opposite. To achieve is to lose. To suppose that you are winning is to be undergoing absolute defeat.[27]

The father, though clearly unwell when he goes to hospital, dies unexpectedly during the first night, falling unseen from his bed and dying, it is supposed, as he lies on the floor, unattended. The evasions of the hospital staff and the autopsy suggest a concern to forestall an allegation of negligence. At the funeral reception the son holds forth with apparent fluency and authority on the subject of the rays and their care. In particular, the question of a suitable 'substrate' for the rays is of paramount importance, given their ironical preference for a *vivisepultural* (buried alive) 'lifestyle':

> The ray is stationary. You wouldn't even register it there, retracted into its environs. It sees you before you see it. The ray lies on the substrate. On it, in it, what you will. The ray is prone, adoringly, to a decent bottom. Without an appropriately sandy, muddy or gravelly one, the ray cannot bury itself, which it does both in self-protection and with a view to prey. Vivisepulture is its lifestyle. Now you see it, now you don't. Then not now again. The ray blends in with the substrate, altering appearance, what is around disappearing into it, eye encrypting camouflage.[28]

The son's concern for a suitable substrate for the rays is echoed in the terrifying 'gravel dream' that appears in part two of the novel: a repeated nightmare in which he alone is left to the enormous task of checking individually and by hand the hundreds of tiny pieces of gravel that line the bottom of the pool, looking out for any sharp edges that might damage the rays' sensitive ventral surface:

> I dream of gravel. I'm going to miss the funeral because of it. Time's recoiled and we are completely lost in the logistics of acquiring the gravel, the agitation about having the right kind.[29]

The dream, like the gravel, is carefully selected for the work it can achieve both in the son's mind and in the text. The likely trend of an interpretation along the lines of the son's grief for his father, combined with his feelings of guilt (that his father's death might have been prevented, that he was too negligent in placing his trust in the hospital's care) is neither repressed, nor hidden. The narrator makes as much clear:

> It's as if I were dreaming intermittently aware that what's happening is an allegory but I keep forgetting this.

I suggest that a metaphor of depth is at work in both the dream of the gravel that provides a substrate for the rays, and in the dream itself, which is recognised consciously as 'allegory', a dream too thin or superficial in respect of a certain Freudian conception of psychoanalysis as 'depth psychology'. Getting to the bottom of the son's dream is not a difficult task. What he finds most disturbing is the idea of 'no substrate at all', or need for one:

> A couple of days after the gravel-dream (which comes back repeatedly over the nights that follow, and which you relate to a disquiet you have about 'no substrate at all')[30]

> This recurrent nightmare proceeds, you believe, from a sense of outrage at the so-called specialists who have the gall to suggest that there is no need for a substrate.[31]

Reflecting on Freud's theory of dream, in which the work of the analyst is to bring to the surface the 'deeper' meaning of the dream, the dream 'substrate', Bion begins to formulate the rudiments of an alternative conception of dreams:

> [Freud] took up only the negative attitude, dreams as 'concealing' something, not the way in which the *necessary* dream is *constructed*.[32]

Pace Freud, Bion emphasises the function of dream-work in transforming reality, O, into experiences assimilable by the mind, which might even intend to render experience *unconscious*, rather than conscious:

> But *Freud* meant by dream-work that unconscious material, which would otherwise be perfectly comprehensible, was transformed into a dream, and that the dream-work needed to be undone in order to make the incomprehensible dream comprehensible [...]. *I* mean that the conscious material has to be subjected to dream-work to render it fit for storing, selection, and suitable for transformation[33]

The dream-work, for Bion, is above all a creative process, though not necessarily a conscious one, that entails 'dreaming' reality in order to integrate it. The narrator's identification of the father with the ray is a part of this creative work, as is the gravel dream. But it is not an unambivalent or linear process. By locating the rays in 'deep time', the father's death takes place in a time horizon so at odds with what is thinkable in the human experience as to segue into the realm of myth. Later in the dream, the son rails against the specialist suppliers whose passion for customer service entails indifference to the ray:

> Then there are the online dealers. Replaceable ray, dish of the day, this one or that! Initially set you back a hundred dollars, my friend, but if it arrives damaged or dead, refund guaranteed, we'll dispatch another within twenty-

four hours! If, on the other hand, you get it home and it acclimatises and seems happy but after three weeks begins to develop fin curl or abrasions from that gravel you selected for the substrate, or if it turns out that the creature never really developed an appetite and has succeeded in starving itself, such apparently suicidal behaviour not unknown, if it dies it dies: just think of it as one of those balloons that go flat, simply pick up the phone or get online and order another one![34]

And yet, as the narrator admits, the ray, or rays – linguistically both singular and generic – are the very figure of a replaceable life form, located in a deep time that is but the 'substrate of the present':

> The ray can be understood generically, as a term for all the rays that ever existed, including the countless millions in deep time, bearing in mind that deep time at once somewhere no one will ever be visiting and, to coin a phrase, the substrate of the present[35]

Transformations, the third of Bion's metapsychological texts, opens with an example of a 'transformation': the painter who transforms an experience of poppies into a painted canvas. The image is a considered one: it recalls both Monet's famous Impressionist painting, *Les Coquelicots*, as well as the poppies of Flanders and Ypres, where Bion served in the First World War. In the case of the painting, Bion writes, it is possible to identify that something – certain shapes, the colour red – remain *invariant* under the transformation, enabling the original form to be recognisable. But what is invariant under one style of painting, or form of art, may not be so under another:

> The invariants depend on the technique he employs: thus the invariants in an impressionist painting are not the invariants of a painting by a member of, say, a realist school of painting.[36]

The psychoanalyst who seeks to understand his or her client is concerned to identify the analysand's transformation of his or her reality in terms both of the *process* of the transformation (that which Bion notates Tα) and the *outcome* of the transformation (Tβ), of which there are several kinds. In the discussion that follows, I follow the categorisation offered by Grinberg et al.[37] to outline four kinds of transformation: rigid motion transformation, projective transformation, transformation in hallucinosis and transformation in O. Bion leaves ample room for the elaboration of many different kinds of transformation in different fields of activity, making possible the development of such locutions as 'transformation *in* writing' or 'transformation *in* poetry':

> Transformation may be a transference of characteristics from one situation to another, from one medium to another, a rigid motion, or a projective

transformation. A musician or artist may transfer or project an emotional experience through Tα to the finished product Tβ, which may be a musical composition or a painting.[38]

The first of Bion's categories, the rigid motion transformation, is the most easily accessible to the reader familiar with classical Freudian theory, implying a transformation of experience in which there is little distortion in form between O and Tβ: Bion includes within this category the typical transference neuroses described by Freud that include anxiety, hysteria and obsessional neurosis.[39] Aspects of *Quilt* lend themselves straightforwardly to a psychoanalytically informed reading along these lines: the son's identification with his father, for example, and the identification of the father with the ray. This latter is apparent in the son's gravel dream, in which he battles extreme odds to master the threat of injury to (and in phantasy undo what has already been suffered by) the sensitive and beloved creature. The dream as it is recounted is an instance of the rigid motion transformation, and an awareness of psychoanalysis seems to inform the narrator 'dreaming intermittently aware'[40] that his recurring nightmare constitutes an allegory of his father's death.

In another passage, implicitly attributed to the son, the phantasy underlying the creation and maintenance of the pool draws attention to the *space* required to safeguard the rays against the contaminant of death:

> Inevitably, in the case of a small aquarium, products of decay from a decomposing body contaminate the water and can rapidly bring about the death of the other creatures, but if you think big, if you can reckon on the worst with a big showcase space, you can have one be dead and decaying for twenty-four hours or more and it have no unduly adverse effect on the life of the other inhabitants.[41]

Thinking 'big' is not, it seems, sufficient to guarantee immunity to death. The narrator (who at this point in the story is the son's partner) adds: 'these are not his words but she extrapolates them, in ironic form, from what he tells her'. The thought is thus presented here at one remove: the partner's extrapolation is also an exaggeration. The image of the ray pool, big enough to survive catastrophe, approximates Bion's description of catastrophic change figured as an 'explosion and its expanding pressure waves' enacting a 'wide externalisation of internal objects'[42] within a mental space correspondingly large, a hyperbolic imaginary. Bion's thinking of hyperbole in *Transformations* enables a critical consideration of the figural aspects of the ray that have to do with time and space. Despite the incongruity of their domestic installation in *Quilt*, the ray are repeatedly located in 'deep time', operating 'incommensurably', located outside any means of chronological or spatial measurement. This word, 'incommensurable', is, I suggest, the token of hyperbole, drawing attention to the mechanism of projection in *Quilt*'s narration.

In a projective transformation, the material that would be 'invariant' under a rigid motion transformation is transformed more idiosyncratically, using the mechanisms not of transference but of splitting and projective identification. Bion suggests that exaggerated and hyperbolic statements signal a projective transformation at work, and may be related to feelings of envy and rivalry, a going beyond, doing one better or 'outdistancing' of material that splits off rivalrous feelings and places them, as in the opening lines of the film *Star Wars*, 'a long time ago, in a galaxy far, far away'. The ray, identified both with the father and the son, are the location of an identification and a relationship that is presented both at infinite remove (in deep time, incommensurably) and *heimlich*. Describing a number of instances of hyperbole, Bion gives the following close reading of an apparently unremarkable statement made by an analysand: 'I knew a woman in Peru, when I was a child, who had second sight'. Taking this statement, with its three distancing aspects (Peru, a country far away from the UK; in a time long ago; the idea of second sight) as the analysand's commentary on the analysis, he writes:

> The goodness of the analyst has been projected a long way in time and place. This is hyperbole; there is something in the experience with the analysand that makes this term suitable for binding the particular conjunction, and none other [...]. The term already marks a conjunction [...] which is present in the conjunction to which I want to draw attention, namely the early meaning of hyperbole as a 'throwing beyond' someone else, signifying rivalry.[43]

In this example, Bion reads an apparently innocuous statement in terms of a projective transformation, suggesting that a way to understand the analysand's statement would be to see it as a hyperbolic transformation of the psychoanalytic situation. In this reading, the incommensurability of the ray conceals an Oedipal story, a way for the narrator to disavow the painful recognition that the father 'is my flesh, so simple, his body mine', a way to re-render the 'rending mystery of [his] father' that threatens a literal 'con-fusion' of the son-father as 'me father' [my father], the father's vernacular at work in the son's language. In the language-world of the ray, the distinction between the particular and the generic is elided, evoking the promise/threat of father/son identity, the son 'of one being with the father', as in the Nicene Creed.

The rays appear in the text as it becomes clear that the father 'doesn't have long by the look of him',[44] that he is 'melting to me all his body mine, mining me, me father'. The ray pool (that is strictly *not*, as the narrator makes clear, a touch pool[45]) creates an *in vitro* environment, a contained space within the house (and in the novel) in which the work of grief in all its permutations – guilt, responsibility, the expiration of a former rivalry – may be progressively achieved. The figure of the enclosed space at work in the ray pool is echoed elsewhere. In an earlier section, the son imagines taking small groups of tourists into a cave in order that they might experience the word 'pristine'. A Platonic-ironic tour-guide, he would 'get their complete attention' by offering to 'reveal the names of everyone in this cave, at the drop of a pin': 'In truth, however, it is an easy thing to do: if you attune your hearing properly in the silence of the caves and listen, most people are speaking a more or less audible version of their name in most of the things they say'.[46] In this way, the cave provides an imaginary location in which it is possible to have an experience of one's self: 'yes, this little outing to the caves is the closest thing that they will ever have of an apprehension of what it is to hear oneself and 'be someone''. This is also explicitly an experience of being born, a being-born-to reality:

> I might very readily proclaim that it is here, in the sonic simplicity and purity of these environs, that it becomes possible to return, yes, for there is always some echo-effect, to return to that conjectural snatch of what it is to be at the very threshold of life, being born, in amniotic oblivion, and in this moment think, and speak.[47]

More specifically, the subterranean experience of the caves ('strange well of feeling, curvature of space') evokes the quality that he associates with his partner: an evocation of that which is both 'fresh and ancient'. He would lead tour groups there, he imagines, in order that the 'angelic oddity' of the word 'pristine' might be 'prised aurally', 'in these delicate clinkings':

> You might think they know you inside out, I begin. In these caves nothing is what you imagine: everything becomes pristine. Listen. *In these delicate clinkings prised,* I add, with a kind of irritating emphasis.[48]

The delicate clinkings evoke a line in Wallace Stevens' poem, 'Description without Place', which draws attention to the way that 'seeming' – the use of words 'for those for whom the word is the making of the world' – creates its own reality. Stevens wrote that the poem's central idea was that 'we live in the description of a place and not the place itself':[49] 'In flat appearance we should be and be/Except for delicate clinkings not explained'.[50] The delicate clink-ings not explained in Stevens' poem thematise an experience of poetry in which description enacts a 'revelation' of the object that is neither 'the thing described, nor false facsimile', and which, moreover, is 'composed of a sight indifferent to the eye', a 'sense to which we refer experience' that is not to be sensuously apprehended. Stevens resonates with Bion's theory of transfor-mation at several points. In 'Making the Best of a Bad Job', his last published essay before his death, Bion quotes Milton in *Paradise Lost*, whose image of inward sight evokes the kind of seeing achieved by psychoanalysis:

So much the rather thou Celestial light

Shine Inward, and the mind through all her powers

Irradiate, there plant eyes, all mist from thence

Purge and disperse, that I may see and tell

Of things invisible to mortal sight.[51]

Bion differs from Stevens in that he does not attribute this 'sight indifferent to the eye' to 'expectation or desire' – Bion is perhaps best known in psychotherapeutic circles for his injunction that the analyst should cultivate the 'ability to banish memory and desire'[52] – but to the nature of O, which cannot finally be apprehended by any relationship to knowledge:

> It is not knowledge of reality that is at stake, nor yet the human equipment for knowing. The belief that reality is or could be known is mistaken because reality is not something that lends itself to being known. It is impossible to know reality for the same reason that makes it impossible to sing potatoes; they may be grown, or pulled, or eaten, but not sung. Reality has to be 'been'; there should be a transitive verb 'to be' expressly for use with the term 'reality'.[53]

The ending of 'Description without Place' nevertheless seems to approach the experiences that Bion is trying to describe. 'The rose *is* itself whatever it may be *said* to be', Bion writes in *Transformations*.[54] A gloss, perhaps, on Gertrude Stein ('a rose is a rose is a rose is a rose'[55]), it resonates with the last line of Stevens' poem, which ends in apparent tautology: 'like rubies reddened by rubies reddening'. For Bion, the tautology, or circular argument, is a necessary step in the development of meaning, only requiring that there be a 'sufficiency of experience' or, continuing the model, adequate diameter, to sustain it:

> The interpretation should be such that the transition from knowing about reality to becoming real is furthered. The transition depends on matching the analysand's statement with an interpretation which is such that the circular argument remains circular but has an adequate diameter. [...] The profitable circular argument depends on a sufficiency of experience to provide an orbit in which to circulate.[56]

The transformation enacted by poetry might, Stevens suggests, be more than metaphor. His line 'There might be, too, a changer immenser than/ A poet's metaphors in which being would/ Come true'[57] seems to describe the kind of change evoked in *Quilt*'s closing pages, where the son seems literally (or *literarily*) to have 'become ray'; that is, to have assumed the experience of his grief, and to have been himself transformed by (rather than only transformed by what he 'knows about') the experience of his father's death. In Stevens' 'potential seemings turbulent', we find, too, an intimation of the catastrophe that becoming O is felt to be.

Foreshadowings of emotional turbulence and potential catastrophe are present throughout the novel. On the day that his father dies, the son 'becomes aware that time has slowed down to a catastrophe', that 'there are all things at once', 'a period of implausible interference'. Royle's description of the experience of grief recalls Denise Riley's account of the experience of losing her son: 'that acute sensation of being cut off from any temporal flow that can grip you after the sudden death'.[58] As the son in *Quilt* awaits his partner at the bus station, the environment takes on a hallucinatory quality. A motorway accident has delayed his partner's arrival:

> He manages to establish that the crash occurred too early for her coach to be involved. He tries to shrug off the thought that the day is imitating itself. It's something quite alien, he thinks, to that falseness in the impressions of external things that Ruskin called pathetic fallacy. It's as if perception itself were a strange mimosa. Everything seems shadowed, shadowing something else.
>
> It should be hallucinational news.[59]

In what follows, the pathetic fallacy (the trope that the external environment described in poetry and literature offers a key to inward mood; the weather, for example, 'coming out in sympathy' to express characters' emotions) is an effect that is both 'uncanny' and 'matter-of-fact':

> The gloom of oncoming buses is repeated in the sky. The brilliant sunshine is inexplicably smacked on the back of the head. Big clouds tumble over, clowns without coherence. The darkness spreads like strong, spilt medicine. Gusts of wind scrap, a chill has crept in. Is this his father's work? There is nothing eerie about it, everything is simple and matter-of-fact.[60]

The narrator's hallucinatory vision brings us to the third kind of transformation, the 'transformation in hallucinosis'. While this is most readily understood as the production of hallucination, Bion's wording – *hallucinosis* – has a subtler implication. To describe it, he has recourse to the poet Shelley's 'formulation of his poetic intuition' as it appears in a footnote in volume seven of Shelley's 'Hellas: A Lyrical Drama': as 'that state of mind in which ideas may be supposed to assume the force of sensations through the confusion of thought with the objects of thought, and the excess of passion animating the creations of inspiration'.[61] Something like this seems to be at work in Royle's motif of the mimosa, which appears on four occasions. Mimosa is so called because the leaves of the plant recoil or 'wizen' in response to touch, and are therefore supposed to mimic or imitate sentient life; the word, 'mimosa', derives from the same etymological roots as 'mimesis'. The etymology also suggests a curious doubling of their mimetic quality: the suffix -osa meaning 'to resemble', the mimosa is that which resembles or mimics a mimesis; the word itself a figure of the *mise en abyme*, the continual dismantling and doubling of that which would guarantee a stable representation. Royle seems to use the word to describe an experience of foreshadowing ('everything seems shadowed, shadowing something else'[62]), of a precocious or uncanny knowledge of what is to come:

That's the wizening mimosa, the madness of the truth, seeping into view before the nurse had even told him what happened, the magisterial, blankety trick-photography of the changing of the light.[63]

As the novel progresses, the son seems to descend into madness or breakdown, his partner finding him increasingly difficult to follow in conversation. Yet the son suggests that he is on the verge of having a new idea about literature and writing:

– Everything is being stripped away. I can't express it. I'm experiencing new, incredible possibilities. It's a kind of magical sharpness, as if shadows have light [...]. It has to do with that mimosa thing I told you about. It's a kind of upside-down space of coincidence, a portal. I can't *stay*...[64]

Grinberg et al. describe 'transformations in hallucinosis [as] a wide range of phenomena that belong to the psychotic part of the personality [...] correlated with a primitive 'disaster' or 'catastrophe''.[65] Yet the transformation in hallucinosis can also seem to have something in common with Bion's fourth kind of transformation: the transformation in O. Put more simply: that which seems simply 'mad' can seem to signal the emergence of the transformation in O that is a break*through* rather than a break*down*. If hallucination is most easily described as 'seeing something that is not there', it is also easy to discern how the transformation in hallucinosis may be mistaken for the emergence of the wild thought, the new thought without a thinker. I want to suggest that Royle's mimosa, trembling on the cusp of a 'foreshadowing', foreknowledge of what is not yet, is the token of the peculiar madness that senses the passage of the transformation in O, or K → O, in Bion's formulation. It is a change preceded by 'psychological turbulence' (compare the son's 'period of implausible interference'). Seeking to characterise this, Bion recalls the Christian mystic, St. John of the Cross, in his description of the three 'dark nights of the soul'. Bion likens the third of these, which 'has to do with the point to which [the soul] travels – namely, God', to the transformation in O. Despite the breakthrough that the transformation in O enacts, the approach to it is experienced in catastrophic terms, since it seems to place the self at risk of a megalomania, a 'becoming' that (as in the religious case above) 'is felt as inseparable from becoming God, ultimate reality, the First Cause', or (in less mystical terms) 'of being responsible, that is mature'.[66]

Catastrophe is also entailed in the projective transformation. Bion describes the case of a man who seems to enact a projection of internal crisis at a particular moment in his treatment:

Then a change: friends or relations who have been denying that there is anything the matter cannot ignore his illness. He has been strange: he spends hours seated morosely in a chair; he appears to be hearing voices and seeing things.[67]

In *Quilt*, the son, too, seems to progress down a path of increasingly strange behaviour and worrying episodes (hallucinating his mother, collapsing, disturbances in his vision) that finally prompt his partner to fly back from the U.S. to see him immediately: 'Something in me gave way. Our separation was no longer to be tolerated'.[68]

Breakdown may be one of the ways in which growth is experienced, Bion suggests, and he reworks Freud's concept of latency, de-emphasising its sexual aspect, in favour of a functional account of latency as that which precedes the irruption of psychical growth. Bion proposes a reconsideration of latency not as a term with a settled meaning but inviting the question: what is latent? For Bion, what is latent is 'emotional turbulence':[69] the felt catastrophe of change and (in)decision that may nevertheless herald the onset of growth. Bion describes the experience of emotional turbulence that may be experienced towards the end of latency via his analogy of the tadpole:

> it is as if a tadpole became very upset because it was turning into a frog. There is nothing abnormal about it; it is not an illness but a change, and the tadpole would like someone to explain what is going on.[70]

In *Quilt*, the curious incident of the frog in the door jamb (following the vicar's visit to discuss funeral arrangements) evokes such a moment of precariousness and vulnerability:

> Then there is the vicar and the frog. [...]

> Only after she has driven away does he look down and see in the jamb, close by the rusty hinge, a frog, or what remains of a frog, with possibly a final throe, the throe as he goes to touch, no, not a throe, a cast of the light, a fantastical last contraction. The vicar killed the frog as she was leaving.[71]

As with the identification of the son with the father, and of the father with the ray, the metaphoricity of the frog story seems evident, not least to *Quilt*'s self-reflexive narrator:

> What is the frog's place in the yarn? What is this leap of faith into the door jamb and wait for the final crunch, as if that frog is indeed another forgery [...]

The narration identifies the son with the frog, enacting the reversal of perspective through the homophony of *throe* with *throw*: the frog's imagined final 'leap' into the door jamb echoed in the son who believes momentarily that he has seen the frog in its 'final throe', and developed further in the description of a precipitous, 'ranarian [frog-like] lucidity' over the events of the day: 'And all the while leaping backwards, in an analepsis of ranarian lucidity, through the entire entraining of funeral arrangements'.

The creature crushed in the door jamb introduces a figure that we will encounter again in a later chapter (about J.G. Ballard): the 'angle between two walls'. A character in Bion's *A Memoir of the Future* also describes the way that the 'angle of the walls' may be a place of both terror and refuge:

> Someone was trying to get me into a corner and club me to death. But thanks to reversed perspective I could cower in the corner where the angle of the walls protected me.[72]

Quilt teems with images of watery life, but it is the son, rather than the father, who seems to suffer a 'sea change'[73] (or at least a change into a creature suited for life around water). In the novel's second part, the narrator recites Clarence's dream from *Richard III*, in which he recalls a terrible dream of 'joining shipwrecked souls that fishes gnawed upon' and the horror of finding oneself

> overboard
>
> Into the tumbling billows of the main
>
> Lord, lord, methought what pain it was to drown:
>
> What dreadful noise of waters in my ears.
>
> What ugly sights of death within my eyes![74]

Clarence's dream offers a vivid, hallucinatory characterisation of the mental turbulence that accompanies the death of a father. Bion suggests repeatedly that this evocation of emotional turbulence may be the central genius of art: he returns frequently to the examples of Leonardo da Vinci's drawings of 'water swirling in turmoil, of hair in disorder',[75] as well as Milton's evocation of 'the rising World of waters dark and deep' that must be 'won from the void and formless Infinite'.[76]

There is a further resonance with Bion. An intriguing narrative digression inserts itself during the narrator's account of his father's funeral. He recalls his father's love of handiwork in an account of something that had taken place twenty years previously. A seemingly abandoned scaffold over the church lychgate had prompted the son to write a parodic history, aided and abetted by his father:

> One day a builder came and erected scaffolding around the lychgate, presumably with the intention of painting or reroofing or otherwise repairing it, but no one ever followed it up, the days passed and the weeks and months and no one came and no one seemed to mind, besides the son who saw it as a daily eyesore and defacement of the church. Eventually he took it upon himself to type out a statement on the subject, on a single sheet of paper.[77]

The text that follows, a text-within-the-text, introduces the curious notion of *excarnation*:

THE SCAFFOLDING [...]

Is the scaffolding now a permanent feature at last, a monument in its own right? And if so, should it be attributed symbolic significance? [...] Suffice to bring to notice the philological endeavours of one local historian who has noted the word 'scaffolding' as etymologically of obscure origin but nevertheless as bearing the less widely known sense of 'a raised framework, as for hunters, or among some primitive peoples for disposal of the dead' (Chambers). Given the etymology of 'lychgate' (Ger. *Leiche*, corpse), the notion of an alternation in church policy, with regard to the practice of excarnation, irresistibly suggests itself.

Excarnation refers to the practice of removing flesh from a dead body (for example, in order to enable the transport of bones), or leaving a body exposed to the elements. It is a funny but disturbing story for a funeral, where the question of how to deal with the remains of the dead is unusually pertinent. The scene is suggestive for a number of reasons. The father (strikingly, referred to impersonally in this scene: 'the dead man screwed down this little text about 'THE SCAFFOLDING' under a carefully cut plastic plinth') is depicted as the arbiter of language, literally screwing down the son's words that have broken free of stable signification since his death. In an earlier passage, the narrator describes his partner in terms of an obscene unmooring: 'The post is past. Words come away. Letters capsize. She is digression, syncopation, asyndeton, ontradiction. Her 'c' curls away invisibly, leaving the shoreline of a new language: *ontra*'.[78]

Throughout the novel, there are unexpected words, suggestive portmanteaus, and near-anagrams – mimosa, mimesis, *mimosaturation*;[79] frogs that are forgeries; 'synapothanumena'[80] – a productive giving way of language in the aftermath of learning that his father has died ('speak English, no, not a word, nary that, all awry, telephoning home, no, never mind, already impossible, hallo, my father has died, he's gone, given the world the slip'.[81] Strangest of all, the son's language is somehow 'wreck[ed]' by the ray itself, with the word, 'ray', prompting the son's invention of the world's first '*dictionaray*'. The partner, now narrating, recounts the moment when she realises that something is wrong:

No, the horrifying conviction comes when he tells me about some writing project he's begun elaborating and proceeds to read it aloud to me over the phone. It is a work of lexicography devoted to the buried life of anagrams and homophones, each word with its own idiosyncratic definition, a dictionaray, yes, as he is pleased to declare: the world's first English dictionaray. It would be a verbal laboratory, a dictionary testamentary to the way the ray leaves its mark in everyday language, a vocabulary that might constitute a new species of bestiary, and generate an altogether other estuary English.[82]

The dictionaray, 'this new English dictionary on hysterical principles',[83] begins with the letter A for 'Airy, Awry, Anniversary, Anteriority, Arraign, Arrange', and fills some 22 pages of *Quilt*. Mad and maddening, it is impossible thereafter not to hear or see the ray in rain, *in medias res*, the middle things become the middle rays, reified: the ray ray-alising language. Bion writes about the way that words and ideas come to be 'constantly conjoined' in a person's mind as the result of emotional experience, enabling meaning to accrete in and around words. Words stabilise meaning, not because there is any necessary connection between signifier and signified, but because the work of naming is the psychical act upon which meaning is based; in the terminology of the Grid, it is the 'definitory hypothesis': 'Once the name has been given and the scattering thereby prevented, meaning can begin to accumulate'.[84]

In a poignant section in *Learning from Experience*, Bion describes this process in detail in regard to the word, 'daddy':

> Let us suppose that the infant repeats an emotional experience in which the following elements are constantly conjoined; the sight of a man, a sense of being loved by the man, a sense of wanting the man, an awareness of the repetition of a phrase, by the mother, of 'That's Daddy.' 'Da, da, da' says the child. 'That's right; Daddy,' says the mother. From the emotional experience the infant abstracts certain elements, what they are depending partly on the infant; these abstracted elements are given a name 'Daddy' in other situations in which the same elements appear to be conjoined; thus a vocabulary is established. This is not a description of fact; I give it the status of a model from which I abstract a theory and expect to find that it is a representation to which some realisation corresponds. The theory I abstract is: 'Daddy' is the name of a hypothesis.[85]

The death of the father threatens to send this process into reverse, to undo meaning, words, the constant conjunction of elements around the idea and the language and the body of the father. The scaffold seems to figure ambivalently the mechanism that enables meaning to accumulate, the constant conjunction of words and meaning that I also liken to the *potence*, the French word used by Perec[86] for the first words in a crossword that are also a gib, or a gallows. Semantically, excarnation suggests itself as an antonym to *incarnation*; the 'word made flesh' through the incarnation of Christ giving way to its opposite, which would be… what? The flesh made word? The body placed outside of itself, exoskeletally, a literal/literary instance of projection? At the lychgate, however, the body has already gone: all that remains is the scaffolding, and 'already it is so long ago that few locals can easily picture the church without its parergonal complement'.[87] That which is secondary, the scaffold, is all that remains: excarnation suggested by an exoskeleton. This section is followed by the first of the book's startling statements about literature: 'Excarnation is literature. Its music strips you. Literature is excarnation'.[88]

Quilt makes a number of statements about literature itself, both in the novel as well as in the afterword. Some, but not all of these, are explicitly voiced through the son's narration: a 'telling' that is also a 'showing', and a kind of intradiegetic, extradiegetic address (or perhaps that which Jonathan Culler has described as the 'extradiegetic homodiegetic narrator display[ing] special knowledge') that might enact a 'vertical' variant on the 'literary telepathy' that Royle has described elsewhere; that is to say, the feeling 'at a distance' passed between narrator, reader, and writer.[89] The declaration that 'excarnation is literature [...] literature is excarnation' might also be re-worded in Bionian terms to the effect that literature enables the *realisation of a pre-conception*: it *realises* an intuition (or intuited knowledge) and enables a transformation of evolving reality, O, along the frontier of the contact-barrier. Put another way, it enables some part of the unstructured, raw 'stuff' of reality ('external' reality, but also the reality of who we are) to become assimilable, knowable, usable. Royle's formulation additionally suggests something negative, that which Bion might call its 'column 2',[90] aspect, since the model of excarnation and a 'stripping' effected by literature implies that something is lost – or, changing the metaphor slightly and using a word that is Bion's own, involves a *denudation* – rather than added.

The scaffold – not strictly a necessary part of excarnation, but foregrounded in *Quilt* – suggests that the vulnerability and exposure that is at the heart of an experience of literature can be mitigated in phantasy by the idea of external structure that does not prevent excarnation, but safeguards the exo-/endo- distinction: an outside *and* an inside. The role of the scaffolding in Royle's formulation of literature might be likened to the self-binding of Odysseus in order both to experience and withstand the music of the Sirens. Bion is deeply alert to the implicit use of models to describe emotional states and psychical processes. His formulation of the container-contained model for learning and growth is derived in part from the ubiquity of conventional statements that model psychical pain as being 'in' something else:

> If a patient says he cannot take something in, or the analyst feels he cannot take something in, he implies a container and something to put in it. The statement that something cannot be taken in must not therefore be dismissed as a mere way of speaking.[91]

Bion returns repeatedly to imagery and phantasy in which visual and verbal descriptions of scaffolding, carapaces, shells and other exoskeletenous structures feature prominently, not least in his own descriptions of his war experiences and his development of the Grid, which might provide, he suggests, a 'mental climbing-frame'[92] for psychoanalysts. Within the process of ideation there is a tension that always risks closing the mind to new and disturbing thoughts, and to the necessity of having to 'think again':

Falling back on metaphor, one could say that when we secrete an idea, or when we produce a theory, we seem at the same time to lay down chalky material, we become calcified, the idea becomes calcified, and then you have another impressive caesura which you can't break out of.[93]

It is a question, for Bion, of the necessary modulation between security and insecurity that a process of creation requires. The scaffolding in *Quilt* is a complex, undecidable figure that simultaneously exposes the body to being stripped and reinforces the body that it surrounds. It can also subject the body within to an unbearable pressure, prove too mighty a shell. The motif of 'a house bigger than a heart' appears on a number of occasions in *Quilt*, seeming to allude to the way that poetical refuge is sometimes inadequate against reality, as well as refiguring the role of the rays within the father's house, with their pools and pumps, as an artificial heart installed to replace 'the heart pulverised, faked within, beyond repair':

Sometimes a house is bigger than a heart, an apparently crazy thought, scarcely stands to irreason: a house is always bigger. But the thinker of the heart knows that in its pull, voracity, embrace and engulfing power it is at least as colossal as the mouth: it sucks up an ocean, casts out decades, burns down at a quiver forest after forest, searing soaring seeking or holding onto its prey, its inseparable maker, in a valley of kings of its own making. But sometimes a house is bigger. You can huff and you can puff but the walls won't give, making the heart collapse, taking it all in at its own pace, a matter of a minute or a year and the house has prised open the heart and built itself so big inside it sprawls out finally standing alone with the heart pulverised, faked within, beyond repair.[94]

Later on, the narrator declares:

There is a new literature. It does something new with people. It has different slownesses and spectralities. It celebrates nanothinking.[95]

'Nanothinking' appears in Royle's essay 'Even the Title: On the State of Narrative Theory Today', where it appears alongside the related word *nanoment*, defined by Royle as 'the literary slowing down of the moment in order to be faithful to its quickness, a written testimony to what might be called the quick fiction of every moment'. Where the nanoment is the 'art of […] taking the moment to pieces', nanothinking evokes, I suggest, the detailed and precarious attentiveness that enables the new thought to come into being. Bion quotes John Keats' famous statement on 'negative capability', that capacity to be 'in uncertainties, mysteries, doubts, without any irritable reaching after fact and reason'.[96] It is the frame of mind able and willing to receive the 'wild thought', the thought without a thinker. The new thought is not a *fait accompli*: it requires a mind – one or several – able to receive and sustain it. What kind of mind is this? It is, perhaps, the mind that dreams:

> We might get a clue [to the question of the wild thought] by wondering in what frame of mind or in what conditions this wild thought turned up and became enmeshed in our method of thinking. It could be that it seemed to occur to us when we were asleep. I am using this expression, 'when we were asleep', because it is a state of mind with which most people think they are familiar, so we can start with this somewhat familiar idea.[97]

Bion suggests that people often dismiss dreams from the altered vantage of the waking state: "Well, of course, I had a dream – but then, it was only a dream". Freud, he writes, 'was one of these peculiar people who seemed to think that dreams are worthy of further consideration'. Like Coleridge's 'Person from Porlock', the waking state tends to interrupt the receptivity of the dreaming mind; yet some aspect of dreaming, Bion contends, remains active even while we are awake. Dream is nevertheless only one word – the most familiar – to describe the many and different states of mind in which the new thought can develop. Elsewhere he writes: 'The night, the dream, is a 'roughness' between the smooth polished consciousness of daylight; in that 'roughness' an idea might lodge'.[98]

The roughness of the dreaming mind suggests a nanoscopic terrain in which a wilder, 'smaller' kind of thinking takes place, a thinking not quite worthy of the name – wayward and untutored, yet unconsciously etymological; the mind of portmanteaus, anagrams, atrocious puns; tmesis and expletive infixation – but nevertheless vital in the creation of new ideas that would find no place in a formal taxonomy. Bion does, nevertheless, attempt one:

> In case one of these strays comes along, I think I shall try to be prepared for its reception by arranging certain categories that might be suitable for placing the stray in a temporary – what? It is difficult to find the word for it. I do not find that the vocabulary that is available to me is very suitable for the purposes for which I want it just now, so I am going to call it a 'box'. The first box I am thinking of is really not suitable for anything so ephemeral as what I usually call a thought, namely, something that is physical; I shall call it a 'beta-element'. I don't know what that means and I don't know what it is, and as it hasn't turned up I am still ignorant. But anyway, there it is, in case that strange creature should exist and should it swim into my ken.[99]

A Bionian nanothinking aims at sustaining the longer-term project of bringing the new idea to a timely maturation that can be foreclosed by premature and excessive scrutiny:

> So you are always under pressure prematurely and precociously to produce your idea. Poor little thing! Pull it up by the roots and have a look at it – it hasn't got a chance. So you have to act as a sort of parent to the idea –

protect it and give it a chance to grow in spite of these pressures; you have to be able to tolerate this state of ignorance.[100]

'A sort of parent to the idea', the writer is cast *in loco parentis*. The final scene of *Quilt* evokes the possibility that the son has undergone not only a breakdown, but a sea-change: that he has in fact become a ray, transubstantiated from human to manta, a wholly efficient transformation with no remainder. Arriving back in the country from the airport, his partner returns to the house, finding not disarray but its eerie opposite: an array of rays, mysteriously multiplied. The original four in the dining room are supplemented by a further installation of eagle rays in the drawing room. Surveying the scene with tears in her eyes, she declares: 'Everyone knows. This is no whodunit', and heads upstairs. The parents' bedroom is the stage for a kind of final-primal scene, in which the achievement of parenthood is the birth of a uniquely fabulous creature:

> As I opened the door of his parents' room the light seemed at once to stream in and hold. Tears were running down my face. It was a translucent cave. [...] The sky had disappeared. It was a manta, the biggest ray, the strangest thing I had ever seen in a house.[101]

The novel's resolution is also a ray-solution: dissolving and resolving the son, who does not reappear after his confession that he has been 'making it up as [he] went along', improvising the dictionaray, *ex tempore*, giving his language over wholly to the morphemic music of the ray as it appears insistently, repeatedly, within the fabric of the English language. In this final scene, the son has possibly fallen out of the novel, beyond language: psychotic, perhaps, or dead; his partner looking 'for some kind of note, a letter, the briefest message', but 'no sign of anything anywhere'.[102] Alternatively he has become the very thing that he has been identified with – his father, the ray, father-as-ray – through the mechanisms of a spectacular transformation in hallucinosis or in O.

In the undecidability of its outcome, the ending of *Quilt* recalls the final scene in Charlotte Perkins Gilman's *The Yellow Wallpaper*, where the female narrator, subjected to a brutally restrictive postpartum rest-cure, becomes one with the woman she sees 'trapped' in the wallpaper, going round and round the room in circles. *Quilt*, which ends not with the curious scene of the parents' bedroom, but with its afterword, closes similarly with a gesture of narrative circling. 'In the middle of the night the phone rings, over and over...'[103] But unlike Perkins Gilman's tale, the ending of *Quilt* is more equivocal in respect of its central character's prospects. The gesture that brings the novel full circle seems rather to inaugurate the possibility of a new cycle of transformation leading to a progressively fuller integration of the emotional experience that is at its heart. For Bion, it is the 'adequacy of the circle's diameter' that makes circularity in thought permissible, the 'sufficiency of experience' that enables meaning to develop. As such, the novel (and the ray pool) can be conceived of as a space of play, a containing space in which grief itself undergoes a transformation. But it is also a birthing pool for the emergence of the new idea: *Quilt* is richly generative in terms of the thinking of new ideas for literary theory. Eschewing the word, 'theory', Bion described his own theory-making as transformation:

> The accounts that I have given, and the one that I am about to give, might be described as 'theories' of what took place. In view of the associations that belong to the term 'theory' I prefer the term 'transformation'.[104]

Quilt performs, I suggest, a number of different kinds of transformations of the emotional experience of grief, staging the complete range of transformations described by Bion. The novel installs a number of identifications – father identified with ray, the son identified with the father – that exemplify the kind of transferential transformation that Bion described as 'rigid-motion'. It also does something more complex, more 'mad', in its development and perseveration of the ray theme: projective transformation. The son's encroaching breakdown entails explicitly hallucinatory aspects (transformation in hallucinosis), and suggests that what the partner encounters in the novel's dénouement may be something too mad to describe, a psychotic reality. But it also holds open the possibility that the son has been transformed, and transformed his experience, in some ineffable but necessary way. Even for Bion, words fail to describe adequately the experience of the transformation in O, which comes at the end of his taxonomy:

> To rigid motion transformations, projective transformations, transformations in hallucinosis, I shall now add transformations in O. That is to say I propose to extend the significance of O to cover the domain of reality and 'becoming'. Transformations in O contrast with other transformations in that the former are related to growth in *becoming* and the latter to growth in 'knowing about' growth; they resemble each other in that 'growth' is common to both.[105]

The transformation in O involves more than 'knowing about' reality; it entails becoming who one is. Of O, he writes: 'the most, and the least that the individual person can do is be it'.[106]

Notes

1 Bion, *Complete Works*, 5:266. (*Transformations*, 156.) Italics mine.
2 Rilke, *Duino Elegies*, 57.
3 Royle, *Quilt*. Subsequent references are to this edition. I am grateful to Nicholas Royle and Myriad Editions for allowing me to use quotations from *Quilt* at length.
4 *Quilt*, 11.
5 *Quilt*, 94.
6 *Quilt*, 149.
7 *Quilt*, 153.
8 Ionescu, "'Cloth Speaks': Cloaks of Telepathy, Melancholia, and the Uncanny in Nicholas Royle's Quilt," 96.

9   Ganteau, *The Ethics and Aesthetics of Vulnerability in Contemporary British Fiction*, 86.

10 *Quilt*, 3.

11 The Latin phrase, '*in medias res*', though it is understood to mean 'in the middle of things', may be translated literally as 'into the middle things'.

12 'The Second Coming', in Yeats, *Selected Poems*, 124.

13 *Quilt*, 3.

14 Bion, *Complete Works*, 10:35 (*Two Papers*, 37).

15 *Quilt*, 33.

16 Bion, *Complete Works*, 5:141 (*Transformations*, 17).

17 *Quilt*, 112.

18 *Quilt*, 5.

19 *Quilt*, 9.

20 *Quilt*, 10–11.

21 *Quilt*, 22.

22 Playfair, "Hutton's Unconformity."

23 *Hamlet*, Act 1, Scene V. Shakespeare, *William Shakespeare: The Complete Works*, 663.

24 *Quilt*, 25.

25 *Quilt*, 26.

26 *Quilt*, 27.

27 *Quilt*, 71.

28 *Quilt*, 32.

29 *Quilt*, 86.

30 *Quilt*, 88.

31 *Quilt*, 91.

32 Bion, *Complete Works*, 11:39 (*Cogitations*: 33).

33 Bion, *Complete Works*, 11:47 (*Cogitations*: 43).

34 *Quilt*, 86–87.

35 *Quilt*, 32.

36 Bion, *Complete Works*, 5:130 (*Transformations*: 5).

37 Grinberg, Sor, and Tabak de Bianchedi, *Introduction to the Work of Bion: Groups, Knowledge, Psychosis, Thought, Transformations, Psychoanalytic Practice*.

38 Bion, *Complete Works*, 5:213 (*Transformations*: 97).

39 Laplanche and Pontalis, *The Language of Psychoanalysis*, 462.

40 *Quilt*, 86.

41 *Quilt*, 51.

42 Bion, *Complete Works*, 5:134 (*Transformations*, 9).

43 Bion, *Complete Works*, 5:271 (*Transformations*, 161).

44 *Quilt*, 7.

45 *Quilt*, 73.

46 *Quilt*, 30.

47 *Quilt*, 31.

48 *Quilt*, 28.

49 Filreis, *Wallace Stevens and the Actual World*, 154.

50 Stevens, *The Collected Poems of Wallace Stevens: Corrected Edition*, 358.

51 Bion, *Complete Works*, 10:139 (*Clinical Seminars and Other Works*, 325).

52 Bion, *Complete Works*, 6:197 (*Second Thoughts*, 160).

53 Bion, *Complete Works*, 5:259 (*Transformations*, 148).

54 Bion, *Complete Works*, 5:251 (*Transformations*, 140).

55 From the poem 'Sacred Emily', in Stein, *Geography and Play*, 178–88.

56 Bion, *Complete Works*, 5:263 (*Transformations*, 153).

57 From 'Description without Place', in Stevens, *The Collected Poems of Wallace Stevens: Corrected Edition*, 358–59.

58 Riley, *Time Lived, Without Its Flow*, 7.

59 *Quilt*, 34.
60 *Quilt*, 35.
61 Bion, *Complete Works*, 5:246 (*Transformations*, 133–4).
62 *Quilt*, 34.
63 *Quilt*, 38.
64 *Quilt*, 95. Also an allusion to *Antony and Cleopatra*, Act 5, Scene 2.
65 Grinberg, Sor, and Tabak de Bianchedi, *Introduction to the Work of Bion: Groups, Knowledge, Psychosis, Thought, Transformations, Psychoanalytic Practice*, 57.
66 Bion, *Complete Works*, 5:269 (*Transformations*, 159).
67 Bion, *Complete Works*, 5:132 (*Transformations*, 7).
68 *Quilt*, 144.
69 Bion, *Complete Works*, 10:113 (*Clinical Seminars and Other Works*, 295).
70 Bion, *Complete Works*, 7:74 (*Brazilian Lectures: 1973 São Paulo, 1974 Rio de Janeiro/São Paulo*, 74).
71 *Quilt*, 50.
72 Bion, *Complete Works*, 12:73 (*A Memoir of the Future*, 73).
73 *The Tempest*, Act 1, Scene 2. Shakespeare, *William Shakespeare: The Complete Works*, 1173.
74 *Quilt*, 85. From *Richard III*, Act 1, Scene 4.
75 Bion, *Complete Works*, 10:113 (*Clinical Seminars and Other Works*, 296).
76 Bion, *Complete Works*, 5:261 (*Transformations*, 151).
77 *Quilt*, 59.
78 *Quilt*, 27.
79 *Quilt*, 52.
80 *Quilt*, 42.
81 *Quilt*, 21.
82 *Quilt*, 121.
83 *Quilt*, 144.
84 Bion, *Complete Works*, 5:74 (*Elements of Psychoanalysis*, 88).
85 Bion, *Complete Works*, 4:334–35 (*Learning from Experience*, 66).
86 See discussion of the French word, *potence*, in chapter two, in relation to Georges Perec.
87 *Quilt*, 60.
88 *Quilt*, 62.
89 Royle, "Even the Title: On the State of Narrative Theory Today."
90 See chapter three for a fuller discussion of the column 2 formulation.
91 Bion, *Complete Works*, 5:11 (*Elements of Psychoanalysis*, 6).
92 Bion, *Complete Works*, 5:99 (*Taming Wild Thoughts*, 5).
93 Bion, *Complete Works*, 9:110 (*The Italian Seminars*: 11).
94 *Quilt*, 76.
95 *Quilt*, 82.
96 Bion, *Complete Works*, 6:327 (*Attention and Interpretation*: 125).
97 Bion, *Complete Works*, 10:175–76 (*Taming Wild Thoughts*: 27).
98 Bion, *Complete Works*, 13:48 (*A Memoir of the Future*: 268).
99 Bion, *Complete Works*, 10:176–77 (*Taming Wild Thoughts*: 29).
100 Bion, *Complete Works*, 9:27 (*The Tavistock Seminars*, 23).
101 *Quilt*, 148.
102 *Quilt*, 149.
103 *Quilt*, 159.
104 Bion, *Complete Works*, 5:178 (*Transformations*, 58).
105 Bion, *Complete Works*, 5:266 (*Transformations*, 156). Italics mine.
106 Bion, *Complete Works*, 5:251 (*Transformations*, 140).

9 Dream I Tell You: Bion's *A Memoir of the Future*

[Freud] took up only the negative attitude, dreams as 'concealing' something, not the way in which the *necessary* dream is *constructed*.[1]

In the last years of his life, Bion wrote his strange magnum opus, *A Memoir of the Future*.[2] Initially published in three parts between 1975 and 1979 (the year of Bion's death), it was supplemented by a key/index section (completed by Francesca Bion) in 1981, and finally published in a single edition in 1991. Part-autobiography, part-Victorian melodrama, part-dream, *A Memoir of the Future* is a disturbing and unclassifiable piece of writing that roves indeterminately between the domains of creative and critical writing. Strange, lengthy, repetitive – replete with idiosyncrasy and personal references – *A Memoir of the Future* was initially dismissed with some embarrassment by many of Bion's peers as evidence of his senility, and it has remained relatively neglected in the now four decades since its original publication (with some notable exceptions within the psychoanalytic community, such as Grotstein, Meltzer and Sandler[3]). The writer and visual artist Meg Harris Williams has also published a poetic and personal appreciation of and commentary on *Memoir* in *Bion's Dream: A Reading of the Autobiographies*. More recently, there has been renewed critical interest in *Memoir* by Jacobus[4], ffytche[5] and Beebe Tarantelli.[6]

My intention in this chapter is to continue the work of exploring *A Memoir of the Future* from a literary and creative perspective via a discussion of the book's major themes: dream, war, death, and the birth of the mind. *Memoir* can be thought of as Bion's 'dream book', recalling the name given to Freud's *The Interpretation of Dreams*.[7] In very different ways, both books elaborate a theory of dreams and involve self-analysis. Bion's experience of war also looms large across its pages: the 'story' recounts the lives of a fractious group of characters during a time of war that seems to reference both the First and Second World Wars, and includes recognisable vignettes of his war experiences (especially the case of the injured private, Sweeting) that appear in his other autobiographical works: *War Memoirs 1917–1919*, *The Long Week-End 1897–1919: Part of a Life*, and *All My Sins Remembered: Another Part of a Life and The Other Side of Genius: Family Letters*. Bion's 'deaths' – the one to come and the psychical 'death' that he describes having experienced during the First

DOI: 10.4324/9781003006619-9

World War – haunt the text. The reader also encounters a fantastical *mise-en-scène* of Bion's birth, as well as the birth of *mind* that is the result of the central group's growing capacity to give birth to the thought without a thinker. It is not possible within the scope of this chapter to do justice to *A Memoir of the Future* in all of its bewildering range and provocation. Nevertheless, I hope to contribute to the re-integration of Bion's neglected text and draw attention to Bion's interest as a creative writer.

Dreams proliferate in *A Memoir of the Future*: characters go to sleep and wake up within their own (or someone else's) dream: there are dreams within dream, dream experiences and dreams recounted, dreams of psychoanalysis and writing, and characters whose dreams are disturbed by unconscious parts of their own self. The first volume, entitled 'The Dream', opens with an unnamed narrator exhausted from an over-full night of dreaming:

> I am tired. It is quite bad enough having a full day's schedule without having a full night's programme too. I do not remember what happened anyway. Something about reversed perspective. I was writing something about it.[8]

The narrator's 'reversed perspective' recalls the mechanism used by patients, in Bion's description, to 'preserve a static hallucination'[9] rather than countenance a new point of view. He gives the example of the popular visual illusions that can be seen in two ways (e.g. the image that can be the silhouette of two faces or a vase) as a model for the way that the discovery of the selected fact crystallises the moment in which a reversed perspective becomes possible. The beginning of *A Memoir of the Future* is an invitation to observe dreaming 'from the inside out':

> Suppose I used my alimentary canal as a sort of telescope. I could get down to the arse and look up at the mouth full of teeth and tonsils and tongue. Or rush up to the top end of the alimentary canal and watch what my arse-hole was up to. Rather amusing really. It depends what my digestive tract felt about having me scampering up and down the gut all night.

Whose dream are we witnessing in *Memoir*? In the prologue, it is the narrator who wakes up after a dream, wondering what Alice has been doing in her sleep. Alice appears in the first chapter, where, like her Wonderland namesake, she is rubbing her eyes and pushing away the shower of leaves which had awoken her: 'I had such a queer dream about the Empress of India'.[10] Unlike Carroll's Alice, she awakes *into* a dream in which an enemy invasion is on the horizon. Her maid, Rosemary, comes to her to beg to be allowed to depart for the final train before it is too late. Imperious and complacent, the upper classes refuse to run away, assuming that their world of privilege and ease will be retained even under enemy rule. 'Now I remember a bit of a dream about

violence and murder', Bion writes in the prologue: 'Something about Albert
and Victoria'. Bion's dream of the dreaming Alice depicts the world into
which Bion was born: one of privilege and class distinction, fuelled by colonial
expansion in India and sustained by the public school system[11] that sought to
create an élite cadre of colonial officers. In the scenes that follow, that world is
turned on its head, with master and servant changing places (Alice becomes
Rosemary's servant on the basis of her sexual submission), and the men of the
old order (chiefly Roland and Robin) unable to subjugate the virile character
of 'Man', who has a gun.

The prologue announces that 'this is a fictitious account of psychoanalysis
including an artificially constructed dream'. This remarkable statement signals
a dream-project markedly different to Freud's. Writing in his journal in 1959,
Bion reflected that Freud 'took up only the negative attitude, dreams as
'concealing' something, not the way in which the *necessary* dream is *constructed*'.
The necessary dream, Bion suggests, is the one that enables the subject to
integrate more of their reality through the successful operation of alpha-
function. For Bion, reality is not chiefly apprehended by the cultivation of
conscious thought, but by expanding the mind's capacity to 'dream', the work
of the mind that he initially calls 'dream-work-α' [dream-work-alpha][12] and
later, alpha-function. The figure of the dream (Fr. *rêve*) is also at work in the
mother's reverie – her capacity to receive and transform the infant's feelings –
setting dream-work-α developmentally in train. James Grotstein has described
the role of the analyst as a 'dreaming co-pilot' who enters the analysand's
'continuing dream [...] in order to complete the dream'.[13] Row C of the Grid
('dream-thoughts, dreams, myths') is 'intended for categories of sensuous,
usually visual images such as those appearing in dreams, myths, narratives,
hallucinations'.[14] The unsaturated dream-*thought* is the basis for creative
dream-*work* that enables the development of meaning and further abstraction.

Thus does dreaming take on a very different role within Bion's metapsychology. For both Freud and Bion, dreams are the object of psychoanalytic enquiry. But unlike Freud, Bion sees the dream as the very location of
psychoanalytic work rather than simply an artefact of psychical process. The
Italian psychoanalyst Antonino Ferro writes 'in praise of row C', characterising
psychoanalysis 'as a particular form of literature'[15] in which both participants of
analysis contribute to the narration – sequencing and elaboration – of the
'narrative derivatives' of alpha-elements that can take place in row C. This
leads to a very different conception of Freud's term, 'dream-work':

> But *Freud* meant by dream-work that unconscious material, which would
> otherwise be perfectly comprehensible, was transformed into a dream, and
> that the dream-work needed to be undone in order the make the
> incomprehensible dream comprehensible [...]. *I* mean that the conscious
> material has to be subjected to dream-work to render it fit for storing,
> selection, and suitable for transformation [...][16]

While Bion's characterisation of Freud is correct, there are hints of a train of thought similar to Bion's within *The Interpretations of Dreams*, which nevertheless comes to be dominated by the theory of repression and the dream as wish-fulfilment. Dreams, he writes, are 'not only reproductive but productive',[17] and can be 'excretions of thoughts that have failed to germinate',[18] a comment that comes very close to Bion's articulation of wild thoughts as seeds seeking germination.[19]

It may be helpful to make a few further remarks of comparison between Freud's and Bion's 'dream-books'. The *Interpretation of Dreams* is Freud's founding document of psychoanalysis, marking the decisive moment, in his early forties, that his researches into psychology and hysteria took on the status of a new clinical field. As he candidly admitted, his book had a 'further subjective significance for me personally – a significance I only grasped after I completed it. It was, I found, a portion of my own self-analysis, my reaction to my father's death – that is to say, to the most important event, the most poignant loss, of a man's life'.[20] The work is notable for its inclusion of Freud's own dreams (such as the dream of Irma's injection) and the analysis of other personal material. By contrast, *A Memoir of the Future* was written in the closing years of Bion's life. Like *The Interpretation of Dreams*, Bion's dream-book is a deeply personal, auto-analytic document that enacts a kind of 'wild' psychoanalysis in concert with the exposition of theory. What differs, I suggest, is the relationship to writing and literature. Bion makes clear that *A Memoir of the Future* is a 'fictitious account of an artificially constructed dream', making of dream itself a kind of mode or genre. It is beset by 'shadowy figures', such as 'Science Fiction', and a proliferation of ephemeral characters (such as 'Sherlock', apparently based on Sherlock Holmes) who lament the inadequacy of their imagination by dreamers on whom their existence depends:

> SHERLOCK (to Watson) Has he gone? It's humiliating to think that dreams are at the mercy of people who dream.[21]

The term, 'dream-imagination', appears seven times in *The Interpretation of Dreams*. Thereafter it disappears entirely from Freud's terminology, while the related term, 'dream-work', remains in use for the rest of Freud's career. Freud attributes the term to K.A. Scherner, who theorised dreams as the product of dream-imagination: a faculty that, free from waking rational thought, was available for the creation of dreams charged with symbolic significance. Freud's reference to the potentially productive quality of dreams comes in a long passage devoted to Scherner, whom Freud credits as having recognised the psychical (rather than purely mechanical) contribution to dreams. A special faculty of mind, the dream-imagination 'never depicts things completely, but only in outline', and 'does not halt [...] at the mere representation of an object [but] is under an internal necessity to involve the dream-ego to a greater or less extent with the object and thus produce an *event*'.[22] I suggest that Freud's term, the 'dream-imagination', has similarities to Bion's conception of the dream-work-α, active equally during waking hours and sleep; the part of the mind that draws, as for Scherner, on 'somatic stimuli' in order to generate unsaturated dream-images (or Ferro's 'narrative derivatives') that are not only representational but actively creative. 'For Scherner', Freud writes, 'dream-formation begins at the point where others believe it dries up'.[23]

Scherner's contribution is important to Freud's thinking on dreams, though subject to Freud's characteristic ambivalence to his intellectual forebears ('I have held fast to the habit of always studying things themselves before looking for information about them in books, and therefore I was able to establish the symbolism of dreams for myself *before I was led to it* by Scherner's work on the subject'[24]). Disparaging Scherner's book as 'written in a turgid and high-flown style [...] inspired by an almost intoxicated enthusiasm for his subject which is bound to repel anyone who cannot share in his fervour',[25] he will nevertheless subsequently credit Scherner as 'the discoverer of dream-symbolism', noting that 'psycho-analysis has confirmed Scherner's findings, though it has made material modifications in them'.[26] Where Freud repudiates Scherner's argument is in replacing 'dream-*imagination*' with the idea of a 'dream-*work*' in the service of repression. Bion's contention that Freud 'took up only the negative attitude, dreams as 'concealing' something' draws attention to the path not taken by Freud when he placed repression at the centre of his theory.

In *A Memoir of the Future*, there are a number of scenes in which what is most striking is Bion's permissive approach to material that is vulgar, bawdy, or low-brow. Indeed, much of the book's capacity to shock and disturb comes from the apparent incongruence between the ostensibly 'respectable' Bion – a former President of the British Psychoanalytic Society – and this other Bion who seemed to break with everything that had come before. Where earlier Bion wrote tersely and in numbered paragraphs, late Bion is prolix. Sex, rarely mentioned in his earlier work, is everywhere in *Memoir*: from Alice's 'rape' by the farm-hand, Tom; and in the discussions of Rosemary's mother, a prostitute. Though Edna O'Shaughnessy finds continuities between the phases of Bion's work, she finds *Memoir* 'less disciplined', 'too open, too pro- and e-vocative, and weakened by riddling meanings', with a tendency of 'sliding between ideas rather than linking them'.[27] Meltzer and Harris Williams, writing together in 1985, described the general reaction to the work as 'one of shocked rejection': 'He was a great man, but he had no experience of writing fiction', a well-known literary critic is reported to have said, declining to review the books'.[28]

The recoil of *A Memoir of the Future*'s early readers is understandable, especially given the way in which the work first appeared. Bion's three volumes of (more or less) conventional autobiography had not been published at the time when the first volumes of *Memoir* came out, and much of the autobiographical detail becomes clearer when it is read in conjunction with these. Moreover, Bion had surprised (and in some measure, rejected) the British psychoanalytic community by resigning his positions of authority in favour of moving to Los Angeles (at the age of 71) to begin anew with clients and teaching. Meltzer and Harris William note wryly that when 'the slim volumes of the *Memoir* began to appear in their shoddy and error-ridden Brazilian edition (1975, 1977) [...], it seemed that perhaps Dr Bion had not left us but, rather, had been kidnapped and was being tortured or degraded, or perhaps was just becoming senile'.[29]

An instance of the work's strangeness is given in the following example. In an early chapter, a character called 'Captain Bion' (who appears only once in *A Memoir of the Future*) launches into a strange soliloquy:

> CAPTAIN BION I stared at the speck of mud trembling on the straw. I stared through the front flap at the clods of earth spouting up all around us. [...] I got out and hovered about six feet above us. I knew 'they' would... and saw trees as wood walking. How they walked – walk! walk! they went like arfs arfing. Arf arf together, arfing's the stuff for me, if it's not a Rolls Royce, which I'd pick out for choice. [...] Cooh! Wot 'appened then? 'E talked a lot more about Jesus and dog and man and then 'e sez, all sudden like, Throw away the uvver crutch! Coo! Wot 'appened then? 'E fell on his arse. And 'is Arse wuz angry and said, Get off my arse! You've done nothing but throw shit at me all yore life and you expects England to be my booty! Boo-ootiful soup; in a shell-hole in Flanders Fields. Legs and guts... must 'ave bin twenty men in there – Germ'um and frogslegs and all starts! We didn't 'alf arf I can tell you. Let bruvverly luv continue. No one asked 'im to fall-in! No one arsed 'im to come out either – come fourth, we said, and E came fifth and 'e didn't ½ stink. Full stop! 'e said. The parson 'e did kum, 'e did kwat. 'E talked of Kingdom Come. King dumb come.[30]

Elements of Captain Bion's remarkable monologue become clearer in the light of the autobiographies. Bion's experiences as a tank command officer impressed him deeply; at twenty years old, he found himself in command of working-class soldiers whose voices he ventriloquises, and a witness to innumerable horrors. The song of the mock turtle in *Alice in Wonderland* ('beautiful soup') becomes a grim elegy to the fallen men of Flanders Field. 'Arf arfer' recalls the young Bion, who confused the 'Our Father' of the Lord's Prayer with an ever-present bogeyman called 'Arf Arfer', threatening punishments for childhood crimes (as recounted by Bion in *The Long Week-End*). In this scene, 'arfing' has been transformed into a verb connoting the monstrous march of dead soldiers and the 'trees as wood walking'. The demotic word play, proliferation of voices, and disarming address recall the experiments of Modernist writers such as T.S. Eliot, whose iconic poem, *The Waste Land*, may also provide the source of one of Bion's best-known clinical recommendations that the analyst should forego 'memory and desire'.[31]

Bion was evidently aware of literary modernism, mentioning Joyce and Pound (though not, in fact, Eliot) on several occasions. In a densely punning, allusive passage, a 'Voice (out of the smoke)' may allude to *Finnegans Wake* (as

'Fin I gain')[32] alongside Marlowe and Coleridge. Throughout *A Memoir of the Future* there is a pressure on language that seems to signal both the irruption of trauma and the possibility of language giving way to new ideas, to thoughts without a thinker. When the character 'Half Awake' launches into a stream of bad puns ('Toot and come again'), 'Paranoid Schizoid' complains:

> PARANOID-SCHIZOID I can't stand this damned noise. It is like being bombarded with chunks of feeble puns, bits of Shakespeare, imitations of James Joyce, vulgarisations of Ezra Pound, phoney mathematics, religion, mysticism, visions of boyhood, second childhood and visions of old age. Possibly, it could be old age itself.[33]

Matt ffytche has commented directly on Bion's apparent 'preference for de-motic, or 'low-brow' genres of writing',[34] and Meltzer and Harris Williams describe *Memoir* as a 'Shavian, Socratic semi-novel, semi-drama'. In *Bion's Dream*, Harris Williams suggests that it was Bion's intention to write a 'por-nographic novel',[35] while Francesca Bion considers *Memoir* a 'psycho-analytically orientated autobiographical fantasy'.[36] Part of what is disturbing about *A Memoir of the Future* is that it resists expectations of genre and read-ability. Who is it *for*? In an epilogue that seems to recall the autobiography of another war writer, Robert Graves,[37] Bion writes:

> All my life I have been imprisoned, frustrated, dogged by common-sense, reason, memories, desires and − greatest bug-bear of all − understanding and being understood. This is an attempt to express my rebellion, to say 'Good-bye' to all that.

Reading *Memoir* in terms of dream enables the reader to account for its ex-cessiveness and repetition, for the absurdity, word play, and the myriad cast of characters and part-characters, and characters drawn from other stories (such as Sherlock and Mycroft). *A Memoir of the Future* can be boring; it does not always 'read well'. Like the critic who refused to review it, the reader may be put off by long passages in which characters circle endlessly in fractious discussions of morality, mathematics, and psychoanalysis. *Memoir*'s readability brings into question the literary and aesthetic value of dream. If, as for Freud, the re-counted dream is 'brief, meagre and laconic'[38] compared to the latent thoughts from which the dream is spun, then Bion's dream suggests a reversed per-spective: the reader encounters the experience of the dream 'from the inside out' in all its repetition and absurdity. Part of the title of this chapter references the book of the same name by French writer and theorist, Hélène Cixous. *Dream I Tell You* is a sample collection of around a hundred 'dreams' derived from Cixous' long-standing practice of recording her dreams in a bedside notepad. A 'book of dreams without interpretation', it offers a provocation to the literary critic: presented 'in their entirety, unpolished, innocent', Cixous' dreams document the mental products of an artist without laying any claim to artistry, describing her dreams as 'larva' that she could 'by brooding on them have transformed [...] into butterflies'. As literary objects, the dreams are of equivocal merit (they bear all the hallmarks of dreams: fragmented, non-sensical, with abrupt changes in place and mood), and as a reader it is unclear whether we should be impressed by the vividness or frequency of her dreams, or admire her discipline in writing them down (she notes that she has perhaps collected some ten thousand dreams in this way). Cixous' dreams are left instead as 'limbo things' that she does not seek to develop into the 'analysis and literature [she has] kept at arm's length'.[39] Bion is doing something very different: he is trying to 'construct' a dream that is 'necessary', in order to make sense of the events of his life as it draws to a close, but it is also an attempt to communicate, a 'public-ation'.[40] The artfulness of Bion's endeavour derives not from *Memoir*'s verisimilitude to the dreams we remember in the daytime but from the attempt to find a form that can give birth to the thought without a thinker; he writes that 'the night, the dream, is a 'roughness' between the smooth polished consciousness of daylight; in that 'roughness' an idea might lodge'.[41]

Meg Harris Williams invokes the idea of 'counterdreaming' in her book *Bion's Dream: A Reading of the Autobiographies*. In his review of it, James Grotstein suggests that 'the task of *Memoir* [is] to 'counterdream'– that is, to 'undream' and then 'redream'' Bion's traumatic war experiences.[42] One incident in particular stands out from the many scenes of death and destruction that Bion witnessed during the First World War. At the Battle of Amiens, Bion finds himself crouching alongside a young tank gunner called George Kitching[43] (whom Bion will lightly anonymise to 'Sweeting') during a shell attack. Amid the noise and confusion, Bion initially fails to notice that Sweeting has been hit. It is only when the young man at his side complains that he cannot 'cough' that Bion realises what has happened. As the enormity of his injury becomes clear, Sweeting awaits death while pleading with Bion to 'write to his mother'. It is a horrible, pathetic scene that Bion will go on to write about on no fewer than four occasions. A brief but politically angry account first appears in his war memoir, written for his parents shortly after the war: 'I mention it in such detail, horrible as it is, because it had a great effect on me. The look in his eyes was the same as that of a bird that has been shot – mingled fear and surprise'.[44]

In *The Long Week-End*, the scene appears again, this time marked sharply by his own self-loathing in his recollection of the anger and disgust he felt at the young man's entreaties: 'Sweeting, *please* Sweeting... please, *please* shut up'.[45] Later on he writes: 'And then I think he died. Or perhaps it was only me', declaring: 'Sweeting. Gunner. Tank Corps. Died of Wounds. That, for him, was the end'. Sweeting is mentioned again briefly in *All My Sins Remembered*, this time under his real name, Kitching,[46] and yet again in 'Amiens', a third-person account 'aroused by [a] train journey in France on August 3rd 1958'.[47] Written forty years after the event, it provides the fullest and most devastating account of the death:

Bion was aware that Sweeting was trying to talk to him. Above the sound of the barrage it was impossible to hear any ordinary speech. Bending his ear as close as he could to Sweeting's moving lips, he heard him say, 'Why can't I cough, why can't I cough, sir? What's the matter, sir? Something has happened.'

Bion turned round and looked at Sweeting's side, and there he saw gusts of steam coming from where his left side should be. A shell splinter had torn out the left wall of his chest. There was no lung left there. Leaning back in the shell-hole, Bion began to vomit unrestrainedly, helplessly. Then, somewhat recovered, he saw the boy's lips moving again. His face was deadly pale and beaded with sweat. Bion bent his head so that his ear came as near as possible to Sweeting's mouth.

'Mother, Mother, write to my mother, sir, won't you? You'll remember her address, sir, won't you? 22 Kimberly Avenue, Halifax. Write to my mother – 22 Kimberly Road, Halifax. Mother, Mother, Mother, Mother.'

'Oh, for Christ's sake shut up', shouted Bion, revolted and terrified. [...]

He fell limply into Bion's arms, now no longer attempting to press himself into the hole. His face, ghastly white, turned up to the sky. The fog swirled as thickly as ever around them. Every moment they seemed to be bathed in showers of bright sparks of red-hot steel from the bursting shells.

Never have I known a bombardment like this, never, never – Mother, Mother, Mother – never have I known a bombardment like this, he thought. I wish he would shut up, I wish he would die. Why can't he die? Surely he can't go on living with a great hole torn in his side like that.

In her companion essay to 'Amiens', Parthenope Bion Talamo notes the way that 'some episodes are carried over almost unchewed and apparently un-digested into *A Memoir of the Future* [...] as though no further working-through were possible'.[48] It is a more compressed version of the Sweeting story that appears in *Memoir*, spoken through the character 'P.A.' [Psycho Analyst], but three details are invariant: the gaping hole in the boy's chest, his entreaties that Bion 'write to [his] mother', and Bion's recoil:

> P.A. A runner who was crouching beside me in a shell hole had his thoracic wall blown out, exposing his heart. He tried to look at the ghastly wound across which an entirely ineffectual field dressing dangled. 'Mother, Mother – you'll write to my Mother, sir, won't you?' 'Yes, blast you,' I said. If I could believe in God I would ask him to pardon me. 'Dieu me pardonnera. C'est son métier.'[49]

Bion marks the date of the Battle of Amiens – 8th August, 1918 – as the day that he, Bion, 'died' (a month short of his 21st birthday), a date that is inscribed, moreover, not within the common era or the 'year of our Lord' but in 'minus-K', in a dimension of time that is 'inchoate, it is not past'.[50] Minus-K appears in *Learning from Experience* as the reversal or dismantling of the K link, where 'K' stands for knowledge or knowing. A relationship in K is one in which someone is 'getting to know about' someone or something else, and its reversal or negative implies a relationship of phantasied mastery over the object that is a species of false knowledge, not in the trivial sense of 'getting the facts wrong', but in the sense that the 'facts' that are 'known' (such as the date of 8th August, 1918) are substituted for the emotional experience itself. Knowledge, for Bion, is always in transit, a refuge but not a terminus:

> P.A. [...] I regard any thing I 'know' as transitive theory – a theory 'on the way' to knowledge, but not *knowledge*. It is merely a 'resting place', a 'pause' where I can be temporarily free to be aware of my condition, however precarious that condition is.[51]

'Of course', Carole Beebe Tarantelli writes, 'we can take Bion's assertion that he had died as a metaphor'. But to do so would not do justice to the meticulous way in which Bion used language: 'Bion used language with utter precision, and he does not say that he almost died, or that he felt as if he had died. He states that he died'.[52] Sweeting's death 'kills' Bion because it is the occasion of an unmasterable trauma in which Bion's alpha-function – his ability to contain, make sense of, and process the event – failed him. The blasted container of Sweeting's thoracic wall is identified with Bion's mind:

> P.A. I am sorry if I am rude; I didn't mean it. I use the saddest words in the language – 'I didn't mean it to happen.' They hang across the gaping wound of my mind like a ridiculous field dressing. August 8, 1918, that was.[53]

The image of a man who cannot be alive with injuries of such severity who yet continues to talk ('why can't I cough, sir?') figures the uncanny horror of being dead and alive at the same time. Bion continues: 'I would not go near the Amiens-Roye road for fear I should meet my ghost – I died there'.

Figures of this post-dead state abound in *A Memoir of the Future*. The character of Roland is shot by Man, but later returns during the Party of Time's Past which precedes the close of the second volume ('The Past Presented'):

> PRIEST [...] One prophet said, 'The Kingdom of Heaven is within you'.
>
> ROLAND Psycho-analysts deprecate these Kleinian statements.
>
> ROBIN Good lord! Don't say you have psycho-analysts in Heaven.

ROLAND You rush to conclusions. I didn't say I was in Heaven – or Hell. I did say I was dead.

ROSEMARY I never regarded physical death as a necessary qualification for being dead.[54]

The collected party find themselves on a train where they are required to change at Purgatory, which is 'some sort of Transit Camp'. The Ghost of Auser, one of Bion's fallen comrades, mistakes P.A., Bion's avatar, for the Ghost of P.A., who declares that 'when you knew me I was a ghost of myself – at Berles aux Bois. I loved you, but I couldn't save you'. The character of Bion the soldier was already the 'ghost of himself' during the war, dead in mind while still alive, wearing his 'Hero dress' but secretly afraid of nervous breakdown, of going 'sane long before the war was over' like another soldier, Gates. A character called Beta identifies the 'alive dead' with *mindlessness*: 'That includes the living who might as well be dead for all the thinking they do and the dead who remain obstinately alive long after it's time they were dead'.[55]

Meg Harris Williams describes Bion's depiction of a 'dinosaur mentality'[56] that threatens to turn the functions of the mind into a carapace: a kind of death-by-mindlessness. The characters of Albert Stegasaurus and Adolf Tyrannosaurus appear in a short early chapter, enacting the failed meeting of two rigid, 'saurian' minds who cannot receive each other's thoughts except as a kind of violent assault:

ADOLF [...] Ow! What's that? You've shoved your thoughts into me, you vile creature.[57]

Images of saurian mentality appear throughout *Memoir*. In volume two, the character of Mycroft sings a bathetic ditty 'as the Saurian lay-a-thynkynge' to the dinosaur mind: 'prettily lay the thought in its shell'.[58] A character called Alpha recalls Bion's description of his own situation as one 'loaded with honours and sunk without trace' prior to quitting his institutional seniority in England for a new life in California:

I knew a delightful old stegosaurus who thought he had found *the* answer to the tyrannosaurus. But the 'answer' was so successful that it turned him into a kind of tyrannosaurus itself and loaded him with such fame – not to mention exoskeleton – that he sank under its own weight. In fact, he was so loaded that the only trace of him left was his own skeleton.[59]

It is the answer, the 'fact' in minus-K, that is, as Bion cites Blanchot, the '*malheur de la question*': the dead thought that kills the question. Established thinking poses a greater danger to the mind than the confusion and projection that occurs in the pre-thinking position of the paranoid-schizoid position, since it threatens to create a suffocating exoskeleton, a death-within-life, that entombs its wearer and entails an extinction analogous to that of the dinosaurs. And yet Bion remains hopeful that even the dinosaur mentality can, with effort, develop afresh the capacity for thinking: 'Yes, but those same dead bones gave birth to a mind'.

Sweeting's entreaty (to 'write to my mother') is what Bion, identified with him, cannot do. The writing *of* trauma that is a writing *to* the mother-mind (the exercise of alpha-function modelled originally on the mother's capacity for reverie) fails in this moment as Bion also 'failed' to contain Sweeting's confusion and distress. It is Bion's recoil – his anger and contempt for Sweeting, the failure of his fellow-feeling, more than the extremity of Sweeting's wounds – that is so profoundly traumatising. Bion cannot 'write' to his own 'mother' and is unable to bring to bear his alpha-function for either Sweeting or himself. In the aftermath of the event, he can only make successive attempts, even some forty years after the event, to attempt to integrate the experience or help him accede to what Bion ironically and ambivalently calls 'the dawn of oblivion' (the title of the third book of *A Memoir of the Future*). The word oblivion, it should be recalled, has its roots in the idea of forgetting. The post-traumatic writer seeks to create the artificially constructed, necessary dream: writing itself constructs the container or the apparatus for the psychical stuff that otherwise comes out, 'unchewed' in Bion Talamo's words, or as 'undigested facts' (beta-elements) in Bion's. 'I have to manufacture the apparatus as I proceed', writes the character 'Bion' in a long monologue on writing in part one:

> BION The whole of this book so far printed can be regarded as an artificial and elaborate construct. I myself, here introduced into the narrative, can be regarded as a construct, artificially composed with the aid of such artistic and scientific material as I can command and manipulated to form a representation of an author whose name appears on the book and now, for the second time, as a character in a work of fiction.[60]

Memoir is also, I suggest, a paradigmatic instance of what Edward Said, following Adorno, has called 'late style'. Said has characterised late style as 'a special ironic expressiveness well beyond the words and the situation'.[61] In the final section of *A Memoir of the Future*, Bion declares that it is his intention to 'write a book unspoiled by any tincture of common-sense',[62] but suspects that he will fail. Adorno declares that 'in the history of art late works are the catastrophes';[63] we must nevertheless remain sensitive to the idiosyncrasies of that catastrophe in each case. Where, in Adorno's study, Beethoven's late works are characterised by the 'abbreviation of his style', Bion's late style achieves a prolixity notably absent from his earlier work. The short epilogue with which the 'Dawn of Oblivion' closes is signalled not once, but four times:

…& Epilogue

…Fugue

...Dona Es Requiem

...Many

Death, of course, is never far away. As Adorno notes, death enters the scene in late style not 'in a refracted mode, as in allegory', but as the limit of an exploded subjectivity that 'disappears from the work of art into truth'. What is interesting about *A Memoir of the Future* is that it occupies the space between two different deaths – the death-in-life constituted by trauma, and the other, biological death, the death 'of the future' that is also the 'dawn of oblivion' in which traumatic material can be laid finally to rest. Bion is also alert to the *deadness* (if not death) of mind that can accompany advancing age. He describes the way that something like a 'psychical osteo-arthritis'[64] can develop as the mind becomes rigid and inflexible: 'I borrow the terms from medical descriptions of arterial degeneration; there is reason to suppose some spiritual counterpart, some unwillingness to entertain new ideas, which is inseparable from advancing physical age'.[65]

Bion's late writing should also alert us – if his laconic formulations in *Experiences in Groups* and the terse, almost programmatic style of *Learning from Experience* have not already done so – to the breadth and interest of his writing style. In a similar vein, Freud's status as a writer, though recognised in some measure during his lifetime,[66] has undergone a significant re-appraisal by those, such as Patrick Mahoney,[67] who have rightly drawn attention to Freud's mastery of rhetoric and the productively circuitous pathways of his thought. Freud, however, rarely strays from a tone of qualified authority – or, what often amounts to the same thing – a perhaps too-insistent sense of his humility in the face of received or anticipated responses to his conjectures.[68] Bion, by contrast, is frank in describing his difficulties in communicating his ideas, as when he writes, in the opening lines of *Learning from Experience*, 'I have experience to record, but how to communicate this experience to others I am in doubt; this book explains why'.[69] Like Freud, Bion communicates almost entirely through the written and spoken word, and yet neglects to attend directly to the question of writing throughout his career, though there are suggestive references to the role played by *words* in his characterisation of even the most rudimentary psychical particles, the beta-elements. The character 'Du' (an unborn, somatic aspect of Roland, who appears in 'The Past Presented', disturbing Roland's sleep) evokes *Hamlet*[70] in his reflection on the constraining relationship of words to the birth of a new thought:

> Words; words; words have no right to be rigid definitory caskets preventing my birth. I have the right to exist without depending on a thinker thinking all day *and* night.[71]

Like Melville's *Bartleby*, Bion declares repeatedly that he would prefer not to write, but does so recognising the responsibility of the writer to 'prevent someone who KNOWS from filling the empty space'.[72] If words risk being 'rigid definitory caskets', which are one kind of container that can prevent the birth of thought, the practice of writing itself can also be a way to hold open and sustain the possibility of thinking, a *containing* that is not a *closing*, a place where thoughts go not to die but to be born, and to be dreamed. The figure of birth is signalled in the opening chapter of the third and final section of *A Memoir of the Future*. A new character, Em-mature, begins:

> This book is a psycho-embryonic attempt to write an embryo-scientific account of a journey from birth to death overwhelmed by pre-mature knowledge, experience, glory and self-intoxicating self-satisfaction.[73]

Em-mature (later 'Em') represents 'Embryonic Maturity', and is one of several pre- and post-natal facets of a central self that enact the life of Bion (and the character, 'Bion'). Em is joined by a host of others – including the ironical Pre-mature (who appears on one single occasion to interrupt Em with 'Get on with it – when were you born?'), Twenty Months, Infancy, Eight Years, Twenty-Four Years, Thirty Years, Forty Years, Forty-Two Years (and so on), for the post-natals; along with Term, Four Somites, Somite Eighteen and a chorus of Somites *en bloc* who speak with exasperation for the pre-natal group whose somatic, intra-uterine preferences threaten to be disregarded by the post-natals: 'We don't want a nipple! We want an erection!'. The caesura of birth provokes a new and uneasy relationship, meanwhile, between the two fledgling personalities of Mind and Body (this latter Em's sequel), who agree to call each other Psyche and Soma respectively and inaugurate an uneasy truce between their competing claims on knowledge:

> EM Now you have muddled me. I shall be body; for ever I shall gird at your mind.
>
> MIND Hullo! Where have you sprung from?
>
> BODY What – you again? I am Body; you can call me Soma if you like. Who are you?
>
> MIND Call me Psyche – Psyche-Soma.
>
> BODY Soma-Psyche.
>
> MIND We must be related.
>
> BODY Never – not if I can help it.[74]

Bion emphasises repeatedly that our conventional date of birth correlates only poorly with the reality of our 'being born'. Being born, for Bion, takes place at innumerable moments unregistered throughout the course of our lives – including our lives prior to birth. P.A. says: 'I don't want to know your birthday because I am sure you will tell me a date which does *not* outrage ideas of genital intercourse, midwifery, surgery. What I want to know is, when was your character or personality born?'[75] In his essay 'Caesura', Bion develops Freud's claim that 'there is much more continuity between intra-uterine life and the earliest infancy than the impressive caesura of the act of birth allows us to believe'.[76] In determining our many births to various aspects of experience, we have to contemplate the possibility of reckoning with precursor, pre-caesural states that bear witness to our history. In one of *Memoir*'s more ex-quisite moments, Em-mature describes a pre-history of vision registered as pressure on the optic pits of the embryo:

> EM I don't know when the amniotic pressure made my optic pits hurt; the stars were so brilliant, I kicked out.[77]

The discussion between the different age-selves is a fractious, uneasy one, though P.A. thinks 'it might some day be possible for them all to be awake and carry on a fairly disciplined debate'.[78] Most of *A Memoir of the Future* is structured as a series of group discussions (in book two, it is primarily the characters of Alice, Rosemary, Roland, Robin and Man, along with Priest and P.A./Bion; in book three the group expands to include the pre- and post-natals), and it should not be forgotten that Bion began his psychiatric career with the study of the *group*. At the end of the first volume, the character 'Bion' declares that the 'idea of the individual being a 'group' – like Hobbes' idea of the group being an individual – could be an illuminating one'.[79] The meeting of Bion's different age-selves effects a dramatisation of a psychoanalysis in which competing 'voices' clamour to have their differing and partial realities acknowledged. In a note on analytic technique made in 1960, he differentiates his view from other theorists: 'Winnicott said patients *need* to regress: Melanie Klein says they *must not*. I say they *are* regressed, and the regression should be observed and interpreted'.[80]

Later on, Robin suggests that these different and competing levels of the personality might be reconciled topographically:

> ROBIN If we could come together we could still preserve our identity – like the hills on a map in which all the same levels could be joined by a contour –[81]

Unlike Freud, focused on an archaeology of the mind, Bion proposes that greater attention be paid to the moment – or caesura – in which the new personality or aspect of mind emerges, and that we develop our imagination in order to be able to investigate both sides of the caesura: the before as well as the after. Noting these changes in state should not blind us, however, to the emotional experience, as the following anecdote, taken from Bion's war ex-periences, dramatises. His twenty-year old self pours scorn on the re-presentative of 'army intelligence' who fails to see the wood for the trees, the deep impact of tank warfare for the change in geological landscape:

TWENTY YEARS [...] You're as bad as our Army Intelligence Officer. When I came out of the Third Battle of Ypres and hardly knew whether I was alive or dreaming, he asked me if I had noticed when the alluvial changed to the cretaceous. I couldn't even laugh.[82]

The character of Alice is identified ambiguously as both Bion's/the narrator's partner (as she seems to be in the prologue) and his mother. At the beginning of 'The Dawn of Oblivion', Alice retorts to the character 'Term' (the foetus at full term) who describes struggling to get out of the uterus that it 'nearly lost me my life'.[83] Later on, she appears to be happily pregnant by her husband Roland, and the world, no longer at war, is returned to rights. Though P.A. is 'sometimes consoled by the possibility that the goodness, the capacity for love and concern for our fellows may be a greater force than hate',[84] 'The Dawn of Oblivion' nevertheless ends on the sombre note that the existence of the mind compels 'the growth of a capacity for discrimination – or catastrophe'. The figure of a nuclear Third World War looms into view in Alice's closing words, a possible outcome of a world in which human beings do not learn to *think*, seeking instead easy 'solutions', 'answers', or 'cures' that are the 'wrong choice'. Book three closes with a declaration by Bion *qua* psychoanalyst (P.A.):

> P.A. There are no labels attached to most options; there is no substitute for the growth of wisdom. Wisdom or oblivion – take your choice. From that warfare there is no release.

So much a part of his experience, war is an abiding metaphor for Bion. In 'Making the Best of a Bad Job', an essay written in the year of his death, he compares the practice of psychoanalysis to the experience of war, reflecting that it is the job of the analyst to be able to think even while under attack by the patient: 'In war the enemy's object is so to terrify you that you cannot think clearly, while your object is to continue to think clearly no matter how adverse or frightening the situation'.[85]

Despite its difficulty, *A Memoir of the Future* stands testament to a mind that is 'senile' (of old age) but by no means 'demented' (indicating a mind – in Latin, *mens* – in decline). The late Bion is at the peak of his powers, finally throwing off the shackles of respectability and drawing the many different threads of his life and work together. He is aware of the risks of his endeavour, but the construction of the necessary dream entails speculative works of imagination. 'I think it is good to give your imagination an airing', he writes, 'Never mind how ridiculous, stupid or intolerable it is. I am not talking about undisciplined, rhapsodical display of just saying anything that comes into your mind. At the same time I do not want to be limited by having to be scientific, precise and exact'.[86] *Memoir* records Bion's playfully serious attempt to bring the creative resources of literature to bear on questions around the birth of the mind and the ability to think, reflecting his understanding that the mind is finally defined neither by a physical boundary ('mind' grows up also in the group and in society) nor by a date. It is also an experiment in form that is 'mindful' (full of mind) through the elaboration and distinction of the many different 'minds' inside his head, and wary of the different aspects of mindlessness at work in the saurian mentality or the unthinking 'Yes I know' response that produces a 'lifeless society'.[87] *Memoir* is also an auto-psycho-biographical attempt to integrate the dead and traumatised parts of his own mind through a post-traumatic writing that draws on art and creativity to create the 'apparatus' of the mind to enact alpha-function. This is not, *pace* Segal, art in the service of the reparation of originary destructive impulses, but art that makes dreaming possible through the construction of the 'necessary dream'.

I want to close with a comment about the mind of the reader. Bion writes suggestively about the possibility of an evocative writing that is able to communicate ideas between the writer and the reader. Two Bionian avatars discuss the point in 'The Dream':

> BION [...] You must often have heard, as I have, people say they don't know what you are talking about and that you are being deliberately obscure.
>
> MYSELF They are flattering me. I am suggesting an aim, an ambition which, if I could achieve, would enable me to be deliberately and *precisely* obscure; in which I could use certain words which could activate precisely and instantaneously, in the mind of the listener, a thought or train of thought that came between him and the thoughts and ideas already accessible and available to him.[88]

His statement echoes the melancholic remark made by the prologue's narrator when he declares that he writes in the absence of another mind: 'If I were there, with the companion to whom I wish to communicate, I could appeal to him to see the evidence I cannot formulate, but on which I wish to build my structure'. The strange – and strangely creative – writing exemplified by *A Memoir of the Future* can be regarded as the deliberate creation of a container that gives birth to the new thought (and attempts to think what was previously unthinkable), while also seeking to evoke the reader-mind able to receive it. Writing as P.A., Bion declares: 'in fact, the greatest thinkers are very difficult to read unless you find great readers to read them'.[89]

Notes

1 Bion, *Complete Works*, 11:39 (*Cogitations*, 33).
2 Bion, *A Memoir of the Future*. The work is also found in volumes 12–14 of *The Complete Works of W.R. Bion*.
3 The Brazilian psychoanalyst Paulo Cesar Sandler has published, at the time of writing, two parts of an introduction to *A Memoir of the Future* (London: Karnac, 2014, 2015).
4 Jacobus, *The Poetics of Psychoanalysis: In the Wake of Klein*.
5 Torres and Hinshelwood, *Bion's Sources: The Shaping of His Paradigms*.
6 Levine and Civitarese, *The W.R. Bion Tradition: Lines of Development – Evolution of Theory and Practice over the Decades*.

7 All references in this chapter are to the *Standard Edition* volumes 4 and 5 except for those from the new translation by J.A. Underwood, published as *Interpreting Dreams*, 2006.

8 Bion, *Complete Works* 12:13 (*Memoir*, 3).

9 Bion, *Complete Works*, 5:52 (*Elements of Psychoanalysis*, 60).

10 Bion, *Complete Works*, 12:16 (*Memoir*, 7).

11 See also note 51 in the first chapter. The term is counterintuitive. In the UK, free-to-attend schools are referred to as 'state schools'. Fee-paying schools are generally called 'private' schools. 'Public' schools refer to an especially prestigious sub-section of these.

12 Bion, *Complete Works*, 11:65 (*Cogitations*, 62).

13 Grotstein, *A Beam of Intense Darkness: Wilfred Bion's Legacy to Psychoanalysis*, 286.

14 Bion, *Complete Works*, 10:7 (*Two Papers*, 3).

15 Ferro, *Psychoanalysis as Therapy and Storytelling*, 27.

16 Bion, *Complete Works*, 11:47 (*Cogitations*, 43).

17 Freud, *Standard Edition*, 4:84.

18 Freud, *Interpreting Dreams*, 92. (In Freud, *Standard Edition*, 4:79, this is given as 'Dreams are excretions of thoughts that have been stifled at birth'. For the purpose of my discussion, I prefer the alternative translation.)

19 Bion, *Complete Works*, 13:8 (*Memoir*, 224).

20 Freud, *Standard Edition*, 4:xxvi.

21 Bion, *Complete Works*, 12:92 (*Memoir*, 96).

22 Freud, *Standard Edition*, 4:84–85.

23 Freud, *Interpreting Dreams*, 98.

24 Freud, *Standard Edition*,14:19. Italics mine.

25 Freud, *Standard Edition*, 4:83.

26 Freud, *Standard Edition*,15:152.

27 O'Shaughnessy, 'Whose Bion?', 1524–25.

28 Meltzer, *Sincerity and Other Works: Collected Papers of Donald Meltzer*, 546.

29 Meltzer, 521.

30 Bion, *Complete Works*, 12:57 (*Memoir*, 54).

31 See Anna Dartington's essay in Mawson, *Bion Today*, 247.

32 Bion, *Complete Works*, 12:126 (*Memoir*, 135).

33 Bion, *Complete Works*, 12:56 (*Memoir*, 51).

34 Torres and Hinshelwood, 175.

35 Harris Williams, *Bion's Dream: A Reading of the Autobiographies*, 30.

36 Bion, *Complete Works*, 1:8 (*The Long Week-End 1897-1919*, 7).

37 Graves, *Goodbye to All That*.

38 Freud, *Standard Edition*, 4:279.

39 Cixous, 7–9.

40 Bion, *Complete Works*, 11:164 (*Cogitations*, 169). See also chapter four where 'publication' is discussed in relation to B.S. Johnson.

41 Bion, *Complete Works*, 13:48 (*Memoir*, 268).

42 Grotstein, 'Bion's Dream: A Reading of the Autobiographies (Review)', 465.

43 George Kitching lies buried in a British military cemetery in Namps-au-Val, France: https://www.cwgc.org/find-records/find-war-dead/casualty-details/38294/KITCH-ING,%20G/ [accessed December 2020]. I was pleased to be able to locate his headstone, and pay my respects, in a small, well-tended military cemetery overlooking fields on the centenary of the Battle of Amiens, in 2018.

44 Bion, *Complete Works*, 3:133 (*War Memoirs 1917–1919*, 127).

45 Bion, *Complete Works*, 1:280 (*The Long Week-End 1897–1919*, 249).

46 Bion, *Complete Works*, 2:46 (*All My Sins Remembered*, 44).

47 Bion, *Complete Works*, 3:214 (*War Memoirs 1917–1919*, 214).

48 Bion, *Complete Works*, 3:307 (*War Memoirs 1917–1919*, 309).

49 Bion, *Complete Works*, 13:37 (*Memoir*, 256).

50 Bion, *Complete Works*, 12:144 (*Memoir*, 155).
51 Bion, *Complete Works*, 14:34 (*Memoir*, 462).
52 Levine and Civitarese, *The W.R. Bion Tradition: Lines of Development – Evolution of Theory and Practice over the Decades*, 48.
53 Bion, *Complete Works*, 13:37 (*Memoir*, 256).
54 Bion, *Complete Works*, 13:176 (*Memoir*, 408).
55 Bion, *Complete Works*, 12:61 (*Memoir*, 59).
56 Harris Williams, 29.
57 Bion, *Complete Works*, 12:82 (*Memoir*, 84).
58 Bion, *Complete Works*, 13:124 (*Memoir*, 353).
59 Bion, *Complete Works*, 12:62 (*Memoir*, 60).
60 Bion, *Complete Works*, 12:84 (*Memoir*, 88).
61 Said, *On Late Style: Music and Literature Against the Grain*, xiii.
62 Bion, *Complete Works*, 14:138 (*Memoir*, 578).
63 Adorno, *Essays on Music*, 567.
64 Bion, *Complete Works*, 14:21 (*Memoir*, 447).
65 Bion, *Complete Works*, 14:109 (*Memoir*, 545).
66 Freud was awarded the Goethe Prize in Literature and was nominated several times, but never awarded, the Nobel Prize for his scientific contributions.
67 Mahony, *Freud as a Writer (Expanded Edition)*.
68 A notable exception appears in his 1916 [1915] essay, 'On Transience', an abrupt tonal change marking the horror of WW1: 'A year later the war broke out and robbed the world of its beauties'. (Freud, *Standard Edition*, 14:307)
69 Bion, *Complete Works*, 2014, 4:263 (*Learning from Experience*, v).
70 *Hamlet*, Act 2, Scene 2. Shakespeare, *William Shakespeare: The Complete Works*, 666.
71 Bion, *Complete Works*, 13:55 (*Memoir*, 276).
72 Bion, *Complete Works*, 14:138 (*Memoir*, 578).
73 Bion, *Complete Works*, 14:5 (*Memoir*, 429).
74 Bion, *Complete Works*, 14:8–9 (*Memoir*, 433).
75 Bion, *Complete Works*, 14:55 (*Memoir*, 486).
76 Bion, *Complete Works*, 10:35 (*Two Papers*, 37).
77 Bion, *Complete Works*, 14:8 (*Memoir*, 433).
78 Bion, *Complete Works*, 14:18 (*Memoir*, 443).
79 Bion, *Complete Works*, 12:199 (*Memoir*, 215).
80 Bion, *Complete Works*, 11:161 (*Cogitations*, 166).
81 Bion, *Complete Works*, 14:40 (*Memoir*, 470).
82 Bion, *Complete Works*, 14:27 (*Memoir*, 453).
83 Bion, *Complete Works*, 14:21 (*Memoir*, 446).
84 Bion, *Complete Works*, 14:134 (*Memoir*, 573).
85 Bion, *Complete Works*, 10:137 (*Clinical Seminars and Other Works*, 322).
86 Bion, *Complete Works*, 15:50–51.
87 Bion, *Complete Works*, 14:68 (*Memoir*, 501).
88 Bion, *Complete Works*, 12:177 (*Memoir*, 191).
89 Bion, *Complete Works*, 13:22 (*Memoir*, 240).

10 Is writing (an) alpha-function?

> He doesn't suggest that you misuse [his concepts]; he suggests you might put them to better use than he does.[1]

The possibilities of an approach to literary criticism drawing on the work of Wilfred Bion are by no means exhausted by the previous chapters. Rather, it has been my experience that Bion's work – his ideas, theoretical models, literary references and turns of phrase – seem ever more richly suggestive. Bringing some of the ideas for which he is best known – such as the container-contained relationship or the thought without a thinker – to bear on thinking about literature can, on occasion, be a project easily enough 'won' (as in the case of *The Unfortunates*, a book literally contained in a box), but other aspects of his work are either theoretically intimidating (the 'algebra' of *Transformations* a case in point) or deeply idiosyncratic (*A Memoir of the Future*). *The Unfortunates* presented itself as an almost perfect illustration of Bion's relational model of a container and its contents, but not only because of the box: the book's themes – of ambivalent relationship, of mentoring, of the value of there being 'two minds' involved in writing a book – also offer a way to understand Bion outside of the narrower clinical or developmental context in which his theory is presented. In other words, the communication between Bion's theory and literature flows in both directions and is mutually enriching; there can be as much a literary reading of Bion as a 'Bionian' reading of literature.

I was fortunate to be briefly in correspondence with the renowned Bion scholar, Dr James Grotstein, in 2012. A practising analyst who was himself analysed by Bion for five years during the 1970s, Grotstein wrote that, while he 'got used to his idiosyncratic style of speech', he was pleased and surprised to discover that Bion was also a 'regular guy' at a dinner party that Grotstein held for Wilfred and Francesca on their last night in Los Angeles. The publication of many of Bion's letters to his wife and children[2] – tender, funny, annotated with doodled pictures – rounds out our picture of a man who can in other contexts appear a remote or detached figure, the exemplar of a certain notion of 'Britishness'. Certainly, I have been struck in conversation and

DOI: 10.4324/9781003006619-10

seminars with non-British colleagues at the way that Bion's striking sense of humour (understated, very dry) may pass unnoticed or come across as downright baffling. This was undoubtedly the case during Joseph Aguayo's discussion panel during the 2016 Bion Conference in Milan, where colleagues of several nationalities discussed Bion's *Italian Seminars*. In the last of these (seminar nine), Bion appears to talk dispassionately about the possibility that a patient 'could resort to throwing himself – or the analyst, of course – out of the window. Therefore, during the time that you are seeing that patient, place yourself between him and the window. It would, in fact, be preferable not to have the consulting-room in such a position that it would be easy for the patient to commit suicide or murder by using the distance between the room and the earth below'.[3] There was some shock at Bion's apparent glibness or lack of emotionality in the face of what must be a terrible, horrifying event were it to occur. But the idea of Bion calmly suggesting that practising analysts re-arrange their furniture to avoid someone hurling themselves (or the analyst) out of the window is also quite funny, absurdist; the dry presentation, I suggest, intended to produce a kind of shock in his listeners and to remind them that the work of psychoanalysis may truly and straightforwardly be a matter of life and death.

Discussing my project with Grotstein, he agreed that the task of connecting Bion's work to creative writing could be worthwhile. He added:

> If I could hazard to guess, I would say that Bion's writing stands on the frontier between the conscious and the unconscious with twists of O contained cryptically within it. In other words, I think his language occupies the contact-barrier which he designates as standing between consciousness and the unconscious and mediates their binary-oppositional function. Bion was fond of word patterns. His language is an attempt to discern and link patterns. Put another way, his writing is very much like a very sparse jigsaw puzzle, which takes considerable patience and profound thinking to put together.[4]

The 'considerable patience' that Bion's work requires is not only due to his frequent recourse to a technical vocabulary (to which the first part of Grotstein's comment abundantly attests), but to his desire that *understanding* his work should be born of an *emotional experience*, provoked by his writing: an experience that may begin as a 'realisation in K' (as he declares in *Learning from Experience*), but become a 'transformation in O' (*Transformations*). Far from the wholly clinical theoretician that he can appear to be, Bion is profoundly concerned with the ways that writing, in particular, has the ability, even a responsibility, to effect transformations in thinking. Where Freud's authoritative style is undercut by the unintended detours of his unconscious, Bion, both as man and theorist, can be seen as someone who writes in the aftermath of trauma, a post-traumatic writer writing in order to rebuild the *possibility* of an unconscious shattered by experiences too awful to be thinkable. Only this could replace the "Yes, I know', 'You know', 'I mean to say" – the linguistic debris of polite conversation – that he identified as a 'modern version of the unconscious', in which 'you can go on like that for ever because you just don't have to *think*'.[5] This concern – the, for him, necessary task of decalcifying a rigidified consciousness, populated by pre-fabricated ideas and cultural cliché – places Bion very readily in conversation with some of the writers explored in this volume, such as Stevie Smith, B.S. Johnson, and J.G. Ballard, but also with many other writers, such as T.S. Eliot and Evelyn Waugh, and indeed with practitioners of other art forms. It also opens a way to connect Bion's ideas to social theory and the examination of how thinking is – or is not – available or effective in helping us to understand or tackle increasingly pressing contemporary questions, such as climate emergency, 'fake news', illiberal democracy, the emboldening of white supremacism, and anti-immigrant politics.

There are also grounds for situating Bion more prominently as a modernist writer. As the late writer and psychoanalyst Anna Dartington has observed,[6] Bion's clinical caution against memory and desire seems to recall the famous opening lines of *The Waste Land*.[7] We do not know whether Bion intended the allusion, or whether he ever read *The Waste Land*. But given his wide habits of reading, and his evident intellectual and cultural curiosity, it seems improbable that Bion would not have encountered Eliot's masterpiece, published in 1922, by the time he first formulated his thoughts on memory and desire in 1965. What is not in question is that Bion shares a number of modernist concerns: the experiments in form, evident throughout his oeuvre, from the austere numbered paragraphs of *Learning from Experience* through to the quasi-dramatisation of *A Memoir of the Future*, which also includes the mixing of ostensibly 'low' and 'high' forms of art, and fragmented, multiple perspectives; a catholic openness to ideas from many different literatures, disciplines, and spiritual traditions; a persistent enquiry into how meaning and truth-telling might be re-grounded in the absence or failure of religious certitude; and a necessary and painful reckoning with the devastation of the First World War. Bion, like Eliot, Pound, Woolf, Joyce, and so many others, shared the experience of living in the aftermath of a catastrophe that left Europe, and much of the rest of the world, dumbfounded; he came of age – both literally and figuratively – at a moment in European history that saw the world, in Freud's memorable formulation, 'robbed […] of its beauties'.[8]

Each of the writers and works brought together in this volume benefit, in different ways, from a reading based on ideas drawn from Bion's work. Along the way, I have tried to showcase the breadth of Bion's writing, and the way that his motifs lend themselves to repeated and different uses. Mindful that Bion is not yet well-known within the English departments of many universities, this book has been written for an audience who may be unfamiliar with Bion's ideas. Therefore the enquiry started in this book is by no means exhausted. Indeed, the resurgence of interest in his ideas over the last few years suggests that Bion may be a writer whose time has now come, fulfilling his own contention that great works of art (in which I would also include great works of theory) may come to be fully appreciated at a later date and by minds (individually, but also societally) only now ready to receive them. The thought without a thinker names a profound – profoundly intimate – alienation at the heart of an experience that we might reasonably consider to be most irreducibly proper to ourselves. The characterisation of beta-elements as potentially – amongst other things – bits of fragmented *language* may offer a powerful way to redescribe our contemporary experience of social media: Tweets, hashtags, memes, along with advertising slogans and empty corporate phrases – bits of sticky, dead, psychical debris that agglomerate to form a background buzz of readymade thoughts, cliché, or pseudo-thinking. Indeed, it is in focusing our attention onto the development of *thinking* (rather than sexuality, *pace* Freud) that Bion's work offers new ways of making sense of contemporary forms of expression and representation.

Bion did not imagine a one-time, conclusive germination of the seeds of new ideas and thoughts, and he was alert to the seduction of concluding thoughts. Indeed he wrote 'I put the term 'conclusion' in inverted commas because I am using it in a special way unrelated to any belief that some discussion has been 'concluded''.[9] His frequent quotation of Blanchot ('the answer is the misfortune of the question') was intended to remind us that conclusions are always liable to harden into dogma, thereby forming another 'impressive caesura' from which we are unable to break free. Instead, he emphasised the ways in which phantasies of conclusion merely allay the anxiety that comes from trying to grasp the 'ineffable experience' of reality that he names O. Where reality exceeds our capacity for alpha-function, we are naturally wont to look to more narrow indicators of our ability to demonstrate that we have understood or achieved something: facts, figures, the delivered deliverable (which in the context of writing this book included deadlines and word counts). As Dave Eggers has written: 'the ceaseless pursuit of data to quantify the value of any endeavour is catastrophic to true understanding'.[10] At the close of *Transformations*, Bion remarks ironically on the tendency to institute a 'premature mathematisation of a subject which is not sufficiently mature for such a procedure', offering as an example the way that the full experience of psychoanalysis is weakly approximated by 'the rules for its practice [...]: 'five times' a week and for '50' minutes [...] readily 'won' from the ineffable experience'.[11] The totality of complex, multisensorial and emotion-filled experience threatens to overwhelm our resources to house O within a containing mind; accordingly, we do what we can with facts and figures to domesticate the wild thought or the emotional experience.

Celebrating Bion's ideas places them at risk of reification, and he stressed repeatedly that 'to allow 'Bion's theory' to operate in a rigid way [...] would be ridiculous'.[12] Incompletion, as he noted in the Author's Note to *Bion in New York and São Paulo*, was to be regarded 'as a virtue' if it stimulated others to go on thinking. On this point, the late Chris Mawson suggested that a 'sign of life in [Bion's] ideas is the fact they can be developed further and not remain static, or stagnate into 'received wisdom'',[13] noting how his ideas have been developed by other psychoanalytic writers. I hope that this book will stimulate a fuller consideration of his work within the fields of literature, literary criticism, and creative writing.

The strange question that opens this chapter recalls an early working title of my original doctoral thesis. The mystery of alpha-function, a term 'intentionally devoid of meaning',[14] offered a productively open way to begin to think about a theorisation of literature and creative writing based on the work of Wilfred Bion. Don DeLillo's suggestive statement that 'writing is a concentrated form of thinking'[15] informed my hypothesis that writing could enact containing and generative elements both in phantasy and reality. Georges Perec's description of the two moments of crossword-setting[16] (an unusual form of writing, but writing, all the same) seemed to describe the way that there could be different kinds of writing that installed aspects of thinking into writing itself.

Another thought along the way was the idea that literary analysis based on Bion's work could be the basis of a 'new' literary criticism, but Bion's late essay 'New and Improved', only recently published as part of the *Complete Works*, sounds an important warning against such a claim. While the prospect of a 'Bionian psychoanalytic literary criticism' does offer new ideas for a field that has been dominated by Lacan and Freud, Mawson reminded us that Bion was alert to 'the silent operation of manic delusions in our field'[17]. He borrowed the phrase 'new and improved' from an advertising slogan for Kellogg's Cornflakes, noting 'it is a very seductive idea – one could almost sum it up in one word – cure. It carries with it a connotation of good times coming, an improvement, *better*'.[18] As noted in my introduction, the very word 'Bionian' is not without difficulty, and I respect the concerns raised in that regard both by Bion's daughter, Parthenope Bion Talamo, and by Bion's editor. There is a risk of making too much of Bion's particular contributions, and, in the process, losing sight of the broader Kleinian and post-Kleinian psychoanalytic context from which Bion emerged: to the detriment, perhaps, of other writers. Mawson (in personal communication) suggested that the contributions of other Kleinian-oriented psychoanalytic thinkers, such as Betty Joseph, Hanna Segal, Paula Heimann, Herbert Rosenfeld, and Elliott Jaques, might be considered equally distinctive. Nevertheless, Bion's remarkable and exciting body of work merits wider discovery and appreciation by students and researchers outside of clinical psychotherapy: here is a rich resource for those of us thinking about literature, writing, and creative process in many fields. Recognition of Bion's importance is also undoubtedly overdue in the country where he spent the majority of his life: at present he remains better known in Italy (thanks to the efforts of his daughter, Parthenope Bion Talamo), and in the various places (especially California and Brazil) where he lived or gave seminars in later life. Bion's work has already been translated into several languages; it is a shame that he is so little known and read in the UK.

Peter Boxall has suggested that scholarship in the humanities is now emerging from a long period in which 'theory' predominated over 'literary value',[19] which came to be associated with the production of bourgeois cultural values and an uncritical 'humanism' that foregrounded romantic conceptions of authorial intent and a naturalised conception of realism to the neglect of textual effects, polysemy, and a critical response to the production of realism. Bion's attention to 'psychotic' modes of thinking, to the thought without a thinker, and to what is inexpressible or unthinkable places a number of tools in the hands of the literary theorist who seeks to relate textual effects to questions of the individual, the group, or society. Questions of plagiarism, for example, that contemporary expression of institutional neurosis, are complicated by Bion's displacement of the *idea* to a transpersonal dimension:

> It may fall to a particular individual to be able to formulate the thought or idea. But I don't think the actual germination of the idea can be attributed to any particular individual. It is very difficult to locate that. It crops up in practice chiefly with people who think that they own ideas and are very sensitive to plagiarism.[20]

In 'New and Improved', Bion described our capacity for talking and discussion as a precarious achievement of humankind, an achievement that 'floats'. 'What does it float on?' he writes, noting tautologically that 'It is a matter of some importance because here in detail we are still floating on the surface of whatever the sea is that we float on'.[21] Writing, I suggest, is another 'floating' achievement. One of the merits of Bion's theory is the way in which it enables us to see more of the psychical work – the alpha-function – enabled *by* writing and enacted *in* writing (as well as in creative expression of many kinds). When it comes to writing, we are liable to at least two distinct seductions: there is the idea of the all-intending author who creates a possibly enigmatic text but one finally closed to creative interpretation; we also imagine texts that 'float', in a different way, entirely free of authorial intent or stabilised meaning. The quotation above reminds us that our floating words are buoyed by processes both turbulent and supportive, as well as by processes that are inter- or transpersonal or which at least imaginatively commemorate previous meetings of minds. Floating also suggests a measure of weightlessness; the opposite of a floating achievement would be a *ponderous* one, reminding us of thinking's etymological freight.[22] The metaphor alerts us to the existence of an exquisitely supportive tension at permanent risk of a preponderance of ready-made or concluded thoughts allowing of no further development. The questions at the heart of this book have been: what supports writing, and what does writing support? What is achieved in and by writing? And where does writing start? Such questions may not admit of 'answers', but Bion's speculative and highly original thinking may enable us to begin our enquiry. There is a word that I borrow from another part of my life that can be helpful to extend the idea of floating: the idea of tensegrity (from *tensional integrity*), sometimes defined as 'floating compression'. Used to describe the way that bodies (and buildings) hang together, the word may be useful to describe the observation that writing holds itself in a kind of tensional support and supportive tension; it creates the space and the structures in which something can be thought and expressed. Thinking about writing in this way enables further questions: how does writing grow? How are ideas scaffolded in order to enable more thinking? If scaffolding suggests an architecture of writing, (what) might we also learn from the very different kinds of writing found in, for instance, computer programming, legal writing, crossword-setting, list-making – or even in the specific forms of writing formed by the constraints and priorities of social media? Each of these non-literary modes of writing speaks to questions around textual resilience, fragmentation, abbreviation, and modularity: the spaces left for more to be said, for other avenues to be explored, for ideas to jump within and between texts and writers; like the cat whose image graces the cover of this book, thoughts without thinkers stealing soundlessly into my mind, or yours.

Notes

1 Bion, *Complete Works*, 8:297 (*Bion in New York and São Paulo*, 61; audience question).
2 Bion, *All My Sins Remembered: Another Part of a Life, and The Other Side of Genius: Family Letters*.
3 Bion, *Complete Works*, 9:181 (*The Italian Seminars*: 90).
4 Personal communication, 24th October 2012.
5 Bion, *Complete Works*, 9:39 (*The Tavistock Seminars*, 36–37); italics mine.
6 Mawson, *Bion Today*, 247.
7 Eliot, *The Waste Land and Other Poems*. The opening four lines cannot be included for copyright reasons; the poem is widely available online.
8 Freud, *Standard Edition*, 14:307.
9 Bion, *Complete Works*, 5:186 (*Transformations*, 67).
10 Eggers, *The Circle*, 485; quoted in Boxall, *The Value of the Novel*, 1.
11 Bion, *Complete Works*, 5:279 (*Transformations*, 171).
12 Bion, *Complete Works*, 10:164 (*The Tavistock Seminars*, 114).
13 Bion, *Complete Works*, 4:252.
14 Bion, *Complete Works*, 4:271 (*Learning from Experience*, 3).
15 Begley, 'Don DeLillo, The Art of Fiction No. 135'.
16 See chapter two.
17 Bion, *Complete Works*, 15:6.
18 Bion, *Complete Works*, 15:49.
19 Boxall, *The Value of the Novel*, 2.
20 Bion, *Complete Works*, 9:67 (*The Tavistock Seminars*, 69).
21 Bion, *Complete Works*, 15:47.
22 The word in English, *pensive*, and the French word *penser* (to think), draw on the Latin words *pensare* (to weigh, consider) and *pendere* (to hang).

References

Adorno, Theodor. *Essays on Music*. London: University of California Press, 2002.

Ballard, J.G. *Miracles of Life: Shanghai to Shepperton. An Autobiography*. London: Harper Perennial, 2008.

Ballard, J.G. *The Atrocity Exhibition*. London: Fourth Estate, 2014.

Baxter, Jeannette, ed. *J.G. Ballard: Contemporary Critical Perspectives*. London: Continuum, 2008.

Begley, Adam. "Don DeLillo, The Art of Fiction No. 135." *The Paris Review* 128 (1993).

Berkeley, George. *The Analyst*. London: J. Tonson, 1734.

Bion Talamo, Parthenope. "Bion: A Freudian Innovator." *British Journal of Psychotherapy* 14, no. 1 (1997): 47–59.

Bion Talamo, Parthenope. *Maps for Psychoanalytic Exploration*. London: Karnac, 2015.

Bion, Wilfred. *All My Sins Remembered: Another Part of a Life and The Other Side of Genius: Family Letters*. Edited by Francesca Bion. London: Karnac, 1985.

Bion, Wilfred. *A Memoir of the Future*. London: Karnac, 1991.

Bion, Wilfred. *Attention and Interpretation*. Karnac, 1970.

Bion, Wilfred. *Bion in New York and São Paulo*. Perthshire: Clunie Press, 1980.

Bion, Wilfred. *Brazilian Lectures: 1973 São Paulo, 1974 Rio de Janeiro/São Paulo*. London: Karnac, 1990.

Bion, Wilfred. *Clinical Seminars and Other Works*. London: Karnac, 1994.

Bion, Wilfred. *Cogitations*. London: Karnac, 1992.

Bion, Wilfred. *Complete Works of W.R. Bion*. Edited by Chris Mawson and Francesca Bion. London: Karnac, 2014.

Bion, Wilfred. *Elements of Psychoanalysis*. London: Maresfield, 1963.

Bion, Wilfred. *Experiences in Groups and Other Papers*. London: Routledge, 1961.

Bion, Wilfred. *Learning from Experience*. London: Maresfield, 1962.

Bion, Wilfred. *Second Thoughts: Selected Papers on Psycho-Analysis*. London: Karnac, 1984.

Bion, Wilfred. *Taming Wild Thoughts*. Edited by Francesca Bion. London: Karnac, 1997.

Bion, Wilfred. *The Complete Works of W.R. Bion*. Edited by Chris Mawson and Francesca Bion. London: Karnac, 2014.

Bion, Wilfred. *The Italian Seminars*. London: Karnac, 2005.

Bion, Wilfred. *The Long Week-End 1897–1919: Part of a Life*. Edited by Francesca Bion. London: Karnac, 1982.

Bion, Wilfred. *The Tavistock Seminars*. London: Karnac, 2005.

Bion, Wilfred. *Transformations*. London: Karnac, 1984.

Bion, Wilfred. *Two Papers: The Grid and Caesura*. London: Karnac, 1989.

Bion, Wilfred. *War Memoirs 1917–1919*. London: Karnac, 1997.

Bion, Wilfred. *Wilfred Bion: Los Angeles Seminars and Supervision*. Edited by Joseph Aguayo and Barnet Malin. London: Karnac, 2013.

Bléandonu, Gérard. *Wilfred Bion: His Life and Works 1897–1979*. London: Free Association Books, 1994.

Blondel, Nathalie. *Mary Butts: Scenes from the Life. A Biography*. Kingston, N.Y.: McPherson, 1998.

Bluemel, Kristin. *George Orwell and the Radical Eccentrics: Intermodernism in Literary London*. Basingstoke: Palgrave Macmillan, 2004.

Boxall, Peter. *The Value of the Novel*. Cambridge: Cambridge University Press, 2015.

Braudy, Leo, and Marshall Cohen, eds. *Film Theory and Criticism: Introductory Readings*. Oxford: Oxford University Press, 1974.

Braybrooke, Neville. "The Return of Jean Rhys." *Caribbean Quarterly* 16, no. 4 (1970): 43–46.

Brontë, Charlotte. *Jane Eyre*. London: Marshall Cavendish, 1986.

Brook, Peter. *The Empty Space*. London: Penguin, 1972.

Butts, Mary. *The Journals of Mary Butts*. Edited by Nathalie Blondel. London: Yale University Press, 2002.

Butts, Mary. *With and Without Buttons and Other Stories*. Manchester: Carcanet, 1991.

Cassin, Barbara. *Dictionary of Untranslatables: A Philosophical Lexicon*. Princeton: Princeton University Press, 2014.

Civitarese, Giuseppe. *The Violence of Emotions: Bion and Post-Bionian Psychoanalysis*. London: Routledge, 2013.

Cixous, Hélène. *Dream I Tell You*. Translated by Beverley Bie Brahic. The Frontiers of Theory. Edinburgh: Edinburgh University Press, 2006.

Cixous, Hélène. *Stigmata: Escaping Texts*. Translated by Eric Prenowitz. London: Routledge, 1998.

Coe, Jonathan. *Like a Fiery Elephant: The Story of B.S. Johnson*. London: Picador, 2004.

Connor, Steven. *Beckett, Modernism and the Material Imagination*. Cambridge: Cambridge University Press, 2014.

Connor, Steven. "Thinking Things." *Textual Practice* 24 (2010): 1–20.

Crary, Jonathan. *Techniques of the Observer: On Vision and Modernity in the Nineteenth Century*. London: MIT Press, 1990.

Derrida, Jacques. "Freud and the Scene of Writing." Translated by Jeffrey Mehlman. *Yale French Studies* 48 (1972): 74–117.

Derrida, Jacques. *Of Grammatology [Corrected Edition]*. London: The John Hopkins University Press, 1997.

de Haan, Eric. Translated by Sue Stewart. *Relational Coaching: Journeys Towards Mastering One to One Learning*. Chichester: John Wiley & Sons, 2008.

'Dr. A.A. Brill Dies; Psychiatrist, 73.' *New York Times*. 3 March 1948.

Douglas, Hazel. *Containment and Reciprocity: Integrating Psychoanalytic Theory and Child Development Research for Work with Children*. Hove: Routledge, 2007.

Eggers, Dave. *The Circle*. London: Penguin, 2014.

Epstein, Mark. *Thoughts without a Thinker: Psychotherapy from a Buddhist Perspective*. London: Duckworth, 1996.

Ferro, Antonino. *Psychoanalysis as Therapy and Storytelling*. Translated by Philip Slotkin. London: Routledge, 2006.

Filreis, Alan. *Wallace Stevens and the Actual World*. Princeton: Princeton University Press, 1991.

Foy, Roslyn Reso. *Ritual, Myth, and Mysticism in the Work of Mary Butts: Between Feminism and Modernism*. Fayetteville: The University of Arkansas Press, 2000.

Foy, Roslyn Reso. "'Brightness Falls': Magic in the Short Stories of Mary Butts." *Studies in Short Fiction* 36, no. 4 (1999).

Francis, Samuel. *The Psychological Fictions of J.G. Ballard*. London: Continuum, 2011.

Freud, Sigmund. *Aus Den Anfängen Der Psychoanalyse, Briefe an Wilhelm Fließ, Abhandlungen Und Notizen Aus Den Jahren 1887–1902*. London: Imago Publishing, 1950.

Freud, Sigmund. *Interpreting Dreams*. Translated by J.A. Underwood. London: Penguin, 2006.

Freud, Sigmund. *The Standard Edition of the Complete Psychological Works of Sigmund Freud*. Edited by James Strachey. London: Vintage, 1966.

Freud, Sigmund. *The Standard Edition of the Complete Psychological Works of Sigmund Freud: Volume I (1886–1899)*. London: The Hogarth Press, 1966.

Frickey, Pierrette, ed. *Critical Perspectives on Jean Rhys*. Washington, D.C.: Three Continents Press, 1990.

Frick, Thomas. "J.G. Ballard, The Art of Fiction No. 85." *The Paris Review* 94 (1984). http://www.theparisreview.org/interviews/2929/the-art-of-fiction-no-85-j-g-ballard.

Ganteau, Jean-Michel. *The Ethics and Aesthetics of Vulnerability in Contemporary British Fiction*. Abingdon: Routledge, 2015.

Graves, Robert. *Goodbye to All That*. London: Cassell & Company, 1957.

Greenland, Colin. *The Entropy Exhibition: Michael Moorcock and the British 'New Wave' in Science Fiction*. London: Routledge & Kegan Paul, 1983.

Grinberg, Leon, Dario Sor, and Elizabeth Tabak de Bianchedi. *Introduction to the Work of Bion: Groups, Knowledge, Psychosis, Thought, Transformations, Psychoanalytic Practice*. London: Maresfield, 1975.

Grotstein, James. *A Beam of Intense Darkness: Wilfred Bion's Legacy to Psychoanalysis*. London: Karnac, 2007.

Grotstein, James. "Bion's Dream: A Reading of the Autobiographies (review)." *American Imago* 67, no. 3 (2010): 463–9.

Grotstein, James. *Do I Dare Disturb the Universe? A Memorial to W.R. Bion*. London: Karnac, 1981.

Harris Williams, Meg. *Bion's Dream: A Reading of the Autobiographies*. London: Karnac, 2010.

Henry, Holly. *Virginia Woolf and the Discourse of Science: The Aesthetics of Astronomy*. Cambridge: Cambridge University Press, 2003.

Hinshelwood, R.D. *A Dictionary of Kleinian Thought*. London: Free Association Books, 1991.

Humm, Maggie. *Border Traffic: Strategies of Contemporary Women Writers*. Manchester: Manchester University Press, 1991.

Hunter, Dianne. *Seduction and Theory: Readings of Gender, Representation, and Rhetoric*. Urbana: University of Illinois Press, 1989.

Ionescu, Arleen. "'Cloth Speaks': Cloaks of Telepathy, Melancholia, and the Uncanny in Nicholas Royle's Quilt." *Meridian Critic* 24, no. 1 (2015).

Jacobus, Mary. *The Poetics of Psychoanalysis: In the Wake of Klein*. Oxford: Oxford University Press, 2005.

Jaques, Elliott. "Disturbances in the Capacity to Work." *The International Journal of Psycho-Analysis* 41 (1960): 357–67.

Jarry, Alfred. *Selected Works of Alfred Jarry*. Edited by Roger Shattuck and Simon Watson Taylor. New York: Grove Press, 1980.

Johnson, B.S. *The Unfortunates*. London: Picador, 1999.

Johnson, B.S. *Trawl*. London: Picador, 2013.

Johnson, B.S. *Well Done God! Selected Prose and Drama of B.S. Johnson*. Edited by Jonathan Coe, Philip Tew, and Julia Jordan. London: Picador, 2013.

Jordan, Julia, and Martin Ryle, eds. *B.S. Johnson and Post-War Literature: Possibilities of the Avant Garde*. Basingstoke: Palgrave Macmillan, 2014.

Klein, Melanie. *The Selected Melanie Klein*. Edited by Juliet Mitchell. Harmondsworth: Penguin, 1986.

Lacan, Jacques. *Écrits: The First Complete Edition in English*. London: W.W. Norton, 2006.

Laplanche, Jean. *New Foundations for Psychoanalysis*. Oxford: Basil Blackwell, 1989.

Laplanche, Jean, and Jean-Bertrand Pontalis. *The Language of Psychoanalysis*. London: Karnac, 1973.

Lee, Hermione. *Stevie Smith: A Selection*. London: Faber and Faber, 1983.

Levine, Howard B., and Giuseppe Civitarese, eds. *The W.R. Bion Tradition: Lines of Development – Evolution of Theory and Practice over the Decades*. London: Karnac, 2016.

Lichtenberg, George Christoph. *The Waste Books*. Translated by R.J. Hollingdale. New York: The New York Review of Books, 1990.

Louvel, Liliane. *Poetics of the Iconotext*. Edited by Karen Jacobs. Farnham: Ashgate, 2011.

Luckhurst, Roger. 'The Angle Between Two Walls': The Fiction of J.G. Ballard*. Liverpool: Liverpool University Press, 1997.

Mahony, Patrick. *Freud as a Writer (Expanded Edition)*. London: Yale University Press, 1987.

Matless, David. "A Geography of Ghosts: The Spectral Landscapes of Mary Butts." *Cultural Geographies* 15, no. 3 (2008): 335–57.

McAfee, Noëlle. *Julia Kristeva*. Abingdon: Routledge, 2004.

McQuillan, Martin, ed. *Deconstruction: A Reader*. London: Routledge, 2000.

Meltzer, Donald. *Sincerity and Other Works: Collected Papers of Donald Meltzer*. London: Karnac, 1994.

Meltzer, Donald. *The Kleinian Development*. London: Karnac, 1998.

Miller, Ian. *Beckett and Bion: The (Im)Patient Voice in Psychotherapy and Literature*. London: Karnac, 2013.

Najarian, James. "Contributions to Almighty Truth: Stevie Smith's Seditious Romanticism." *Twentieth Century Literature* 49, no. 4 (2003): 472–93.

O'Shaughnessy, Edna. "Whose Bion?" *International Journal of Psychoanalysis* 86 (2005): 1523–8.

Parrinder, Patrick. "The Novels of B.S. Johnson." *Critical Quarterly* 19, no. 2 (1977): 45–59.

Perec, Georges. *Les Mots Croisés*. Paris: Éditions Gallimard, 2012.

Phillips, Adam. *On Flirtation*. London: Faber and Faber, 1994.

Playfair, John. "Hutton's Unconformity." *Transactions of the Royal Society of Edinburgh* V, no. III (1805).

Poincaré, Henri. *Science and Method*. London: Thomas Nelson and Sons, 1908.

Pope, Alexander. *The Major Works*. Edited by Pat Rogers. Oxford: Oxford University Press, 2006.

Rainey, Lawrence, ed. *Modernism: An Anthology*. Oxford: Blackwell Publishing, 2005.

Raiskin, Judith. *Snow on the Cane Fields: Women's Writing and Creole Subjectivity*. Minneapolis: University of Minnesota Press, 1996.

Ramazani, Jahan. *Poetry of Mourning: The Modern Elegy from Hardy to Heaney*. Chicago: Chicago University Press, 1994.

Rhys, Jean. *Wide Sargasso Sea*. Edited by Angela Smith. London: Penguin, 1997.

Riley, Denise. *Time Lived, Without Its Flow*. London: Capsule Editions, 2012.

Rilke, Rainer Maria. *Duino Elegies*. London: Enitharmon Press, 2006.

Rose, Jacqueline. *On Not Being Able to Sleep: Psychoanalysis and the Modern World*. London: Vintage, 2004.

Rose, Jacqueline. *Why War? Psychoanalysis, Politics and the Return to Melanie Klein*. Oxford: Blackwell, 1993.

Royle, Nicholas. *Quilt.* Brighton: Myriad Editions, 2010.

Royle, Nicholas. *The Uncanny.* Manchester: Manchester University Press, 2003.

Rudnytsky, Peter L., ed. *Transitional Object and Potential Spaces: Literary Uses of D.W. Winnicott.* New York: Columbia University Press, 1993.

Sacks, Peter M. *The English Elegy: Studies in the Genre from Spenser to Yeats.* Baltimore: The John Hopkins University Press, 1985.

Said, Edward. *Beginnings: Intention and Method.* London: Granta Books, 1985.

Said, Edward. *On Late Style: Music and Literature Against the Grain.* London: Bloomsbury, 2006.

Sandler, P.C. *A Clinical Application of Bion's Concepts. Volume 3: Verbal and Visual Approaches to Reality.* London: Karnac, 2013.

Sandler, P.C. *The Language of Bion: A Dictionary of Concepts.* London: Karnac, 2005.

Sartre, Jean-Paul. *Being and Nothingness: An Essay on Phenomenological Ontology.* London: Routledge Classics, 2003.

Segal, Hanna. "Notes on Symbol Formation." *International Journal of Psychoanalysis* 38 (1957): 391–405.

Shakespeare, William. *William Shakespeare: The Complete Works.* Oxford: Oxford University Press, 1988.

Smith, Stevie. *Novel on Yellow Paper, Or, Work It out for Yourself.* Repr. Virago, 1980.

Solms, Mark. *The Feeling Brain: Selected Papers on Neuropsychoanalysis.* London: Karnac, 2015.

Solms, Mark, and Michael Saling, eds. *A Moment of Transition: Two Neuroscientific Articles by Sigmund Freud.* London: Karnac, 1990.

Spalding, Frances. *Stevie Smith: A Critical Biography.* London: Faber and Faber, 1988.

Stein, Gertrude. *Geography and Play.* Boston: Four Seas Co., 1922.

Sterne, Laurence. *The Life and Opinions of Tristram Shandy, Gentleman.* Ware: Wordsworth Classics, 2009.

Stevenson, Sheryl. "Stevie Smith's Voices." *Contemporary Literature* 33, no. 1 (1992): 24–45.

Stevens, Wallace. *The Collected Poems of Wallace Stevens: Corrected Edition.* Edited by John N. Serio and Chris Beyers. New York: Vintage Books, 2015.

Stonebridge, Lyndsey. *The Destructive Element: British Psychoanalysis and Modernism.* Basingstoke: Macmillan Press, 1998.

Swift, Jonathan. *The Poetical Works of Jonathan Swift: Volume 1.* London: William Pickering, 1833.

Tew, Philip, and Glyn White, eds. *Re-Reading B.S. Johnson.* Basingstoke: Palgrave Macmillan, 2007.

Torres, Nuno, and R.D. Hinshelwood, eds. *Bion's Sources: The Shaping of His Paradigms.* London: Routledge, 2013.

Tredell, Nicolas. *Fighting Fictions: The Novels of B.S. Johnson.* Nottingham: Paupers' Press, 2000.

Verne, Jules. *Twenty Thousand Leagues under the Seas.* Oxford: Oxford University Press, 1998.

Vidler, Anthony. *The Architectural Uncanny: Essays in the Modern Unhomely.* London: The MIT Press, 1992.

White, Glyn. *Reading the Graphic Surface: The Presence of the Book in Prose Fiction.* Manchester: Manchester University Press, 2005.

Yeats, W.B. *Selected Poems.* London: Penguin, 1991.

Index

Printed in Great Britain
by Amazon

23270115R00110